W9-DJM-984

DILEMMAS

From the Library of
David B. Miller
AMBS
dbmiller@ambs.edu

DILEMMAS

A Christian Approach
to Moral Decision Making

Richard Higginson

Westminster/John Knox Press

LOUISVILLE, KENTUCKY

First published in Great Britain 1988
Hodder & Stoughton Limited, London

© 1988 Richard Higginson

All rights reserved—no part of this book may oe reproauced in any form
without permission in writing from the publisher, except by a reviewer who
wishes to quote brief passages in connection with a review in magazine or
newspaper.

Unless otherwise stated, scripture quotations are from the Revised Standard
Version of the Bible, copyrighted 1946, 1952, © 1971, 1973 by the Division
of Christian Education of the National Council of the Churches of Christ in the
U.S.A., and are used by permission.

First American edition

Published by Westminster/John Knox Press
Louisville, Kentucky

PRINTED IN THE UNITED STATES OF AMERICA
9 8 7 6 5 4 3 2 1

Library of Congress Cataloging-in-Publication Data

Higginson, Richard.
    Dilemmas : a Christian approach to moral aecision making / Richard
Higginson. — 1st American ed.
        p.   cm.
    Includes index.

    ISBN 0-664-25068-8 (pbk.)
    1. Christian ethics. 2. Decision-making (Ethics) I. Title.
BJ1251.H54 1989
241—dc19   88-29755
                                                                CIP

CONTENTS

ACKNOWLEDGMENTS

I am grateful to Gerald Duckworth and Co., publisher of Alasdair MacIntyre's *After Virtue*, and A. and C. Black, publisher of Helmut Thielicke's *Theological Ethics*, for permission to quote from these works.

The place of publication of books which have been cited is London unless otherwise stated.

There are several people whom I would like to thank for their part in the production of this book. Colleagues at St John's College, Durham covered for my absence on sabbatical in the summer term of 1986, when the substantial part of *Dilemmas* was written. David Wavre of Hodder and Stoughton has been consistently encouraging and helpful. David Field kindly invited me to contribute to the series he is editing and made some very constructive criticisms of my first draft. Last but not least, my wife Felicity has offered constant and patient support to me in all my writing endeavours. To each of them, many thanks.

Richard Higginson

DILEMMAS

INTRODUCTION
WHAT THIS BOOK IS ABOUT

This book is an exploration of the subject of moral dilemmas. It attempts to bring together the realms of the theoretical and the practical, and of moral philosophy and Christian theology. It outlines some influential approaches to moral decision-making, subjects them to criticism and then suggests an alternative way forward. Above all, I hope that it stimulates readers to think afresh about moral dilemmas for themselves.

   In the course of these pages I touch on many different types of moral dilemma: some of the major topical issues of our day (e.g., nuclear deterrence, the care of the dying); some of the agonising decisions which confront individuals in extreme and unusual situations (e.g., in Nazi prisoner-of-war camps); and some much more typical everyday problems (e.g., what to teach very young children about sex). I have included a good share of the third type, since this – strangely enough – is the category on which books on ethics often have least to say. But it would be a mistake to expect the entire spectrum of ethical issues to be canvassed here, or to anticipate a comprehensive treatment of any one moral dilemma. Other books can deal with particular issues in greater detail. I have used the specific dilemmas as illustrative material in order to make points about moral decision-making which have wider relevance. It is the factors which are relevant across the whole range of moral dilemmas which I have been principally concerned to identify. At times I have offered a judgment on a particular moral quandary; sometimes I have sketched an approach to questions such as abortion and war; other issues I have simply been content to raise, or left it to readers to guess what my opinion would be. But my hope is that even readers who disagree with some of my specific views will find the basic approach outlined here instructive and illuminating.

A heartening development of recent years has been the appearance of a number of good introductory books on Christian ethics. I should like to pay particular tribute to Arthur Holmes's *Ethics* (IVP, 1985), David Brown's *Choices* (Blackwell, 1983) and Michael Langford's *The Good and the True* (SCM, 1985), all of which contain significant points of agreement with this book. It seems to me that Christian ethicists are currently engaged in the constructive business of building on each other's insights, rather than being engaged in demolition work!

One further point about what this book is not highlights an area where we do need fresh Christian thinking and writing. Coming to a right judgment on a moral issue is one thing, and that is this book's major concern; shaping or adapting the laws of the country in which we live is another matter, and that is an area into which I have had little space to venture. But it is very important. To what extent can Christians expect their convictions to be accepted and find expression in the legal framework of an increasingly pluralistic society? It is a question on which updated perspectives are needed. In this book my aim has been to help Christians become clearer about what their views are and why, and I trust that this will make them better equipped to take part in this wider debate.

1

DILEMMAS GREAT AND SMALL

Dilemmas

Dilemmas come in all shapes and sizes. In the course of this book I shall say something about many of the major topical issues of our time: abortion, war, strikes, capital punishment, and so on. But the dilemmas which confront most people in the everyday course of their lives are of a much more mundane character. Indeed, some of them are so matter-of-fact that they are scarcely recognised as dilemmas.

A recurrent theme in many dilemma situations is that of honesty. A man who applies for a job is asked if he has ever been under psychiatric care. He saw a psychiatrist for depression eight years previously. Need he feel that he has to mention this? A bank clerk makes an expensive error at her work, and finds that a fellow-employee is blamed for it. Should she own up? You know that the car you are trying to sell has a faulty gear-box. Do you give prospective buyers any hint of this? My child has dropped the telephone and I have to call out the phone engineer. Do I admit how it was broken and incur a charge that I would avoid if I said that I didn't know how it had been damaged?

Sometimes these situations are compounded by the fact that other people encourage us in our or their dishonesty – especially financial dishonesty. A solicitor may encourage us to exaggerate the extent of our injuries so that we can get a larger settlement after a car accident. A shop-girl offers to accept coupons for goods which we have not in fact bought. A decorator asks us to pay cash rather than by cheque, so that he

can avoid paying VAT when he declares his earnings. There
seems to be an implicit assumption that it is all right to try to
'fiddle the system'.

Another area into which we stray repeatedly is that of
minor illegality: parking on a double yellow line; photo-
copying written material without asking for permission; driving at 80 mph on the motorway rather than at 70 . . . in many
such cases, the offence seems trivial, and it is tempting to take
the risk and see if we can get away with it – especially if we feel
that the law in question is a bit silly.

When we stop and think about many of these situations,
however, they don't really involve much by way of a *moral*
dilemma. In other words, it's actually quite obvious what we
should do: we ought to be honest, or we ought to abide by the
law. But because of the personal inconvenience involved, or
because the matter seems unimportant, or because we don't
want to appear moralising and 'holier-than-thou', or simply
because we are weak-willed and sinful, we do not do what we
know we ought to do. And by negligence of this kind, we
probably contribute, little by little, both to our own moral
deterioration and to the decay of our society. Petty dishonesty
leads to a loss of trust between people, and petty illegality
makes society function less smoothly and may actually harm
somebody. But we subconsciously banish such thoughts to the
back of our minds!

However, there are other everyday situations where closer
examination leaves us genuinely unsure about our duty.
Dishonesty is clearly wrong where it's simply to protect my
own skin or to forward my own interests, but what if it might
compensate for a wrong which I believe I have suffered?
Perhaps I have recently been refused an insurance claim for a
lost camera, which I believed to be covered by my policy. The
company do reimburse me for a watch lost at the same time.
Shortly afterwards I find my watch. Should I return the
money, even though it's roughly the same amount as the
worth of the camera? Alternatively, the local garage mech-
anic forgets to charge me for the new windscreen wipers that
he's fitted during a car service. I feel that his labour charges
are unreasonably high, and I'm annoyed that he didn't get the

service done on the day that he promised. Do I point out his omission? Is there a natural justice in keeping quiet about the wipers, or is it true that 'two wrongs don't make a right'?

Another type of quandary is where we are tempted to omit doing something in order to spare both ourselves and other people hurt and embarrassment. Bob finds it terribly difficult to end a romance with Karen, who loves him far more than he loves her, and will be deeply upset by his telling her that he doesn't think their friendship has any long-term future. A mother accidentally lets her 4-year-old son's hamster escape, and has the opportunity to replace it without telling him. Under the watchword of 'ignorance is bliss', should she refrain from telling him that he's now got a different hamster? Might a similar justification excuse a devoted husband's concealing of the fact that he secretly enjoys dressing up in his wife's underwear – because he fears that she won't understand? Dilemmas like these pose important questions about the nature of relationships and what really makes for a healthy relationship.

There are also dilemmas which are deeply agonising and involve an enormous amount of heart-searching. Individuals find themselves tossing arguments backwards and forwards, feeling convinced first by one point of view, then the other. They may consult endless numbers of people; they may struggle with a particular problem alone. Peace can ensue when a decision is finally made, but there is no guarantee of that.

In the paragraphs that follow, I outline three imaginary situations involving individuals grappling with the more momentous type of dilemma. One depicts a couple facing up to a topical biomedical issue which has profound personal implications for them; another portrays a businessman confronted by a typical problem in his field of work; the third involves two would-be politicians discussing the morality of defence policy. I shall then use these situations as illustrative material for presenting important features about moral dilemmas in general.

Alan and Tricia

Alan and Tricia are childless. They have been married for eight years and have been trying to conceive for the last six. Infertility tests eventually revealed that Tricia suffers from damaged Fallopian tubes. This is probably, but not definitely, the result of infection following an abortion Tricia had when she was a teenager, before she ever knew Alan. In past years this discovery would have represented the end to the couple's hopes of having their own children, but now the development of *in vitro* fertilisation (IVF) offers the prospect of bypassing Tricia's problem. They have heard of other women with the same problem who have successfully conceived through this method, and they start to save up the £1,400 which is the going rate for participation in the IVF procedure. Since they both work and have well-paid jobs, this doesn't take them all that long.

When they go to the IVF clinic, the doctor explains what the procedure involves. And for the first time, Alan and Tricia start to think about aspects of IVF which up till now they had brushed to one side. The doctor explains that to increase the chances of fertilisation it is usual for female patients to be given fertility drugs, so that as many as six eggs would be extracted from Tricia's ovary and mixed with Alan's semen. Two or three would then be transferred to her womb, and hopefully at least one would implant and develop. Of course, if they all implanted successfully, Tricia might end up with twins or triplets! Alan asks what would happen to the embryos that weren't put back inside her. The doctor says that he would like to ask the couple's permission to use them for 'important research', which may help the clinic to find out if cells from a tiny embryo can be grafted into patients with bone-marrow problems. The clinic is very keen to use 'spare embryos' for this purpose, but as the doctor explains, 'Of course we wouldn't dream of doing that without your consent.'

'That means the embryo will die, doesn't it?' says Tricia.

'Yes,' says the doctor, 'but of course it will anyway if we just leave it in the laboratory. The only way it can stay alive outside your body is if we put it in a freezer. We could do that, of course. Then if you want another baby at a later stage we could implant that embryo, rather than making you go through all the superovulation and laparoscopy again.'

Although Alan accepts all these possibilities readily enough, Tricia begins to feel rather uneasy about the whole business. Sure, it would be nice to help bone-marrow patients, but is it right to allow lethal experiments on an embryo created from their flesh and blood in order to do so? Isn't that embryo a human being, albeit a very tiny one? And the thought of storing an embryo in a deep-freezer doesn't exactly appeal to her either. What if something was to go wrong with it while it was there? Nor does she like the idea of taking fertility drugs. The whole IVF procedure seems to involve doing so many things which are peculiar and, as she sees it, 'unnatural'. And yet she and Alan both desperately want a baby. A thought occurs to her.

'Do I have to be superovulated?' she asks the doctor. 'Wouldn't it be possible just to take the one egg from my natural cycle and fertilise that, so that we don't have the complication of the spare embryos?'

'That could be done,' says the doctor, 'but we would strongly discourage it. You see, your chances of successful implantation would be greatly reduced. You could be coming back to this clinic time after time before we got an embryo to develop and a pregnancy to develop. That could boost the cost for you astronomically. And in a sense you'd be wasting our time because we wouldn't be carrying out the IVF process as efficiently and economically as we can.'

Alan and Tricia nod. The doctor suggests that because they're obviously harbouring uncertainties, they go away and think about things before making a definite start on treatment for Tricia. And Tricia for one feels caught on the horns of a dilemma. The guilt which she has often experienced about that teenage abortion rises to the surface again. Often since then she has felt that her infertility is a punishment for going through with the abortion. At the time everyone who knew said it was the sensible thing to do. But ever since then she has felt that the life of the embryo is something one ought, wherever possible, to respect. And now the technique which promises an end to her infertility problem seems to involve doing away with, killing off, still more embryos on the side . . .

Bill

Bill is the chief sales executive of a large motor company. The firm has not been doing very well recently, for a variety of reasons. A series of small-scale but niggling strikes has reduced output and led to the loss of some anticipated orders. The government has withdrawn certain subsidies as part of its 'let-industry-stand-on-its-own-feet' policy. One particular model is flagging badly in competition with an outstanding rival. And Bill's firm, like many another, is suffering in a general way from the world recession. There is a real threat of the firm's having to make a substantial cut in the workforce – maybe up to 15,000 redundancies.

But now a shaft of light has appeared on this gloomy horizon. In the face of considerable competition, Bill's sales team has negotiated a major contract with the government of an African country. The contract is for the sale of lorries and buses to this country and is worth £400 million. This looks like being a real life-line to Bill's firm: it should mean that most if not all of those 15,000 jobs can be saved.

Yet only days after the contract has been negotiated in draft form, Bill's joy turns to fury. The government agent starts sounding less enthusiastic about the deal. Bill discovers that a rival motor company has offered the agent 10 per cent of the contract's value if that firm is given the contract. On being confronted with this discovery, the agent says that he is open to higher bids from Bill's firm.

Bill is not surprised. He has done business with this and neighbouring African countries before and he knows that such payments ('commission', as they are sometimes called) are a normal part of economic transactions. Never before, however, has Bill been confronted with a demand for a payment *this big*. He desperately wants to clinch the deal. He genuinely believes that his firm make better lorries and buses than their rival, that they deserve to win the contract. At the same time he resents bitterly having to out-bribe the competitor: Bill is unable to call what goes on by any name other than bribery.

Bill feels himself to be in a quandary. There are many aspects of his job that he likes, and he feels that he is good at it, but he detests being a party to this sort of deal. He knows that if he is not prepared to match the rival's bribe, his firm will almost certainly lose the deal, and the consequences could be horrendous: 15,000 employees might lose their jobs. Some of them live in his vicinity, and if they were to find out that he could have saved their jobs, they could make life quite intolerable for him. He would probably lose his job himself, being either sacked by the management board or feeling obliged to resign when the circumstances of the missed deal became clear. Yet if Bill does what is 'necessary' and pays the bribe, he feels that the increasingly corrupt cycle of trade relations with that part of the world will only become more corrupt. If firms like his participate in a crooked set-up, its crookedness can only increase, and they will end up having to pay even bigger bribes. Yet countries like that represent a corner of the trade market which it is simply not financially viable to ignore . . .

Linda and Tom

Linda and Tom are political researchers. They are members of a political party of centrist tendencies and they have been saddled with the responsibility of drafting a discussion document on the party's attitude to nuclear defence. The party contains a clear divergence of opinion on this issue, including both staunch defenders of nuclear deterrence and advocates of nuclear disarmament. Although not whole-heartedly committed to either position, Linda and Tom find that these differences are reflected in their own discussions on the issue.

'Nuclear weapons are immoral,' says Linda. 'They're not

only immoral, they're pointless. If the Russians did drop a nuclear bomb on us, what would be the point of dropping one on them? It would only serve the purposes of revenge. It would kill thousands of innocent people who bear no responsibility for the Kremlin's attacking us. And it wouldn't put an end to the conflict. Because neither side has first-strike capacity, it wouldn't eliminate the Soviet capacity to hit us again and almost certainly would encourage them to do so. And if using these wretched weapons can't be justified, what's the point of having them?'

'Hold on a minute,' says Tom. 'The whole point about possessing nuclear weapons as a deterrent is that if they work, you don't have to use them. We threaten to use them in order not to use them. I admit it's difficult to visualise circumstances in which using them would be justified. I'm very unhappy about the prospect of NATO forces using them as a first-strike weapon, should Communist forces invade through central Europe, and the likelihood of hitting purely military targets without killing civilians and inviting an escalation of conflict seems pretty remote. But hopefully, simply by possessing these horrible things, we stand a good chance of avoiding such situations. The two power blocs have been locked in a state of nuclear deterrence for forty-odd years now, and so far it's worked.'

'Yes, it's worked so far,' admits Linda, 'though only at the cost of America and Russia working out their aggression towards each other in other places at other countries' expense. But that apart, what assurance can we have that it will go on working? Isn't there bound to be a complete breakdown in relations eventually? Or perhaps some minor crisis that gets blown up out of all proportion? If deterrence fails, what then?'

'Well, if it fails', replies Tom, 'which I don't think is likely, then we ought not to use nuclear weapons. If it came to the crunch, I would rather be red than dead – or, for that matter, rather be taken over by the Communists than support the killing of innocent women and children. The gamble of deterrence is that we avoid *both* being red *and* being dead.'

'Ah, so you admit it is a gamble now. But let's think

carefully about what you've just said. If you support the possession of nuclear weapons but you're not actually prepared to use them, then how are you going to deter the Russians? The weapons won't deter unless you show every indication that you're ready to use them. And if you're not prepared to use them, isn't it really a waste of money making and keeping them? There are a thousand and one causes on which the money could be better spent.'

'It's not as simple as that,' replies Tom. 'I admit that what I'm advocating is essentially a bluff position. But possessing weapons may still deter because we do everything possible to ensure that the potential enemy doesn't know we don't intend to use them. The fact that we do not so intend would have to be hidden from everyone except the very highest level of political and military command. And for that reason it certainly couldn't be a declared part of our party policy!'

Linda certainly isn't silenced by this line of argument. 'But that poses further massive problems,' she points out. 'It means not only that we're trying to deceive the Russians, but that we're involved in deceiving our own people and party as well. We try to get elected on the basis that we are prepared to use nuclear weapons, when all the while we're not! We expect the electorate to support something we ourselves know to be immoral and pretend isn't immoral. If we're prepared to take part in that sort of mass deceit, are we really any better than the Communists with all their lies and propaganda? Can we honestly then say that our political system is any better than theirs?'

'Yes, I see your point,' Tom says. 'I hadn't thought of that aspect before. Let's try another tack. Maybe we ought to be perfectly open about this. Maybe we should keep *some* nuclear weapons – I'm sure we could reduce the number – but at the same time disavow any intention to use them. We make no attempt to deceive either East or West. I know what you're about to say, in that case why bother to keep them at all? Because the Russians might still not be sure we mean what we say. Simply because we've got the weapons, we might create sufficient uncertainty in their minds that they're deterred from attacking us. Effectively we're saying: we have no intention of using these weapons, but you'd be unwise to provoke us by taking advantage of that.'

'Brilliant but crazy,' objects Linda. 'How on earth are we going to get that over to the electorate? And surely there's a basic flaw in it – your strategy works on the assumption that the Russians will mistrust us and not believe what we say. We trade off their mistrust. But if they started trusting us and believing us, then they might take advantage of us and attack us, and your deterrence policy would have failed.'

'Your non-deterrence policy is even more open to that risk. Nuclear disarmament provides no credible defence option whatsoever,' says Tom. 'Oh dear, I don't think we're ever going to get this discussion paper written . . .'

Crucial Nature

Clearly all three of the dilemmas described above are of a crucial nature. The decisions made will alter the course of people's lives significantly. In the first two cases, the effect will directly concern the individuals taking the decisions. If Bill decides that he cannot go through with the deal, he will probably have to resign. If Tricia and Alan decide that they cannot stomach the thought of experiments on live embryos, they will probably have to abandon their desire to have a child. The achievement or frustration of deeply-felt personal ambitions and hopes may well be at stake in resolving a moral dilemma. It is important to face up to the implications of this. The fact that we have so much personally at stake should make us suspicious about the impartiality of our reasoning in deciding one way or the other. If we stand to lose a lot by deciding in a particular direction, even though we may convince ourselves that we are acting on other grounds, self-interest *is* likely to be the determining factor. This is not to say that fulfilling personal hopes and ambitions is necessarily wrong. It is simply to warn that we have a great capacity for self-deceit.

Most dilemma situations are complicated, however, by the fact that other people are involved, too. And depending on which way a decision goes, some will almost certainly gain, others will equally probably lose. The employees in Bill's car firm will gain through his winning the contract, and so will the agent – but his and other firms also lose money in the long term through the perpetuation of a corrupt trading practice. Human embryos will suffer (though probably not *feel* suffering) through being subjected to experiments, but sufferers from bone-marrow complaints, hereditary genetic disorders and mysterious infertility problems may one day benefit. Avoiding a nuclear holocaust is clearly of crucial importance to all of us; but reducing the threat of a Communist takeover matters much less to groups of an extreme left-wing persuasion than it does to the majority of people in the West. So moral dilemmas raise questions not only about our responsibilities to ourselves, but also about responsibilities to other people. It is not infrequent that we wonder to which group of people we owe the primary responsibility.

Cultural Influences

A second important factor is that our perspective on moral dilemmas is strongly influenced by the particular culture of which we form a part. The three situations I have described all involve people in the West, probably – though not necessarily – British. Since this book is written with a Western audience principally in mind, I make no apology for that. But undoubtedly our Western perspective affects not only the choice of issues we consider important, but also our way of looking at them. Thus there are many Third World countries where having a child would matter even more to a married couple than it does to Alan and Tricia; and yet we in the West, with a culture suffused by the spirit of technology, are probably far more ready to use artificial techniques to achieve that desired end than they would be. Linda and Tom have clearly been conditioned, rightly or wrongly, into thinking of Russia as a threat. It is not simply *right-wing* political thinkers in the West who see a takeover by a Communist regime as a fate to be avoided at almost any price. If we lived in a part of the world where we had been subjected to the extremes of the political right, or where a Marxist government had handled power in an appreciably more humanitarian way than we perceive to be true of Soviet Russia, then our perspective would be altered.

The fact that different cultures vary in their perspectives has a crucial effect on our understanding of moral concepts and the connotations which attach to certain words. Bill instinctively feels that having to outbid the rival firm in its offer to the government agent amounts to bribery. To him bribery is a dirty word with thoroughly undesirable connotations and he wants to have nothing to do with it. But in the country with which he is dealing, the same word would not be used and the practice carries none of the same 'vibes'. Rather it is seen as part of a way of life where bargaining infuses every financial deal. The agent may actually consider that he has a *right* to the payment which he is demanding. But few cultures embody one culture in a monolithic way. There may well be *some* individuals in the agent's country who disapprove of what he is doing, who think that the quality of the lorries and buses offered should be the determining factor for him rather than his own personal aggrandisement.

Similarly, Tricia feels that the early embryo is a human being, a term she equates with that of a person, and that it has a right to life which should be respected. But many people in our Western culture would challenge this assumption. They would define a person as an individual with a developed capacity for rational agency, i.e., a member of the human species with powers of thinking, responding and communicating. This means that the crucial factor for determining the status of human life is when the brain attains a certain degree of capability. In fact, according to the above definition, one cannot really be said to become a person until some way into childhood. Most people shy away from that conclusion, because it conflicts with the attitude that they customarily adopt towards young babies. They may then opt for the mediatory, not entirely logical position that it is the beginnings of brain functioning (at about six or eight weeks into pregnancy) which are the vital watershed after which we should start thinking of the embryo as a person, with most or all of the rights that status usually entails. And so, when Tricia had an abortion (which she had ten weeks into pregnancy) she may well have been involved in killing a human person, but in allowing research to be done on a spare embryo, she is not. However, it should be noted that the above case depends heavily on an emphasis on human *rationality* as the criterion for determining human *personhood*. This is symptomatic of a post-Enlightenment culture like ours which places great stress on human reason and takes considerable pride in it; but it is a stress which is open to question, and as Tricia's reaction shows, another view of the worth of the embryo is possible within that same culture.

Compromise

Of the three dilemma situations outlined, one (Alan and Tricia's) might be described as fundamentally a question of *personal* ethics, while the other two encroach into the area of *social* ethics. Bill on the one hand and Linda and Tom on the other are members of big organisations, with many people looking to them for guidance, leadership and protection (in the case of Linda and Tom, this level of responsibility would obviously increase if their party was to come into power, or they became Prime Minister and Defence Secretary). Of course, questions of personal ethics rarely involve only one or two people – other people might benefit from embryo research, while public funding of IVF raises important questions about priorities in medical spending – but a rough-and-ready distinction between personal and social ethics is possible and helpful. Because the sphere of social ethics carries more overtones of responsibilities to other people, it does appear that individuals come under greater pressure to compromise their ethical ideals. They decide and act with a greater sense of their choices having been restricted, their hands having been tied.

The principal reason for this is that areas of life like economics and politics have come to be viewed as autonomous spheres, which have rules of conduct different from those that apply in personal life. As a private citizen, the prospect of threatening individual Russian citizens with nuclear destruction is horrific, and we instinctively recoil from it, yet it becomes a tolerable possibility when transferred to the political scene. The capacity to defend one's country is seen as a primary responsibility of government, and therefore, even if that end can only be achieved by the crudest and most immoral of threats, the threat is rendered acceptable. Nuclear deterrence is a fact of life in a nuclear age – so the argument runs. The phrase 'fact of life' represents an unconscious attempt to rule *moral* questions about nuclear deterrence out of order.[1] The notion of certain means being necessary to achieve desired ends is probably even more endemic to economics than to politics. Thus it is significant that moral stances *are* sometimes taken in politics: normal diplomatic and political relationships may be broken off in protest at a dastardly act or policy perpetrated by a particular regime, but usually when that occurs *economic* sanctions are the last thing to be considered seriously. The relationships of Western countries with South Africa, Soviet Russia and Libya over recent years reveals this tendency repeatedly.

One of the most striking facts about Bill's situation is that he is an unusually scrupulous sales executive to be experiencing the pangs of conscience that he is. However much they might privately deplore bribery, however disturbed ·they might be if contracts in this country were negotiated in a similar way (though of course business lunches and Christmas hampers can represent inducements on a smaller scale!), the vast majority of sales managers would not think twice about doing what was 'necessary' to outbid the competitor. Indeed, bribery practices of this kind are such an established part of trade with certain countries that the negotiated price often includes a 'bribe margin'. If Bill was a more run-of-the-mill sales executive, there is little doubt that he would see his immediate responsibility to his company, its shareholders and its employees as outweighing any wider responsibility to the international community for the conduct of world trade and therefore as excluding *moral* as opposed to *technical* considerations.

It is, I believe, inadequate simply to bemoan this widespread tendency to compromise in the social sphere, a compromise which appears to involve the suspension of moral standards that would normally be accepted in the personal sphere. The realities and responsibilities with which businessmen and politicians are confronted need to be taken seriously. It is disturbing when the stripping of areas of their moral dimension has reached the stage where participants no longer see that a dilemma is involved, but it is a genuine dilemma – paying the agent his bribe, threatening a nuclear strike are plausible options – and it is salutary for those of us who work in more sheltered occupations to remember that.

In the personal sphere, the pressure to compromise will also be experienced. Even if Tricia remains convinced that an embryo is a human person, external pressure from the doctor or Alan and internal pressure from her own longing to have children may still lead her to undergo treatment for *in vitro* fertilisation. A couple may have strong beliefs in the indissolubility of marriage, yet the misery of their own marriage or the attractions of another partner may become so predominant in their minds that they consent to its dissolution. But as in the social sphere, the decision will be made easier, and peace of mind appear more easily attainable, if they can be convinced that moral claims on one side can be discounted. If Tricia no longer believes that the embryo is a person, or if the marriage vows are no longer seen as awesomely binding, the dilemma loses much of its moral edge.

Choices

Thus far I have spoken consistently of dilemmas, as if the options open to people were always two. But analysis of the situations described shows that this is not usually the case. Most moral dilemmas are really more like multilemmas – we need to invent a new word! – because there is a variety of choices involved.

Thus, strictly speaking, Bill does not have only two choices,

to bribe or to quit the business world. He could attempt a deal
with the agent whereby he offered the lorries and buses at a
reduced price (£360 million?), but paid the agent nothing.
This is unlikely to work, because the agent would not prosper
personally, but if Bill detected any sign of manoeuvrability or
moral scruple in his make-up it might be worth trying. Bill
could allow the rival firm to clinch the deal and then publicly
disclose the means it had used to do so, hoping that the
ensuing indignation would lead to that firm's being dis-
credited and his own firm making up lost ground and winning
contracts. Again, this is unlikely to work, because public
indignation over crookedness in business soon blows over,
but there are times when sentiments are unusually sensitive
about this. Alternatively, Bill could stomach his scruples and
go through with the deal on this occasion, but try to organise a
get-together of all interested parties (rival firms, government
officials, etc.) to eradicate the practice of bribery and re-
establish trade on a reformed footing. Or else he could pursue
a strategy of exposure and attempted reform from a vantage-
point outside the firm from which he has resigned . . .

Similarly, participation in the *in vitro* technique does not
necessarily commit Alan and Tricia to consenting to experiments on *their* embryos. They could request that all the
fertilised eggs be replaced in Tricia (and take the double risk
of a multiple pregnancy or losing them all), that the spare
ones be kept in a frozen state (despite Tricia's initial revulsion
at that prospect), or that she should not be given any fertility
drugs. The clinic is unlikely to be happy with the first or third
alternatives, but it may be flexible and accede to the couple's
requests. Opposition to embryo research does not always go
hand in hand with opposition to IVF *in toto*.

On the question of nuclear deterrence, many of the different possibilities have already been canvassed in the course of
Linda and Tom's discussion. Possessing nuclear weapons with
a readiness to use them; possessing them as a bluff; possessing
them while disowning any intention to use; not possessing
them at all – all these options arose as they spoke. There are
further subtle variations one could add. Distinctions could be
made between readiness to use nuclear weapons in a first- or

second-strike capacity, or to use tactical but not strategic weapons (or vice versa). Possessing weapons while remaining unsure about whether one would or would not use them is another possibility (this is not as silly as it sounds, for it is unpredictable how those in high command would act in an actual state of emergency). Furthermore, if one is committed to disarmament, there are many different ways in which one might go about this: some favour a strictly multilateral process by which each side abandons precise equivalents in strike power at the same time, others favour a significant unilateral gesture to evoke trust and get the painfully slow process going. Unilateralism may be staged and lengthy, or it may be thoroughgoing and immediate.

This point about the variety of options usually open to us is often forgotten and needs emphasising. When confronted by an apparent dilemma, we need to be open to its complexity and manifold possibilities. We need to exercise creativity and imagination. We allow ourselves to be impaled on the horns of a dilemma all too easily.

All the same, it is understandable that the word dilemma has not been replaced. Although there are often a number of possible options, they frequently do boil down to two main ones. Bill could try to unhook himself from his painful choice, but one's initial impression at least was that none of these apparent alternatives was very promising. Tricia could undergo IVF without consenting to embryo research, but if she did not she would still have to live uneasily with the knowledge that IVF would never have reached its present sophisticated level of performance if hundreds of embryos had not first been sacrificed in perfecting the technique. It is possible to attempt a middle way between a full-blown nuclear deterrence policy and one of unilateral disarmament, but the mediatory positions are strewn with problems. Linda exposed serious difficulties that are implicit in the so-called bluff position. So often there do appear to be only two plausible alternatives, but we must not allow ourselves to be pressurised into assuming that this is always the case.

Christian Uncertainty

The situations I have described are those in which people of a whole variety of beliefs, religious or secular, Christian or non-Christian, might find themselves. And the presence or absence of Christian belief would not by itself decisively resolve the dilemmas for the individuals involved. Indeed Alan and Tricia in the first case, Bill in the second, and Linda and Tom in the third, might or might not be Christians. Nothing which they have been described as thinking, saying or doing clearly establishes that likelihood one way or the other. Along with many other moral dilemmas, the issues described are very open ones for Christians – the Christian community has not delivered a clear and uncontested verdict on any of them.

Perhaps the most one might say is that the greater the degree of moral scruple and sensitivity shown by the individuals involved, the likelier it is that this points to a Christian influence. Bill *is* probably more likely to feel unhappy about bribing an agent, Tricia to register concern about the fate of the spare embryos, Linda to be aghast even at simply threatening (without intending) a nuclear strike, if they are Christians or the products of a Christian upbringing. But that serves only as a broad generalisation. Bill may well have a Christian colleague who has no scruples about paying the bribe. Alan and Tom respectively could well lack some of the scruples harboured by Tricia and Linda while remaining Christian men of good standing and clear conscience.

When confronted by moral dilemmas, Christians are often advised to consult various sources of guidance which have, traditionally, been thought to hold authoritative status. The sources which are usually cited are the Bible, Christian tradition, the teaching of the Church (or, more accurately, churches), natural law, and the Holy Spirit. Obviously, these different sources overlap and interrelate. All, I believe, are of inestimable value; and on some issues they speak uncontroversially and with a united voice. But on many issues the testimony they give is varied or ambiguous. There are differences in emphasis, differences in starting-point, differences in reasoning process, differences in conclusion. In addition, Christians from one tradition or another vary in how much weight they put on the different sources.

Certainly there is no Christian consensus with regard to the three situations which I have outlined. *In vitro* fertilisation and nuclear deterrence are of course two twentieth-century developments on which it would be quite unreasonable to expect the Bible or Christian tradition to say something specific. The Bible and Christian tradition (which includes a natural law tradition) do handle issues which are relevant to these recent developments, notably war, deterring potential evil-doers, the status of the human embryo and the relationship between sexual activity and procreation. But on all these issues we encounter a mixed tradition; and even if it did speak with one voice, there would still be scope for argument about its application to new phenomena. And so the teaching which the churches provide on these issues to guide contemporary Christians tends to be either tentative and provisional, in which case it leaves them in a state of considerable uncertainty, or (less often now) dogmatic and definitive, in which case it tends to provoke reaction and dissent!

In this book, my prime aim is to help Christians in their state of uncertainty. Despite the problems mentioned above, I shall not be afraid to appeal to these traditional Christian sources, acknowledging that they can be interpreted in different ways, but arguing that some ways are more persuasive than others. Above all I look to the Bible with confidence. This is not to commend a simplistic use of the Bible, where a moral case is constructed simply by stringing together a collection of Biblical verses with no attention to their context, or its dissimilarity from our own. For instance, biblical condemnations of bribery nearly always have corruption in the law-courts in view, so it should not be assumed too quickly that they 'settle' Bill's business quandary.[2] What I do believe is that where the Bible is studied carefully, with close attention to detail, and applied thoughtfully, with sensitivity and imagination, it repeatedly proves its relevance to moral issues – even those of which it makes no *direct* mention. We need to consider the biblical witness in its entirety, and seek a proper balance in noting contrasting strands within it. We need to spell out the more general themes and principles to which particular blocs of ethical material or resolutions of dilemma situations in the Bible point. Above all we need to keep our minds open to a *method*, an overall line of approach which can be applied to dilemma situations in all their profusion.

There may also be some who are not Christians who have picked up this book, or with whom Christian readers are engaged in debating moral issues. Christians and non-Christians are confronted by many of the same dilemmas, and the latter as well as the former experience bewilderment and disagreement. Appeal to the Bible and other specifically Christian sources of authority may carry little weight with them. But it may still be possible to commend to them an approach which emerges from these sources as reasonable and constructive; in short, I remain hopeful that I may be able to persuade a non-Christian reader some of the way along the road with me. We may be able to agree on some of the principles which should underlie moral decision-making, though in the majority of cases the principle will be reinforced by a specifically theological consideration.[3] The non-Christian may respect the principle, but not give it as much force as I would because of this additional theological factor.

Consequences and Rules

One final reflection on the different dilemmas described leads straight on to a major preoccupation of this book. Many moral dilemmas are, consciously or unconsciously, resolved by an underlying philosophical presumption which exists in the mind of the participant. For some people an evaluation of the likely *consequences* is what sways them in one direction or the other. For others it is more important that they stick to a well-established *rule* which carries considerable moral weight for them.

When discussing the fact that moral decisions can have crucial effects on people, the evaluation of consequences inevitably comes into play. If Bill allows simply consideration of consequences to govern his thinking, he will almost certainly pay the bribe – because the consequence of 15,000 redundancies is a most unpleasant prospect. The consequence of bringing relief to bone-marrow patients, as well as fulfilling their own desire to have children, may sway the decision of Alan and Tricia. The consequences of Russia's holding the world at ransom leads many, like Tom, reluctantly to support nuclear deterrence – though others would argue that by possessing nuclear weapons ourselves we make their eventual use more likely. The oft-asked question 'Would you rather be red than dead?' then raises the question of which of two undesirable consequences we find most undesirable!

There are clearly problems with a purely consequential method of resolving dilemmas – the most obvious being that consequences are often difficult to forecast accurately, and different answers may be arrived at depending on whether short-term or long-term consequences are given greater prominence. Of these I shall say more in a later chapter. In the face of these difficulties, the person who favours the rule-based approach is inclined to say: 'Never mind the consequences, unpredictable and imponderable as these are. Simply be content to do the right thing.' And often, though not always, this will mean *not* being prepared to do something, i.e., steering clear of anything that is morally dubious. So Bill, if he followed this approach, would not be prepared to pay the bribe; Tricia, with her respect for the embryo, would not be prepared to submit to IVF; Linda, in drafting party policy, would not be prepared under any circumstances to support retention of an intrinsically immoral weapon. For the consequentialist, the end can and does justify the means, nasty and regrettable though these often may be. For the person who sticks to rules, the end does not justify the means. The purity of one's means matters, and if unfortunate ends sometimes result through abiding by one's principles, that's just too bad. Being moral involves making sacrifices – for oneself and others. The consequentialist would then retort that it is making sacrifices on behalf of other people that casts doubt on whether the rule-based approach is as moral as it claims.

Throughout Christian history, throughout the overlapping but distinguishable history of Western moral thought, there has been a debate going on as to which of these two approaches is right. The debate has not always been explicit, it has often carried on below the surface of argument, and it has been couched in a variety of moral language, but it has been there all the same. It does not exhaust the categories of moral thought, and it can be argued that neither of the two approaches is satisfactory, and that we ought to look for a third approach which bypasses the problems of both. I shall look at some of the alternative approaches suggested in Chapter 6. Although I believe that these alternatives have important things to contribute, I do not believe that they succeed in bypassing the two mainstream approaches which I have outlined; and therefore I make no apology for conducting my analysis of moral dilemmas mainly in terms of these two approaches.

Notes

1 Another striking example of this attitude was seen during a TV interview of Foreign Office minister Timothy Renton, when questioned about British support for the US air attacks on Libya. He said that he preferred not to think of this as a moral question.
2 See e.g., Exodus 23:8, Deuteronomy 16:19, or Amos 5:12.
3 For instance, the widely accepted conviction that human beings possess dignity and deserve respect is reinforced – for the Christian – by the belief that God has made man in his own image. I develop this theme later in the book.

2

TWO ETHICAL THEORIES

The Consequentialist View

There is little doubt that in the modern, increasingly secularised West, the consequentialist approach to moral decision-making has become increasingly dominant. This does not of course mean that rules have now been discounted, or dispensed with. But life has become less governed by rules, certainly by absolute rules; one could say that the status of many rules has been relativised. And whenever a case is being made for keeping a rule or ignoring it, the likelihood is that evaluation of consequences will feature prominently, if not exclusively, in the argument.

Some years ago, when he was leader of the Conservative Party, I recall that Edward Heath was asked on a television interview whether he was in favour of the restoration of capital punishment. His reply was that while he could see plausible arguments for and against, the main consideration for him was whether the presence or absence of the death penalty could be shown to have a significant effect on the numbers of murders committed. If abolition of capital punishment could clearly be shown to have led to an increase in the number of murders, he was prepared to support its restoration; if the figures did not show this or were ambiguous, he was against restoration. Consequences – at that time, at any rate – were the decisive criterion for him on this issue.

Talk of consequences inevitably raises the questions: 'What sort of consequences?' 'What are to count as good consequences and what as bad?' The philosophical idea which, implicitly or explicitly, has dominated consequentialist thinking in the West is Utilitarianism. According to this school of thought, consequences should be calculated in terms of utility, or usefulness. But again we have to ask a further question: 'What sort of usefulness?' and the answer given is in terms of whether actions produce pain or pleasure, suffering or happiness.

Bentham

Utilitarianism in one form or another has been around for a long time, but as a clearly and consciously articulated philosophy it is reckoned to have started with Jeremy Bentham (1748–1832). Bentham reacted strongly against the rule-based morality of his age by which certain actions were considered to be *intrinsically* right or wrong. He dismissed the concepts which were used to justify such thinking (like 'man's moral sense', 'eternal and immutable rules of right', or 'a law of nature') as empty and meaningless. To him they represented an evasion of human responsibility to provide a single, scientifically objective standard of morality.

Bentham's *An Introduction to the Principles of Morals and Legislation* begins thus:

> Nature has placed mankind under the governance of two sovereign masters, pain and pleasure. It is for them alone to point out what we ought to do, as well as to determine what we shall do.[1]

Bentham's basic argument is that whether we intend to or not, we all invariably seek to maximise our pleasure and minimise our pain; and because this is our central preoccupation it is misguided and futile to base an ethical system on any other principle. Even when man thinks that he is seeking other goals, he is really seeking his own happiness or satisfaction. Presumably the miser or martyr is simply seeking happiness in some rather unusual ways. Bentham then moves swiftly from the starting-point that we all desire our own happiness to the premise that we should wish to see happiness distributed as widely as possible, so that the guiding goal of Utilitarianism is not a maximising of individual pleasure, but the attainment of the greatest possible amount of happiness for the greatest possible number of people. The task of a country's laws, therefore, is to increase the likelihood of achieving this – hopefully making individual happiness coincide with universal happiness as much as possible.

Bentham devised the idea of a hedonic calculus – a pleasure-calculator! – listing all the criteria of pleasure which should be taken into account when assessing the consequences of an action, or for that matter a piece of legislation. He thought that pleasure could be calculated in terms of its intensity, duration, degree of certainty that it will occur, how soon it will occur, its capacity to engender further pleasure, how free it is of accompanying pains, and how many people it affects. Pains should then be calculated in like manner. It is unlikely that Bentham thought that *exact* calculation of future effects could be calculated in this way. He concedes: 'It is not to be expected that this process should be strictly pursued previously to every moral judgment, or to every legislative or judicial operation'.[2] But he thought that the calculus gave a good general outline, and should always be kept in view.

Bentham went on to specify the things which, in his view, bring pleasure and pain. He lists 14 'simple' pleasures (e.g., the senses, wealth, skill, friendship) which he then subdivides to provide further detail. Twelve pains are listed in the same way. Some things, like the senses, feature in both lists, because they are clearly double-edged.

Bentham was adamant that all types of pleasure and pain could be measured on the same scale. In other words, they can be compared *quantitatively* because there is no *qualitative* difference between them. He once said that 'quantity of pleasure being equal, push-pin is as good as poetry'.[3] Actually Bentham had little time for poetry, criticising it as misrepresentation (one can see that it ran counter to his calculating outlook) and this is one area where John Stuart Mill, the most important of his utilitarian successors, parted company with him.

Mill

Mill (1806–73) was the son of James Mill, a friend of Bentham, and came under the latter's influence a great deal as a boy. This influence prompted a dual response of loyalty and reaction on Mill's part. Alasdair MacIntyre has commented:

> Mill's whole tenor of thought is that of a utilitarian who cannot avoid any of the difficulties which this doctrine raises, but who cannot conceive of abandoning this doctrine either.[4]

Thus Mill applauded Bentham's questioning spirit, which had done much to break down the static conservatism of his day, and which had led to important reforms in the parliamentary and penal systems. He agreed with Bentham in his basic view that the rightness of actions should be judged according to whether they contributed to the general happiness, not only indeed of mankind, 'but, so far as the nature of things admits, to the whole sentient creation'.[5] However, he produced a more sophisticated version of Utilitarianism. He found Bentham 'one-eyed' in a number of respects. Thus Mill, who was lifted from a period of deep depression by his discovery of Wordsworth, appreciated poetry and more generally the arts in a way that Bentham never did. He emphasised the pleasure of freedom (a quality surprisingly missing from Bentham's list) and wrote an important essay 'On Liberty'.[6] Most importantly, his method of calculating pleasures was not merely quantitative. He regarded intellectual pleasures as qualitatively superior to physical ones, arguing that the pleasures of the intellect, the imagination and a clear conscience are more valuable and desirable than those of man's animal nature.

> It is better to be a human being dissatisfied than a pig satisfied; better to be Socrates dissatisfied than a fool satisfied. And if the fool or the pig are of a different opinion, it is because they only know their side of the question.[7]

He is assuming that the educated person, who has been both educated and uneducated, who has experienced the pleasures of both body and mind, would definitely opt for the pleasures associated with his education. Problems and pains the latter may also bring, but the benefits, in Mill's view, more than compensate. Indeed, they are such as to rank on a different qualitative scale altogether.

The Scene Today

The thinking of both Bentham and Mill is open to question at many points. Philosophers both in their day and since have exposed various obscurities and non sequiturs. I shall consider some of these myself at a later stage. In the forms in which they expounded it, Utilitarianism is clearly inadequate, and it is fashionable in some quarters to debunk it wholesale. All I wish to emphasise at present is its abiding significance. On the philosophical scene its star has risen, fallen and experienced a partial resurrection. On the social and political scene it has made much steadier progress. In raising questions about whether people benefit and how many people benefit from a particular practice or institution, the utilitarian spirit has waged war on selfish privilege and inefficient bureaucracy. It has led to an expansion and wider distribution of social, medical, educational and many other services which we now take for granted. Of course, happiness is a difficult thing to evaluate on an overall graph, and individuals do discover their pleasures in different ways, some refusing what others assume are good for them, but in many areas there is a working consensus about what makes for a happier life and what doesn't. The spread of utilitarian ideas seems to have instilled into the British people at least a greater sense of urgency about reducing human misery. For this it surely deserves credit.

Utilitarian thinking is perhaps most explicit today when we talk of costs-benefits analysis. Like Bentham, we recognise that some courses of action can bring pleasure *and* pain, desirable consequences and undesirable ones. Like him, we attempt to analyse the costs and the benefits, whether we are contemplating the effects of closing a school, resiting a factory, or redistributing resources in the health service. Again and again we try to arrange things so that human happiness is maximised or, where circumstances dictate for the worse, so that human suffering is minimised.

Nevertheless, it would be quite misleading to say that all moral judgments are of this costs-benefits type. Consequentialist thinking in general and utilitarian assumptions in particular are widespread, but they do not rule the roost completely. There is another sort of moral language in use which does not speak principally, if at all, in terms of consequences. Another leading politician who was interviewed in the context of a more recent parliamentary debate on the restoration of capital punishment is Roy Hattersley. Having briefly discussed consequential considerations, he announced that he had a more fundamental objection to capital punishment, one of 'principle'. This amounted to the fact that the practice was in his view *barbaric*, an affront to civilised values.

While Mr Hattersley did not spell out the content of his understanding of 'barbaric' in any detail, it was clear that he meant something other than that hanging people had undesirable consequences. Clearly he found something spine-chilling and offensive in the very act of killing someone in this cold-blooded way. The thought of the act appeared to provoke in him an intuitive reaction of 'that's disgusting!'. While we may or may not concur with this particular judgment of Mr Hattersley's, all of us find ourselves reacting in a similar way over one type of action or another.

Another striking feature about the use of language in contemporary moral discussion is the readiness with which people appeal to their *rights*. It is not always clear what they mean (or that they themselves know what they mean) when they speak of rights, and the fact that these rights are sometimes asserted to be 'self-evident' makes one wonder how secure is the ground on which they are claimed. The rights to life, liberty and estate claimed by Locke and echoed by the American founding fathers have been supplemented of late in ever increasing detail.[8] The 'right' to take advantage of the new artificial techniques for creating children has been

claimed not only by infertile married couples (and incidentally infertile unmarried couples), but also by some single
people and homosexual couples of both sexes. However, the
connected facts that talk of human rights can be carried to
ridiculous extremes and that the arguments used to support
specific rights are often non-existent or weak should not lead
us to dismiss the concept *per se* as a piece of self-delusory
nonsense. There is a rationale behind the language of rights,
and it comprises something different from 'you have the duty
to make me as happy as possible' (in other words, it is not
simply the other side of Utilitarianism). Asserting my human
rights reflects a deeply-felt conviction that there is something
endemic to my humanity which gives me a claim to be treated
in a certain sort of way, and with that a claim not to be treated
in other sorts of way. At its very least, I have a right to live,
positively speaking, and a right not to be killed, negatively
speaking. This claim appears to be based on something
special about human beings. Such a view clearly diverges
from a philosophy based solely on feelings of happiness,
which animals appear to experience as well as humans, so that
their sensations might feature as equally significant on a
hedonic calculus.

The Deontological View

Specific rules about how human beings should and should not
be treated often flow from recognition of human rights. And
though Utilitarianism is not incompatible with strongly-held
rules, the language of rights tends to invest these rules with a
greater aura of inviolability. Because the human person is
regarded in a special light – even, in some versions, as
someone *sacred* – anything which might be construed as
'violating' him is to be avoided at all costs. According to this
way of thinking, ethics should be construed not in consequentialist terms but deontological ones. The word *deontology*
is derived from the Greek for necessary ('what ought
to be'). Some states of being simply ought to be, others
ought not. The overriding stress is on doing one's *duty*.

Certain attitudes and actions invariably constitute one's duty; they find expression in laws (e.g., do not commit adultery), principles (faithfulness in marriage) or institutions (marriage itself). Violation of these laws, principles or institutions would amount to dereliction of one's duty. As George Eliot once said when walking in the Fellows' Garden of Trinity College, Cambridge, duty is 'peremptory and absolute'.[9]

Those who support this line of ethical thought do not entirely agree on the content of these overriding duties. Actions which have been regarded as unthinkable at certain times and in certain places have been viewed in a far more tolerant light centuries on or centuries back. The notion of possessing another human person, which is fundamental to the institution of slavery, is as abhorrent to twentieth-century Westerners as it was inoffensive to most of our forefathers of the eighteenth century. A brilliant ethical thinker like Aristotle was able to relegate slaves to the category of non-person. Nevertheless, cultural relativity can be exaggerated. If we take four of the prohibitions which appear in that corner-stone of the Judaeo-Christian moral heritage, the ten commandments, 'do not murder', 'do not commit adultery', 'do not steal', and 'do not commit false witness', it is striking how often these crop up in one culture after another.[10] They may be defined in different ways, and they may be enforced with varying degrees of rigour, but the widespread respect for human life, marriage, property and truthfulness which they indicate is surely significant. They tend to feature prominently in lists of prohibited actions detailed by thinkers of a deontological type. So while there is certainly scope for argument about how fundamental some rules are, others appear to be assured of a central place.

However, the rule-based approach to ethics does not only prompt the question: 'What are these things which always constitute one's duty?' It also invites the query: 'How do we *know* that certain things are always our duty?' Put another way, what is the basis for describing a practice as barbaric, or for claiming a human right? This question is answered in different ways by different writers.

The Will of God

First of all, there are some religious thinkers (and here I am thinking of strands within Judaism and Islam as well as Christianity) who would reply simply in terms of certain attitudes and actions being the revealed will of God. God has laid down his laws, and it is not for human beings to argue with them. Often we can perceive something of the purpose behind these laws (we can see, for instance, that observation of the commandments cited above is likely to increase people's capacity to get on with each other), but even where we cannot, we should be content simply to abide by our God-given duty. The underlying assumption is that God is good and God knows best.

Intuition

Second, there is a school of thought which makes little or no attempt to answer the question. Some thinkers argue that moral duties are discerned directly by human *intuition*, a faculty which bypasses the normal reasoning processes. Actions which constitute one's duty may indeed make for human welfare and add to human happiness, but as a leading intuitionist philosopher, W. D. Ross, put it, 'that is not the whole truth'.[11] A widely recognised duty like keeping promises wields a force and authority quite independent of consequential considerations. It is impossible to *prove* why actions like keeping promises constitute such an inviolable duty, but our intuitions tell us that this is in fact the case. Goodness and rightness are 'givens'; they are apprehended directly in a way comparable to e.g., the yellowness of a daffodil or the three-sidedness of a triangle.[12] We *know* that daffodils are yellow; we know that we should keep our promises. These are not matters open to proof or disproof. The founding fathers appear to have been implying something similar when they claimed that certain rights are self-evident.

Reason – and Kant

It is understandable that both the first and second answers to the question concerning the ground of our duty leave the consequentialist type of thinker baffled and irritated. He has asked for an answer and been given no answer or, as he sees it, only an answer which appeals to a higher authority: the will of God in one case, intuition in the other. But there is a third sort of answer which attempts to supply rather more in the way of solid reasons. This answer seeks to establish rational grounds for the assertion of particular duties. The foremost thinker of this type has been the great German Enlightenment philosopher, Immanuel Kant (1724–1804).

Kant made a distinction between two types of moral statement, hypothetical imperatives and categorical imperatives. 'You ought to deal honestly as a tradesman, otherwise you will gain a bad reputation' is an example of what he meant by a hypothetical imperative. In essence it says: *if* you do (or don't do) such a thing, you will regret the consequences. The motive appealed to is one of *prudence*. In Kant's view, a prudential consideration amounted to a selfish inclination, and made the motive less than pure. In contrast, categorical imperatives are statements which do not depend on such motives. They appeal to disinterested goodwill. They are purely rational.

Moral statements can be tested as to their categorical nature in two different ways. The first is whether they pass the test of *universalisability*:

> Act only according to that maxim by which you can at the same time will that it should become a universal law.[13]

In other words, we should act only in a way in which we can consistently wish all other people to behave. This will root out our all-too-human tendency to make special exceptions for ourselves. Kant takes the example of whether in a difficult situation it could be right to make a promise with an intention not to keep it. He says that when one then asks: 'Can I will that everyone in a similar situation would do the same?',

I immediately see that I could will the lie but not a universal law to lie. For with such a law there would be no promises at all, inasmuch as it would be futile to make a pretense at my intention in regard to future actions to those who would not believe this pretense, or – if they over-hastily did so – who would pay me back in my own coin. Thus my maxim would necessarily destroy itself as soon as it was made a universal law.[14]

Kant uses similar arguments to justify certain other 'universal' duties, such as repaying borrowed money.

One's initial impression is that Kant's *second* formulation of the categorical imperative has little to do with the first. This runs:

Act so that you treat humanity, whether in your own person or in that of another, always as an end and never as a means only.[15]

This is an extremely important principle, the intention and effect of which is to safeguard individual human dignity. If one has sexual intercourse with another person, it is possible – and objectionable – to use that person simply as a means to satisfy one's desires or ease one's frustrations. Probably those elements will be present in any act of sexual intercourse, but if one's intention is also to express love to that person, considering her interests and welfare as well as one's own, the act assumes a different – and morally defensible – character.[16] The principle comes into play (and often runs counter to utilitarian calculations) when treating one or some individuals as means appears to offer the prospect of bringing benefit to a large number of individuals. If embryos are counted as part of humanity, then Kant's principle protects them from being used *simply* as research fodder for the good of other people.

Kant's two apparently unconnected formulations of the categorical imperative seem to be united by the underlying concept of man as a rational being. It is man's reason which gives him his dignity, and it is man's reason to which one is appealing in insisting that people should think about situations in a universal context, not simply a local or individual one. Although Kant was well aware that human beings frequently act from baser instincts, he treasured an impressive ideal of humanity using reason impartially – and possessing great dignity because of that.

What follows is only a preliminary analysis of these two contrasting ways of thinking, the consequentialist and the deontological. But in it I seek to establish two crucial points. The first is that both types of thinker, the consequentialist and the deontologist, experience great difficulty in sticking consistently to one type of thought. Without usually realising it, each borrows from the other in a substantial and significant way. There is also a greater degree of convergence between the two approaches in *practice* (i.e., in terms of the practical guidance for action which they provide) than one might superficially have expected from the differences in *theory*. The second point is that both approaches, if they *are* pursued rigorously and consistently, end up with morally unacceptable conclusions. In short, both consequentialism and deontology on their own are inadequate and undesirable.

Inconsistencies

Alert readers may have spotted points where neither school of thought is internally consistent. Bentham and Mill both make a big logical jump from their starting-point, that human beings seek individual happiness, to the linchpin of their system, that human beings ought to support what makes for happiness in general. They assume that we should treat other people's desire for happiness as counting just as much, on a quantitative scale, as our own. But hidden behind this assumption seems to be the presupposition that human beings should be treated impartially, i.e., I have a duty to respect their desire for happiness just as much as I heed mine. Yet this presupposition does not follow from the utilitarian starting-point, one of individual hedonism; not all single-minded pleasure-seekers are utilitarians, and though we may justly accuse them of selfishness, it is not clear that we can charge them with logical inconsistency. The utilitarians' concern for impartial treatment seems rather to flow from a conviction that *beneficence* – seeking the welfare of others – is a fundamental human duty, and one suspects that the roots of this conviction are to be traced either to intuition or religious belief. Utilitarianism is thus a more complex philosophy than its leading spokesmen have realised.

A similar point emerges from Mill's attempt to supplement Bentham's quantitative distinctions between pleasures with qualitative ones. This *sounds* like a more sophisticated and satisfactory version of Utilitarianism; in fact it creates more problems than it solves. The philosopher G. E. Moore showed why.[17] When Mill said that some pleasures are more valuable and desirable than others because of their superior quality, this must mean one of two things. One is that 'superior in quality' means having *more* of the property which is common to all pleasures. If Mill meant that, he was still using a quantitative notion: 'more' measures quantity. The other, more likely, interpretation is that Mill meant that some things are intrinsically *better* than others, i.e., it is better to retain one's noble character, love of liberty and appreciation of aesthetic and intellectual pursuits, even if one might be happier in a state of addiction to 'inferior pleasures'. But if Mill meant that, he was actually abandoning the utilitarian principle. Mill actually appears to have felt *called* to follow the path of an educated aesthete – just as a Christian might say he feels called to be a disciple of Jesus – irrespective of the sacrifice of pleasures this involves. His talk of quality indicates that a higher criterion than happiness or pleasure is being called into play.

When we turn to the most famous exponent of the deontological view, Kant, his debt to the viewpoint he is attacking is more obvious still. Kant's reasons for affirming the universality of certain laws clearly take consequences into account. His claim to distinguish categorical imperatives from hypothetical ones breaks down. If breaking promises became a universal habit the result would be a loss of trust in each other's word: this is nothing if not a prudential consideration. Kant does not even limit himself to describing the undesirable *general* consequence of social chaos, but laments the effects of this on one's own person: 'they would pay me back in my own coin'. When the deontologist ventures beyond the protection of divine revelation or intuition and tries to establish plausible reasons why certain things should or shouldn't be done, it appears to be impossible not to appeal to favourable or unfavourable consequences at some point in the argument.

Convergence

It appears, therefore, as if neither type of thought can survive without the other. There is a crucial area of overlap. And although differences between the two approaches do tend to make for divergence in conclusion with regard to the most difficult cases of moral dilemma, they frequently point in the same direction when it comes to commonplace, everyday morality. Driving a car when drunk, for instance, stands condemned both as a dereliction of duty, and for the danger it poses to life and limb. It is easy to see that the ethical maxims which have stood the test of time are those which, generally speaking, produce desirable consequences. The deontologist will want to say that is not the only reason for abiding by them; the consequentialist will be quite content to say that it is; but either way they are likely to agree that murder, rape and treachery are wrong, and that treating our fellow-humans with kindness and respect is right.

Indeed, there is one version of Utilitarianism which regards basic moral rules as every bit as binding as do Kant and the intuitionists. Here we must take note of a distinction which can be made between act-utilitarians and rule-utilitarians. An act-utilitarian seeks to evaluate each act by the extent to which it will contribute to overall happiness. He will regard such actions as stealing, breaking promises, or killing the innocent as wrong in almost all cases, but he will probably think that they might be justified in some exceptional circumstances. The peculiarity of the circumstance is such that breaking the conventional rule is likely to maximise happiness rather than the reverse. The rule-utilitarian may well concede this, but still feels it is better to adhere to the rules even in this peculiar circumstance. This is because he feels that sticking by the rules consistently is likely to boost the overall quota of happiness in the long-term. Once one starts admitting that these rules can be broken, one is liable – through personal weakness or because of poor judgment – to consent to their violation in many situations where things would not work out well by a utilitarian yardstick. Therefore, although this will prove unjust to particular individuals and be inappropriate to particular situations seen *in isolation*, it is better to remain loyal to a rule which generally does serve the interests of humanity. So a rule-utilitarian *might*, for example, support a strict divorce law, recognising that some individuals who are trapped in unhappy marriages suffer a great deal of misery thereby, but believing that the floodgates are opened to much more human misery and much less overall happiness if the law is loosened.[18]

John Stuart Mill was a man of sensitive conscience; it is obvious from his writings that he has a strong temperamental aversion to violating any of the conventional standards of right and wrong. He speaks glowingly of the importance of telling the truth, and warns firmly against temptations to deviate from the truth for reasons of personal expediency. However, this at least was a rule which he thought allowed of occasional exceptions:

> the chief of which is when the withholding of some fact (as of information from a malefactor, or of bad news from a person dangerously ill) would save an individual (especially an individual other than oneself) from great and unmerited evil, and when the withholding can only be effected by denial.[19]

Interestingly, Mill claims that such exceptions would be acknowledged by all moralists, but in this he was mistaken, because Kant explicitly considered the first situation and judged that lying would still be wrong. It is to the *reductio ad absurdum* of both the rule-based and the consequence-based approaches that I now turn.

Follies

Kant wrote an essay entitled, 'On a Supposed Right to Tell Lies from Benevolent Motives'.[20] In it he poses the dilemma of what we should do if a murderer asks whether our friend, of whom he is in pursuit, has taken refuge in our house (he has). Kant claims that the duty – established by the universal-isability test – to tell the truth in all situations still applies in this instance. He also (confirming the irony I noted earlier!) brings in a prudential consideration. If the householder lies and turns the murderer away, he might run into his intended victim who is at that moment escaping from the house. In that case, the householder would both be guilty of lying and, in Kant's view, bear partial responsibility for the murder.

Kant's example may appear far-fetched, but doubtless in violent parts of society this sort of scenario actually happens. Citizens in occupied Holland and other countries who shel-tered refugee Jews were faced with an equivalent type of situation when Nazi soldiers arrived on their doorstep asking after them. Although concealing their presence obviously exposed the householders to personal danger, if the Jews hiding in their secret rooms were discovered, even the most conventional and law-abiding among them do not seem to have hesitated to lie. (One thinks of the father of Corrie ten Boom, made famous through the book and film, *The Hiding Place*.) And Mill is not *far* wide of the mark when he says that moral thinkers have been united in their judgment on this sort of case – a judgment different from that of Kant.

What the situation described by Kant confronts us with is the problem of a conflict of duties. The normal duty to tell the truth here comes into conflict with the duty (also normally recognised) to try to save life. On most people's scaling of values, the duty to preserve life overrides the duty to tell the truth. Telling the truth is an excellent general rule, but Kant's mistake was to universalise the rule in that general state. One could perfectly well have a universal rule about truth-telling which said, 'Always tell the truth except . . .' and circum-stances in which it is necessary to lie to prevent unjustified killing might constitute a clearly identified exception.

If Kant's famous example shows the deontological approach at its most extreme and most vulnerable, it isn't difficult to imagine cases where thoroughgoing utilitarians might justify actions which are morally outrageous. Let us consider an all-too-familiar situation: a bomb has gone off in a crowded pub, leaving fifteen people dead and fifty injured. A well-known terrorist organisation claims responsibility. A number of its members live close to the scene of the incident. The local police try to interview them, and intercept three men at the nearest railway station as they are seeking to leave town. This and other bits of circumstantial evidence suggest that these are the terrorists responsible for the bombing. In such a situation the police experience tremendous public pressure to find the culprits and bring them to justice as quickly as possible. Although they harbour doubts as to whether the three arrested men really are the bombers, the detectives leading the case bring charges against them. The trial is conducted in an emotive atmosphere, and the three men – who are actually innocent – are jailed for life, the judge's firm recommendation being that 'life really means life'. No more terrorist acts in that town ensue.

A couple of years after the trial, with the convicted men still maintaining their innocence, questions begin to be asked about whether justice has really been done. An appeal is lodged, and in turn dismissed, by a leading judge. He argues that this appeal cannot be allowed to succeed, because if it did it would cause great loss of public confidence in both the police force and the judiciary system. While admitting that the evidence against the three men was somewhat thin, the judge regarded the public's level of satisfaction and sense of security as the paramount considerations.[21]

An out-and-out utilitarian could hardly object to what has happened in this case. True, the three imprisoned individuals were not in fact guilty of this particular crime. But they were members of a notorious organisation, and could be presumed to harbour intentions likely to take violent effect sooner or later; the severe punishment which has been meted out appears to have had the effect of deterring the real perpetrators of the crime from repeating it; and the public does feel much more secure – and much more 'avenged' – because individuals have been found to bear the blame.

Yet whatever the utilitarian pay-off, framing citizens innocent of the particular offence of which they are being accused is still an action quite abhorrent to the majority of people (once they are convinced that it is happening). A case like this touches a raw nerve which is frequently exposed by dilemma situations. What if a particular course of action means that blatant injustice is being done to one or more specific individuals? Of course, the content of the notion of 'justice' needs to be unpacked; but we all know – even the detectives and the judge, deep down, would probably agree – that what has happened to these three men is not just. However committed they may be to the aims and methods of the terrorist organisation, they do not deserve to receive life imprisonment for crimes which they have not committed. Granted that the police were under tremendous pressure, and that the fears which the judge harboured were realistic, they still had a duty to ensure that these men were not convicted on unsatisfactory evidence. They had a responsibility to try to unearth the real truth about the crime – and find the people actually responsible.

Utilitarianism thus has a tendency to justify the reaching of desirable ends by morally unacceptable means. Costly though it may be in terms of time, money or effort, there can be a moral obligation to seek the solution of problems by other means. Tying babies to our car bumpers might make us all drive much more slowly, and thereby reduce the number of traffic fatalities very considerably, but that does not make it acceptable.[22] It would be cruel and potentially lethal to the babies involved, and it is up to us to find alternative ways of making motoring a safer business.

In view of the unpalatability of both the consequentialist and deontological approaches when taken to their logical extreme, it is not surprising that most moral thinkers avoid these extremes, preferring a modified version of either or some sort of mediatory position. Henry Sidgwick, professor of moral philosophy at Cambridge from 1883 to 1900, sought to reconcile Utilitarianism and Intuitionism. R. M. Hare, holder of a similar post at Oxford since 1966, has combined a Kantian stress on universal prescriptions with a utilitarian concern to maximise satisfaction.[23] But enough has been said for the moment about the philosophers. What of the Christian contribution to this debate, of which little has been said so far? Do Christians believe in absolute rules, or do they place a premium on human happiness? What type of moral thinking is reflected in the pages of the Bible? It is to that question that I now turn.

Notes

1 These are the opening words of Bentham's *An Introduction to the Principles of Morals and Legislation*. Chs I–V may conveniently be found in John Stuart Mill, *Utilitarianism*, Collins Fontana, 1962, p. 33.

2 *Op. cit.*, p. 66.

3 John Stuart Mill quotes Bentham as saying this in his essay 'Bentham', *Utilitarianism*, p. 123.

4 Alasdair MacIntyre, *A Short History of Ethics*, Macmillan, 1966, p. 235.

5 John Stuart Mill, *Utilitarianism*, p. 263.

6 This is also included in the Fontana collection *Utilitarianism*.

7 *Op. cit.*, p. 260.

8 E.g., the *United Nations Universal Declaration of Human Rights* runs to thirty articles.

9 This comment is cited by Lionel Trilling in *Sincerity and Authenticity*, Oxford University Press, 1972, p. 118.

10 In this connection, C. S. Lewis once spoke of 'the triumphant monotony of the same indispensable platitudes which meet us in culture after culture'.

11 W. D. Ross, *The Right and the Good*, Clarendon Press, Oxford, 1930, p. 39.

12 These were illustrations used by the intuitionist philosophers G. E. Moore and H. A. Prichard respectively. But Moore was a curious mixture: he believed that the *good* was known intuitively but that a *right* course of action was a matter for utilitarian calculation.

13 Immanuel Kant, 'Foundations of the Metaphysics of Morals', *Critique of Practical Reason and Other Writings in Moral Philosophy* (ed. Lewis W. Beck), University of Chicago Press, 1949, p. 80.

14 *Op. cit.*, p. 64.

15 *Op. cit.*, p. 87.

16   For further elaboration of this see pp. 115–7.
17   G. E. Moore, *Principia Ethica*, Cambridge University Press, 1903, pp. 78–9.
18   It is a debatable question whether in Britain the passing of the 1969 Divorce Reform Act has led to that.
19   John Stuart Mill, *Utilitarianism*, pp. 274–5.
20   *Critique of Practical Reason and Other Writings in Moral Philosophy*, pp. 346–50.
21   What I have described is, of course, a thinly disguised account of what some people believe to have happened in the case of the 1974 Birmingham pub bombing. I am in no position to say whether those convicted in that case were in fact innocent. What *is* clearly questionable is whether they have been shown to be guilty.
22   I have borrowed this example from Daniel Maguire, *The Moral Choice*, Winston Press, Indianapolis, 1979, pp. 156–7.
23   See Hare's books *The Language of Morals*, Oxford University Press, 1952; *Freedom and Reason*, OUP, 1963; *Moral Thinking*, OUP, 1981.

3

BACK TO THE BIBLE

In an essay entitled 'Morality: Religious and Secular', first published in 1961, the humanist philosopher P. H. Nowell-Smith criticised Christian morality as essentially infantile.[1] He thought that the underlying theory (though not necessarily the practice) of Christian morality is similar to the type of moral thinking found in children between the ages of 5 and 9. This is a thinking which is based on rules, rules that are regarded as sacred and inviolable; the authority of the rules is grounded in the authority of the teacher (parents in the case of children, God in the case of Christians); and neither questioning about the purpose of the rules nor flexibility in the application of the rules are seen as permissible. Nowell-Smith, in contrast, favoured a type of moral thinking which set much less store by rules, which freed human beings to decide moral issues for themselves rather than be dependent on others, and which aimed at increasing human satisfaction in an integrated sort of way.

In characterising Christian morality as he did, Nowell-Smith argued that Christianity is essentially Hebrew in type. He thought that it reflects the strongly deontological view of morality found in the Old Testament. He described the New Testament as less deontological in character, but obviously considered that Christians have lived more according to the old covenant than the new. Nowell-Smith admitted that these were oversimplifications, but was clearly prepared to stick by them as broad generalisations.

In a recent major study, Thomas W. Ogletree, Professor of

Theological Ethics at Drew University in New Jersey, evaluates Biblical materials in terms of different ethical approaches in more detail.[2] The three perspectives which he considers are the deontological, the consequentialist and the perfectionist. I shall say more about what is meant by the perfectionist perspective in due course. He concludes that deontology is more to the fore in the Old Testament, perfectionism is more prominent in the New (though the deontological component is still strong there), and consequentialism is little in evidence in either. Nowell-Smith and Ogletree would certainly appear to agree, then, as far as the Old Testament is concerned. In fact, they use the word 'deontology' in slightly different senses. Nowell-Smith understands by it reliance on an authority which is not called to justify its commands. Ogletree detects *reasons* behind the commands which are codified in unalterable rules, namely, the need to provide a context of security and mutual respect within which people can interrelate. He draws heavily on Kant for his perception of a deontological approach and, as we have seen, Kant's reasons for declaring certain rules universal do take consequences into account.

In this chapter I shall argue that the Bible includes a wide diversity of moral reasoning. Consequential considerations are not as rare as either Nowell-Smith, of the Old Testament, or Ogletree, of both parts of the Bible, allege. I shall analyse representative sections of ethical material in terms of these different types of approach, and go on to suggest distinctive and illuminating features which emerge from the Biblical picture.

Deontology in the Old Testament

As we come to consider the nature of the ethical material in the Old Testament, the great profusion of statements which take the form of divine commands is a very striking feature. It has been calculated that there are 613 commands in the Mosaic law – 248 prescriptions and 365 prohibitions. They include laws of many different types: criminal, civil, family,

cultic and charitable.[3] *Charitable* law is not law at all in a
judicial sense: what I have in mind here are the many instructions to act protectively, generously and sensitively towards
poor or vulnerable people. These laws encompass an extraordinary variety of situations, and often the different types
are muddled up in a seemingly bizarre manner. Thus in
Leviticus the seminal command 'Love your neighbour as
yourself' is followed by the apparently trivial and obscure
'You shall not let your cattle breed with a different kind; you
shall not sow your field with two kinds of seed; nor shall there
come upon you a garment of cloth made of two kinds of stuff'
(19:18–19).

This is an example of a command where the rationale is not
given and is difficult to guess. But often reasons are given,
albeit in a kind of shorthand. For instance, a whole variety of
female conditions, skin diseases, bodily discharges and sexual
practices are described as *ritually unclean*, implying that they
are either forbidden or that those affected by them require
purification. Sometimes we can understand why the particular condition or action carried connotations of uncleanness,
but not always. The mystery is perhaps greatest in relation to
animals, as to why they either are or are not labelled as
unclean: locusts, crickets and grasshoppers pass the test, as do
winged insects that hop, but not any other winged insects,
with special reference to those that crawl! (Lev. 11:20–3).

A word which often seems to serve as a synonym for
unclean in these cultic passages is *abomination*. It suggests
something that is utterly loathsome to God. But this word is
used in a wider context than that of ritual uncleanness. A
notable example is the command to use 'honest' weights and
measures. Those who act dishonestly are 'an abomination to
the Lord your God' (Deut. 25:16).

Just as it appears to be considered self-evident what the
Lord hates, so positive commands are frequently explained
by a simple reference to God's character and the nature of his
actions in the past:

You shall not pervert the justice due to the sojourner or to the
fatherless, or take a widow's garment in pledge; but you shall

remember that you were a slave in Egypt and the Lord your God redeemed you from there; therefore I command you to do this (Deut. 24:17–18).

The Israelites' attitude to those vulnerable to oppression was to be modelled on God's attitude to them when they were being oppressed.

The central message of the Old Testament prophets is God's outcry against his people for proving unfaithful to this calling. Despite God's goodness to the Israelites in redeeming them and revealing his will to them, they had spurned that goodness and brought themselves under the lash of divine judgment: 'You only have I known of all the families of the earth; therefore I will punish you for all your iniquities' (Amos 3:2). The prophets' complaints against the Israelites were many and various. But certain themes emerge again and again. The Israelites were repeatedly guilty of the most direct form of disloyalty to God, breaking the first two commandments: 'You shall have no other gods before me. You shall not make for yourself a graven image . . .' (Deut. 5:7–8). This apostasy, which often took the form of Baal-worship, is metaphorically described in terms of adultery and harlotry. But disobedience to the ten commandments had certainly not stopped there. As they catalogue the vices of Israel the prophets – consciously or unconsciously – echo the second half of the Decalogue: '. . . there is swearing, lying, killing, stealing and committing adultery; they break all bounds and murder follows murder' (Hos. 4:2; cf. Jer. 7:8–9).

These activities seem to be singled out as especially heinous, as particularly instrumental in the breakdown of social order and the estrangement of the people from their God. But there are also transgressions of other specific laws on which the prophets repeatedly focused. Neglect of the widow and orphan; dishonesty in commercial transactions through the use of false weights and measures; bribery affecting the dispensation of justice – all these come under regular critical scrutiny. Disobedience to God's laws is seen by the prophets as a matter of utmost seriousness.

The deontological strand in Old Testament teaching comes

out even more strongly in some of its narrative sections. Not infrequently God is portrayed as extremely intolerant of the slightest disobedience to his commands, an attitude apt to be conveyed through spectacular divine interventions! Nadab and Abihu, the sons of Aaron, are consumed by fire when they presume to anticipate their father's priestly duties (Lev. 10:1–2). Moses is told to stone a man for gathering sticks on the Sabbath (Num. 15:32–6). Perhaps most difficult to accept, Uzzah is struck down for touching the sacred ark of the covenant when the oxen carrying it had stumbled, and he was presumably trying to stop the ark from falling (2 Sam. 6:6–7). What is striking in this latter instance is the apparent irrelevance of the *circumstances* in which an offence is committed. Mitigating circumstances here appear to be an unknown concept.

Deontology in the New Testament

Is the New Testament ethic less rule-centred than that of the Old Testament? Nowell-Smith and many others have certainly thought so. Here, surely, we see the triumph of love over law, of principles over rules, of grace over merit. Christ sets people free from bondage to legal minutiae and fiddling regulations. The new covenant carries a very different flavour from the old. True as these all are as broad assertions, their breadth obscures as much as it reveals. It is a mistake to imagine that the deontological style of thinking is absent from the pages of the New Testament. There are limits to the process by which rules are relaxed and law left behind.

For instance, in one controversial area, that of divorce, Jesus appears to move radically in the direction of tightening up a rule. Deuteronomy 24:1–4 assumed the permissibility of divorce, with Rabbinic schools differing as to the breadth with which 'some indecency' (detected in the wife by the husband) should be understood as a sufficient ground. Jesus undercuts this debate by describing Moses' allowance of divorce as a concession to human 'hardness of heart', and by proclaiming

the permanence of the marital union in terms of the picture of
man and woman as one flesh described in Genesis 2:24. He
goes on to say that human beings should never put asunder
what God has joined together. It is true that an 'exception'
clause is included by Matthew in his version of the incident,
apparently bringing Jesus into line with the interpretation
favoured by Rabbi Shammai (viz., that divorce is permissible
on the ground of adultery);[4] nevertheless, the thrust of
Jesus's remarks remains clear. He intended to recall his
contemporaries to a high ideal of marriage which had been
lost. Effectively he was saying: 'Stop looking for ways to
justify forsaking your obligations and be faithful to the marriage covenants into which you have entered.' There is a
toughness here more reminiscent of the deontologist than the
consequentialist.

The teaching of St Paul is full of paradoxes. They reflect the
character of the man himself: a complex thinker who was at
the same time deeply sensitive and fiercely emotional, an
idealist who had been caught up into paradise, who was also
extremely practical and down-to-earth. Certainly, Paul
stressed the importance of being released from the law, a
sense of liberation from its bondage, the new-found freedom
which comes with being a Christian. Keeping the law must
never again be conceived as an instrument for earning salvation. But Paul also recognised, increasingly perhaps in his
later years, that there was still a place in the Christian life for
law – as long, that is, as its subordinate position was understood. God's law remained an invaluable guide in depicting to
ignorant, often weak-willed converts what forms of behaviour
were acceptable to God and what were not. Paul was therefore not averse to *laying down the law* on occasion. He gives
detailed guidance on specific moral issues which troubled
different churches.

In his first letter to the Corinthians, Paul comes out with
some very decisive statements categorically forbidding certain types of behaviour, especially in the sexual realm. He
reacts with shock to a reported case of a Corinthian Christian
living with his stepmother; he does not explain why this is
wrong, but the fact that it was behaviour 'of a kind that is not

found even among pagans' doubtless reinforced his conviction (1 Cor. 5:1). Homosexual activity is clearly regarded as incompatible with inheritance of the kingdom of God (1 Cor. 6:9), Paul's reasons being explained in Romans 1 where he talks about those who exchange natural sexual relations for unnatural. He discourages resort to prostitutes with a complex of overlapping arguments: our bodies are members of Christ, and it should be unthinkable – 'Never!': 1 Cor. 6:15: – that they should be made members of a prostitute; a sexual relationship is meant to imply a union operative at all levels of life (as in marriage), which is clearly not true of a liaison with a prostitute (6:16); and the fact that Christians have been 'bought with a price' (6:20; Christ's own blood) may well be meant to strike a telling comparison with the shoddy price paid for a prostitute's services. These are all reasons very much bound up with the nature of the act: Paul does not here appeal to adverse consequences which may follow from a life of sexual licence, but reminds his readers what redemption means – being *delivered* from a sinful background; see 6:9–11 – and why that is incompatible with a casual expression of one's own sexuality.

However, Paul had sharp words for other failings besides sexual sin. He laments all signs of unnecessary *divisiveness* in church life. Again this is because he saw churches falling short of his visionary ideal, namely, the church as a united body in which racial, sexual and social barriers were broken down. He describes this in Galatians 3:28: 'There is neither Jew nor Greek, there is neither slave nor free, there is neither male nor female; for you are all one in Christ Jesus.'

Paul was unusually clear-sighted among the first generation of Christians in his grasp of the truth that Christ had established a community of equals among culturally diverse peoples. Unhappily, the reality often failed to reflect this. The Corinthian Christians revealed disunity over numerous issues, from questions of leadership to the relative importance of spiritual gifts (chs 12–14). In his criticism, Paul again draws in the image of the *body* of Christ, a notion which he uses in subtly different ways. Thus whoever eats the bread of

the Lord's Supper in an unworthy manner is guilty of profan-
ing the body and blood of the Lord (1 Cor. 11:27). Whoever
promotes the importance of his own spiritual gifts to the
detriment of others is guilty of disrupting the body of Christ
seen in terms of the church – a body in which different
individuals have different gifts, and all of them make an
invaluable contribution, just like the different parts of a
human body (12:14–26). Understanding the nature of the
church (just like understanding the nature of marriage)
should set definite constraints on human behaviour.

Consequentialism in the Old Testament

The fact remains that not all ethical reasoning in the Bible is of
the type described so far. The Biblical writers often seem to
work on a notion of actions being *intrinsically* right or wrong,
but not always. Let us return first to the Old Testament law.
Consideration of beneficial or adverse consequences is a
factor in the explanations which are given for various laws.
Utilitarians like Bentham or Nowell-Smith should surely purr
with satisfaction at Deuteronomy 24:5:

> When a man is newly married, he shall not go out with the army
> or be charged with any business; he shall be free at home one
> year, to be happy with his wife whom he has taken.

Even when the penalties stipulated by the law appear harsh,
part of the rationale for the severity of the punishment is the
valuable deterrent effect it will have on the rest of the
community. And sometimes the consequences which are a
spur to obedience take the form of God's promising personal
prosperity or longevity in return for obedience to his commands; see, for instance, the command to honour one's
parents: 'that thy days may be long in the land which the Lord
your God gives you' (Exod. 20:12), or in general terms the
charge to obey God's commandments in the promised land,
'And you shall eat and be full . . .' (Deut. 8:10).
Mention of the Old Testament Wisdom literature is also

relevant in this context. Only rarely does it take the imperative form (an exception is Proverbs 22:22–9, which are probably a father's instructions to his son). We do not hear the
thunder of 'thus says the Lord' at every step. Instead, in
Ogletree's words, we find 'pithy sayings expressing a kind of
practical wisdom about the good life'.[5] Admittedly, this
wisdom is still God-centred ('The fear of the Lord is the
beginning of wisdom': Prov. 9:10) and certain things – no
surprises here – are described as an abomination to him.[6] But
its leading tenor is one of reflection about life's experiences,
musings on what works for the best and what doesn't. Moral
points are made through juxtaposing pictures of the worker
and the sluggard, the wise man and the fool, the just man and
the crook. Sexual sins are warned against not through laying
down the law against adultery, but through unveiling the
loose woman for the evil person that she is and describing
the dangers which ensue from seduction to her lures. Conventional morality is here being taught in a more pragmatic,
consequentialist vein than is found in most of the Old
Testament.

Earlier, I said that the moral teaching conveyed through
the medium of Old Testament narrative sometimes carries a
strong obey-the-rules-at-all-costs flavour. But this is by no
means the whole story. Let us take the matter of honesty. The
commandment not to bear false witness, strictly applicable of
course to the law-court, may be said to be symptomatic of a
wider concern on God's part that we be truthful in our
relations with our fellow-humans. A 'lying tongue' is an
abomination to him (Prov. 6:17); dishonesty is another peren-
nial complaint of the prophets. Yet various incidents in the
Old Testament narratives suggest that it would be a mistake
to view the prohibition of lying as an absolute which allows of
no exception.

In Exodus the Hebrew midwives, who 'feared God', dis-
obeyed Pharaoh in allowing the sons of Hebrew women to
live, and when called to account claimed that 'the Hebrew
women are not like the Egyptian women; for they are vigor-
ous and are delivered before the midwife comes to them'
(Exod. 1:19).

In Joshua 2, Rahab, who is commended in the New Testament both for her faith and her works, told the king of Jericho's messengers that she had sent Joshua's spies on their way when they were actually hiding under her roof. In 1 Samuel 16 God tells Samuel to visit Jesse of Bethlehem and anoint one of his sons as Israel's future king; Samuel, afraid of Saul's reaction if he hears of it, is instructed to give as his reason for the visit 'I have come to sacrifice to the Lord' (v. 2). Samuel duly carried out the sacrifice, but it was hardly the main purpose of his visit, so that what is at best a half-truth is portrayed here as carrying divine authorisation. Finally, in 2 Kings 6, Elisha misleads the Syrian soldiers who had come to the city of Dothan to capture him. He successfully petitions God to smite them with blindness as they arrive at the gates, and then tells them: 'This is not the way, and this is not the city; follow me, and I will bring you to the man whom you seek' (v. 19). Elisha then leads them to Samaria, where their eyes are opened, but no longer in a position where they can inflict any harm on him.

There is a feature common to all these cases of apparently justified deception. In each case life was imperilled if the truth was told. The Hebrew midwives, Samuel and Elisha feared for their own skins, Rahab for the lives of the spies. This common feature distinguishes their behaviour sharply from the deception perpetrated by e.g., Jacob, when he pretended to be Esau in order to wrest the coveted blessing from Isaac (Gen. 27). The duty to preserve life outweighed the duty to tell the truth in the former cases. These situations (Rahab's in particular) are closely comparable to the imaginary one described by Kant, where I have already argued that his unbending adherence to the truth-telling principle is wrong. Circumstances, and that involves a calculation of likely consequences, make a difference.

Consequentialism in the New Testament

Returning now to the teaching of Jesus, there is one obvious area where his approach was much more flexible than that practised by his contemporaries. On the question of what one was and wasn't supposed to do on the Sabbath, Jesus displayed a radical liberalism of practice which the Pharisees found deeply shocking. This is not to deny his faithful attendance at the synagogue for worship on the Sabbath. But Jesus clearly diverged from other Jewish teachers in the way that he interpreted the fourth commandment. He defended his disciples' act of plucking corn on the Sabbath, citing David's act of eating the sacred bread as a precedent (another example of a more flexible attitude to laws in the Old Testament; see Mark 2:23–6 with its reference to 1 Samuel 21:1–6). He went out of his way to heal people on the Sabbath, not waiting for the individuals concerned – a man with a withered hand, a woman with a bent back, a man suffering from dropsy – to request his aid.[7] He encouraged his hearers to think of the Sabbath as a positive opportunity for helping others, not as an imposition prohibiting all activity: 'Is it lawful on the Sabbath to do good or to do harm, to save life or to kill?' (Mark 3:4). In those famous words 'the Sabbath was made for man, not man for the Sabbath' (Mark 2:27) we could not find a clearer expression of the view that the purpose of God-given laws is the meeting of human need and the fulfilment of human welfare. It is not surprising that Nowell-Smith heartily endorses this slogan, as he calls it![8]

Just as Jesus's teaching shows contrasting ethical emphases, so too does Paul. In contrast to his views on issues discussed earlier, Paul's advice is sometimes more provisional, more tentative, and in the process more consequential. Consider his treatment of the vexed question of whether Christians should eat food which had been sacrificed to idols in pagan temples. Paul was adamant on one point: the Christian must not indulge in idolatry, a practice which features prominently in his lists of vices. Those who believe in a God revealed in Christ believe in a God who has no rivals: 'we know that "an idol has no real existence," and that "there is no God but one"' (1 Cor. 8:4). Precisely because these idols do not really exist, Paul's basic (or starting) position is that there is no need to worry about eating food which, before being sold on the market, had been used in pagan sacrifices.

The meat is neither better nor worse through such an association; the Christian ought to be able to regard it just as part of
the earth's produce, the good gifts of God.

But Paul was well aware that not all Christians saw the issue
that simply. For some, the meat was 'tainted' by its use in
pagan worship. They could not get its association with idols
out of their minds: 'But some, through being hitherto accus-
tomed to idols, eat food as really offered to an idol' (8:7). This
danger was particularly acute where the meat was being eaten
at table in a pagan temple (8:10), presumably in a case where
a Christian had been invited to a feast by a non-Christian.
Paul thought such a situation so full of misleading implications that he advised the Corinthian Christians not to partake
of such meals, though he thought it perfectly acceptable to eat
meat unquestioningly with non-Christians on a private occasion in their own home (10:27). In theory Paul was completely
libertarian on this question; but in practice he was prepared to
advise compromise, depending both on the particular situation in which food was being eaten and on who was present,
i.e., whether there were young Christians present who might
interpret the mature Christian's action in the wrong way and
think that some sort of syncretistic religion was acceptable.
The conscience of the weaker brother is to be respected.
Unnecessary offence should not be given on an issue not
central to the Christian Gospel.

The consequential thrust of Paul's advice is evident: the
immature Christian may jump to the wrong conclusions, he
may be sucked back into idol-worship, the body of Christ is
broken as a result. We see here something like the 'thin-end-
of-the-wedge' argument which often crops up when the consequences of an action or decision are being calculated.
'There is nothing wrong with such-and-such, but if that is
allowed, something that is undoubtedly reprehensible is likely to follow.' Arguments against the legalisation of cannabis
usually concentrate not on the – apparently negligible – harm
which it causes but on the fact that it would legitimise the
taking of drugs, and in turn lead many on to 'harder', definitely harmful drugs such as heroin and LSD. Clearly this type
of argument has its force and needs to be taken seriously. But

ıt also has its dangers. It may lead to a failure both to make and to stick by appropriate *distinctions*. Respect for a weaker brother's conscience can become a strait-jacket. Paul himself was clearly aware of this danger when he asked 'why should my liberty be determined by another man's scruples?' (1 Cor. 10:29). And in this context it is interesting to note that the conscience described as *weak* is actually an overscrupulous one – not, as we should tend to use the word, a conscience which is lax.

Paul's advice also conveys something of a tentative air when he discusses questions of marriage and singleness in 1 Corinthians 7. He advises believers who are married to unbelievers to stay with their partners, though not to stand in the way 'if the unbelieving partner desires to separate' (v. 15). He recommends that those who are single should remain as they are (vv. 25–6). But in each case it is a matter of 'I say, not the Lord' (v. 12); he is conscious that his opinion does not necessarily carry divine authority, though he regards himself as 'one who by the Lord's mercy is trustworthy' (v. 25). Paul cites various reasons why the single state compares favourably with the married, but it appears that his then current belief in an imminent end of the world was a crucial factor. Paul speaks of the 'present distress', says that 'the appointed tıme has grown very short' and regards the 'form of this world' as 'passing away' (vv. 26, 29, 31). His sense of the critical nature of the present state of affairs leads Paul to be more discouraging about taking on the responsibilities of married life than he might otherwise have been.

Eschatology, the belief of the early Christians that God will bring the world to an end and may do so at any moment, undoubtedly has an effect on New Testament ethics. It is, as Ogletree observes, a feature which 'does not easily translate ınto the categories of Enlightenment ethics'[9] – one might add any ethics in our modern world, where perhaps none but the Christian sects lives with the same intense expectation of a sudden wrapping up of the world order.[10] Yet the impact of the eschatological dimension varies. In the teaching of Jesus, ıt goes hand in hand with a sharpening of moral demands: the Sermon on the Mount challenges us to make no concession to

human evil, so that we are even told not to resist it (Matt.
5:39). In 1 Corinthians 7, it leads Paul to discourage Christians from participation in a perfectly natural and legitimate
human activity – entering into marriage. Eschatological
urgency may also help to explain why Paul was not particularly radical in his approach to the social order: for all the
revolutionary potential contained in Galatians 3:28, he
advised slaves to obey (rather than demand freedom from)
their masters, and was generally cautious about allowing
women a prominent role in church life. Because time was
short, he may have felt that Christians should get on with the
urgent task of spreading the Gospel rather than pursuing
long-term social goals. Clearly belief in Christ's imminent
return produces a tension in the life of the Christian. He has
been called to live out the standards of a new age – eternal
life and the Kingdom of God are *present* realities – yet
because he still lives in a sinful age, whose structures are
unjust and where Christians often comprise a minority with
negligible influence, he also has to make concessions to
the old age. This helps to explain why the New Testament
contains both a visionary, idealistic strain and a much
more pragmatic approach to certain issues. Paul's writing
shows that he felt the eschatological tension as much as
anyone.
    There is another way in which thoughts of the end affect
action. The picture of God as judge is a spur to obedience and
a warning against departure from the path of discipleship.
Although Paul believed in justification by faith, he did not
think that meant exemption from the coming judgment of
God. Christians would still have to give account for the way
that they had lived. He is therefore not averse to mentioning
this sober prospect as an inducement to his readers to live in a
manner worthy of the name of Christ.[11] Jesus frequently
spoke, too, of the rewards and punishments of the after-life.
The person who passes through the wide gate rather than the
narrow one will be led to destruction (Matt. 7:13). But the
person who is living in readiness for his return, using his
talents in God's service, and acting lovingly and mercifully
towards those in need will receive eternal life (see the three

parables in Matthew 25). One could describe this as consequentialism carried to an ultimate extreme. But that description is subject to two massive qualifications. First, the decisive thrust of New Testament teaching remains the fact that we cannot earn our own salvation: although our behaviour matters, we remain persistent sinners ultimately dependent on God's grace. Second, the consequences of what happens in a future existence are consequences of a different order from how events may turn out in this life. When one is assessing what may imperil one's state of salvation, one is doing something significantly different from calculating which actions will lead to most human happiness here on earth.

Analysing Biblical material on ethics in the way that I have thus far has its limitations. The Bible resists straightforward categorisation in terms of ethical theory. Neither the deontological nor the consequentialist approaches are found in a 'pure' form in the Bible. What I have traced are simply *tendencies* in one direction or the other. Does this mean, then, that Christians are justified in taking *either* a predominantly rule-centred approach *or* a primarily results-oriented tack – or alternatively may feel justified in oscillating between the two? That would be a premature and mistaken conclusion. The Bible provides more constructive help than that. First, it introduces a distinctive element into considerations about morality, that of personal imitation. Second, it suggests a route through and beyond the rules-consequences impasse, in focusing upon certain key qualities and in hinting at an order of priorities.

A Life of Imitation

Reference has already been made to the way in which God presents his own character and gracious activity towards Israel as a model for the Jews to emulate in their relationships with fellow-humans. 'The God who brought you out of the land of Egypt' serves as a kind of moral shorthand, a folk-memory recalled to instruct and to inspire. In Isaiah 42, God portrays his people Israel as a servant who will 'bring forth justice' (v. 1) and be 'a light to' (v. 6) the nations: this could only come about if their lives exhibited the same qualities as God's own character.

In actual fact, only Jesus proved able to fulfil this prophecy fully; only he is the perfect human model of God in action. But Jesus, too, called his followers to a life of imitation: 'You, therefore, must be perfect, as your heavenly Father is perfect' (Matt. 5:48). The passage from which this verse comes, the Sermon on the Mount, makes clear the demanding standard involved. Jesus spoke of purity in thought as well as action, chastity in mind as well as body. God's enquiring gaze pervades even the most private areas of our lives. No wonder, then, that Ogletree detects a strong perfectionist strand in New Testament ethics. Perfectionism, in contrast both to deontology and consequentialism, denotes a primary concern with the formation and development of persons. Jesus opened people's eyes to the fullness and the richness of what God intended them to be – but left them with no illusions about the suffering and persecution this might entail.

In the Christian's search for what is Godlike, the Gospel stories about Jesus are a great visual aid. Jesus said that 'the Son can do nothing of his own accord, but only what he sees the Father doing' (John 5:19), and he calls on his disciples likewise to emulate *his* actions. A vivid example of this is his washing of the disciples' feet: 'If I then, your Lord and Teacher, have washed your feet, you also ought to wash one another's feet. For I have given you an example, that you also should do as I have done to you' (John 13:14–15).

This does not mean that Christians should necessarily go around copying the precise action of foot-washing. The imitation of Christ is not to be practised in a wooden and legalistic way. The lesson to be learnt from this story is that Jesus performed a deed of breathtaking humility, which cast an entirely new light on relations between those in and under authority. There is still a time and place for such actions, especially by those in 'top' positions. Indeed, they may sometimes provide the way out of a deadlock or the key to a reversal of deteriorating relationships. There are many other actions of Jesus which have an illustrative or *paradigmatic* relevance for our lives today. I shall not be hesitant about drawing on his example at later stages of this book.

Within Jesus's teaching, as I indicated earlier, he applies rules strictly at some points and treats them much more flexibly at others. But the essence of his moral teaching consists neither in unswerving allegiance to God-given laws, nor calculating assessment of favourable consequences, but in challenge to be Jesus's faithful co-workers in the service of the Kingdom of God. Because so much of this teaching is given through the media of pointed story and telling image, its content is extremely difficult to summarise in terms of a few basic maxims. Jesus's technique is to provide us with pictures of how a disciple does and does not behave: a widow persisting with her petitions until a judge relents, a servant released from a great debt refusing to write off some trifling sum owed by a fellow-servant (Luke 18:1–8; Matt. 18:23–35). Jesus lays down the conditions of service ('*unless* you turn and become like children, you will never enter the kingdom of heaven'; '*whoever* loses his life for my sake and the gospel's will save it'[12]) and thereby challenges rather than commands individuals to be his disciples. Even the teaching which takes the imperative form – such as many of the instructions in the Sermon on the Mount – cannot be categorised as clearly defined laws in the way that the Pentateuchal material can. Commands to cut off one's right hand or turn the other cheek certainly need to be taken seriously, but that is most unlikely to mean literally. Jesus paints vivid portraits of what a disciple modelled on his own character might do, but there is something of the cartoonist in him: the features which emerge assume a pointedly exaggerated form!

Inevitably, teaching of this type does not provide immediate answers to most of our modern-day dilemmas. Jesus delivered very few decisive verdicts on conflict situations faced by a later generation, or even for that matter his own. Even where his words and example *seem* to point clearly in one direction, reason for doubt may remain. For instance, the non-resistance teaching of the Sermon on the Mount and Jesus's own lack of resistance in the face of arrest and crucifixion appear to indicate an opposition to violence in all

its forms. But legitimate doubt remains about whether turning the other cheek was meant to apply to governments in the
way that it does to individuals as private citizens; and Jesus
himself used violence when he purged the temple of its
money-grabbing traders. Again, on the question of allegiance
to an occupying nation, Jesus's 'Render to Caesar the things
that are Caesar's, and to God the things that are God's' (Mark
12:17) *appears* to support payment of the tribute claimed; but
it may well be that Jesus was intending to leave open the
question of exactly what was justly owed to Caesar. It was for
his questioners to decide that, not for him to tell them. A
more trivial case where he clearly refuses to take individuals'
decision-taking responsibility away from them is found in
Luke 12:13–14:

> One of the multitude said to him, 'Teacher, bid my brother divide
> the inheritance with me.' But he said to him, 'Man, who made me
> a judge or divider over you?'

The resolution of the correct division of their inheritance is
left in the lap of the two brothers. What Jesus does do is
narrate a telling parable which warns them of the sin of
covetousness.[13]

Key Themes

For all the enigmatic aspects of Jesus's teaching, certain
important themes can still be identified. There are distinctive
qualities which are hallmarks of the Christian disciple. They
flow from the central Gospel message of Jesus, that God is
merciful to sinners and that now is the day to receive his
salvation. Would-be followers, mindful of the cost of discipleship, need to act urgently and change their ways. In
response to God's mercy they should approach God humbly
and can do so trustfully. They should forgive as he forgives;
their love for other people should extend far beyond the
conventional understanding of a neighbour as a fellow-Jew
and a respectable one at that; they should be ready to serve

other people and slow to judge them; they should cast off worldly attachments like wealth which both compete with God for allegiance and deprive society's poor of a decent existence.

Above all, Jesus highlights the importance of love. In response to a lawyer's question: 'Which commandment is the first of all?', he does not reply with one of the ten commandments, as the lawyer might perhaps have expected. Instead he recasts the Old Testament law in its entirety in a positive, summarised form:

> Jesus answered, 'The first is, "Hear O Israel: The Lord our God, the Lord is one; and you shall love the Lord your God with all your heart, and with all your soul, and with all your mind, and with all your strength." The second is this, "You shall love your neighbour as yourself." There is no other commandment greater than these' (Mark 12:29–31).

Both the commandments to love God and to love one's neighbour were there in the Old Testament, but Jesus gave them a new prominence and a fresh significance.

It is clear that in Jesus's view certain aspects of the law were more weighty than others. They contained what we might call 'the heart of the matter'. In response to the Pharisees' nit-picking Jesus twice quoted the prophet Hosea: 'I desire mercy, and not sacrifice'.[14] Mercy here is symptomatic of qualities which Jesus epitomised and to the central importance of which the Pharisees were sadly blind. In identifying key themes in this way, Jesus was following faithfully in the tradition of the prophets. For the prophets saw that even when the Israelites were carrying out the rituals of worship in a formally correct way, blatant abdication of responsibilities to their fellow-men meant that they were completely out of joint in their relationship with God. There are many examples of this.

In Isaiah 1:14 we read that God *hates* the 'new moons and your appointed feasts' of a sinful people. He will not accept their burnt offerings, cereal offerings and peace offerings 'but let justice roll down like waters, and righteousness like an everflowing stream' (Amos 5:24). The use of the words justice and righteousness is significant. In Old Testament prophecy we see the emergence of certain key words denoting qualities which reflect the character of God and encapsulate the demands of God upon his people: justice, righteousness, mercy, holiness, peace. For all the minutiae of God's legal and ritual requirements, it is with these qualities that he is principally concerned. Micah sums up this prophetic shift in perspective in the famous words, 'He has showed you, O man, what is good; and what does the Lord require of you but to do justice, and to love kindness, and to walk humbly with your God?' (Mic. 6:8).

If the prophetic teaching strikes a similar chord to that of Jesus in many respects, so, too, does that of Paul. Like Jesus, Paul focuses far more on what Christian believers should be like than on what they should do. Like Jesus, he is principally concerned with portraying a distinctive Christian character, outlining the shape to which all Christian lives in one way or another should conform. And as with Jesus, the ethics is intrinsically linked to the theology; the moral teaching flows naturally out of the Gospel message.

Of course, in Paul there is a different perspective on the Gospel than with Jesus. Jesus's words were uttered before his death and resurrection, whereas Paul's were written after. The good news preached by Jesus, that God was visiting his people with salvation and offering mercy to the most wretched of sinners, had been dramatically fulfilled in Paul's eyes first and foremost through Calvary and its sequel. Jesus's resurrection vindicated his claim both to be God's Son and that through his death he was offering a 'ransom for many' (Mark 10:45). But the events of the first Easter did not simply convince Paul of God's love for humanity. The images of death and resurrection took on a fundamental significance for Paul's understanding of the Christian life. In baptism a Christian *died* to sin and *rose* to new life in Christ. Christians are a *new creation*; they have passed from *darkness* into *light*.[15] All the metaphors used of what it means to become a Christian have this stark, powerful and dynamic quality. And because Paul was convinced that something momentous did happen when a person became a Christian – as was so obviously the case in his own life – much of his moral teaching is couched in the indicative, not the imperative form. The impact of Pentecost gave Paul confidence in this respect. The apparently impossible ideals with which Jesus challenges us could be realised through the power and grace of the Holy Spirit: 'those who live according to the Spirit set their minds on the things of the Spirit' (Rom. 8:5), and

> the fruit of the Spirit is love, joy, peace, patience, kindness, goodness, faithfulness, gentleness, self-control; against such there is no law. And those who belong to Christ Jesus have crucified the flesh with its passions and desires (Gal. 5:22–4).

The placing of love at the head of that list is no accident. Like Jesus, Paul regarded love as the most important and most inclusive commandment, a summary of the law (Rom. 13:9) and the quality without which the most outwardly impressive of actions remains worthless: 'If I give away all I have, and if I deliver my body to be burned, but have not love, I gain nothing' (1 Cor. 13:3).

A Scale of Values

If we now retrace our steps and go back to the Mosaic law, we find evidence of a *scale* of values implicit even in the law. While it is true that contravention of any of God's laws is depicted as serious sin, it is significant that different punishments are legislated for different offences. Among the ten commandments 'do not kill' and 'do not steal' stood together as two of the corner-stones of Israel's ethical system. They enshrined respect for human life and personal property respectively. But violation of these commandments did not carry equal penalties: killing was punishable by death, whereas stealing was not. The only type of theft which was a capital offence was stealing a person (i.e., kidnapping).[16] While we might take this ordering of priorities for granted, Israelite law here stood in contrast to many other Middle Eastern law codes. Property offences were regarded as serious, since an Israelite's sense of identity and dignity was very much tied up with his piece of land and personal possessions, but not so serious as to warrant the ultimate punishment.

Furthermore, the fact that capital punishment *was* prescribed for murder, kidnapping, adultery and a variety of other offences against the person points to something else important: that the command 'do not kill' (*rasah* being a word which simply denotes violent slaying) is not to be interpreted in a blanket way which excludes all killing, but itself allows of certain exceptions. From the mass of surrounding legislation it is clear that killing was permitted, first as punishment for the most serious offences, and second in times of war. We find here an example of a rule which is of fundamental importance and which is generally binding, but does admit of exceptions in some clearly defined situations.

These findings fit in with my earlier observation about some of the Old Testament narratives. There are unusual situations, situations where two moral duties which normally hold good come into conflict, and where one may rightly be seen as outweighing the other. An underlying scale of values helps to determine which takes precedence.

Taken as a whole, then, the Biblical writers do offer a helpful lead. They suggest what sort of ethical approach is appropriate for the Christian – even if a lot of the detail remains to be filled in. It is an approach which partakes both of deontological and consequentialist characteristics, but conforms closely to neither, and to some extent transcends both. Yet the fact is that Christians often *do* appear to have conformed closely to one or other of these two key models. It is interesting that Nowell-Smith, a humanist, saw Christianity as having been far more influenced by the Old Testament – as he saw it, deontological – type of thinking than the New. And even Christian philosophers who criticised Nowell-Smith's essay were obliged to admit that Christian morality has often been untrue to the spirit of Christ, and hence has been unduly rule-bound. But what of the great Christian thinkers down the centuries? Have they thought in terms of inviolable duties, or have they been much more flexible and pragmatic? We must not imagine that we are the first generation of Christian people since Bible times to have grappled seriously with moral dilemmas!

Notes

1   This is most easily found in Ian T. Ramsey (ed.), *Christian Ethics and Contemporary Philosophy*, SCM, 1966, ch. 5.
2   Thomas W. Ogletree, *The Use of the Bible in Christian Ethics*, Fortress, Philadelphia, 1983.
3   Here I follow the classification of Christopher J. H. Wright, *Living as the People of God: The Relevance of Old Testament Ethics*, IVP, 1983, ch. 7.
4   The school of Shammai was in dispute with the school of the Rabbi Hillel, who thought that a man could divorce his wife on grounds as trivial as dissatisfaction with her cooking.
5   *The Use of the Bible in Christian Ethics*, p. 78.
6   Proverbs 6:16–19.
7   Mark 3:1–6, Luke 13:10–17 and Luke 14:1–6.
8   *Christian Ethics and Contemporary Philosophy*, p. 99.
9   *The Use of the Bible in Christian Ethics*, p. 71.
10   This is not to deny that orthodox Christians look forward to Christ's second coming. But it is sects like the Jehovah's Witnesses which are preoccupied with the end of the world and with trying to set a date to it.
11   E.g., Romans 13:11–14; 2 Corinthians 5:10–11.
12   Matthew 18:3; Mark 8:35.
13   The parable of the rich fool, Luke 12:16–21.
14   This verse, Hosea 6:6, is quoted in Matthew 9:13 and 12:7.
15   Romans 6:1–11; 2 Corinthians 5:17; Colossians 1:11–14.
16   Exodus 21:16.

4

WHAT HAVE CHRISTIANS SAID?

Augustine

If I start my discussion of the Christian tradition with St Augustine, this is not only because of his undoubted importance in Christian history and theology, but because his writing exhibits the tension between different ethical approaches which I have been considering in a very clear way. Augustine has been hailed as an ally both by those who insist on the absolute nature of fundamental moral rules and by those who regard them as possessing only relative significance. The variety of arguments which he employs brings to light different sources of moral authority in Christian ethics. And at least in one important area of human activity, that of war, we see him lending his weight to an influential theory which aims to provide guidance over that recurring and perplexing human dilemma, whether and in what circumstances it is right to fight.

There is in Augustine a stress on right intention which appears to relativise sharply the significance of any particular action. This strain in his thought is encapsulated in his oft-cited words: 'Love, and do what you will.' The context of this phrase was Augustine's attempt to justify the use of force against a dissident church group, the Donatists, in order to compel them to remain part of the Catholic Church. The relevant passage is worth quoting at some length:

> When we look at differing actions, we find that charity may cause a man to be fierce, and wickedness to speak smoothly. A boy may

be struck by his father, and have fair words from a slave dealer
. . . it is charity that strikes, and wickedness that ingratiates . . .
Some actions may seem harsh or savage, but are performed for
our discipline at the dictate of charity. Thus a short and simple
precept is given you once and for all: *Love, and do what you will.*
Whether you keep silence, keep silence in love; whether you
exclaim, exclaim in love; whether you correct, correct in love;
whether you forbear, forbear in love. Let love's root be within
you, and from that root nothing but good can spring.[1]

The last two sentences echo St Paul in 1 Corinthians 13, both
in the lyricism of their tone and in their assertion of the
primacy of love. Augustine directs attention to the motive, or
mainspring, of an action. At the same time, he clearly thought
that one could evaluate the motive only when one considers
the consequences, or intended result, of the action concerned. A boy can be struck lovingly by his father where the
father has in view the disciplined, respectful young man
whom it is hoped he will become. Coercion of the Donatists
may be deemed an act of love because Augustine believed it
was best both for them and the Catholic Church that they
remain a united part of it.

Another striking instance of Augustine's emphasis on intention occurs in his discussion of the morality of suicide. He
considers the question of whether women who are threatened
with rape or who have been subject to rape are justified in
taking their own lives. He argues thus:

'But,' it will be said, 'there is the fear of being polluted by
another's lust.' There will be no pollution, if the lust is another's;
if there is pollution, the lust is not another's . . . [Since purity] is a
quality of the mind, it is not lust when the body is violated.
Indeed, when the quality of modesty resists the indecency of
carnal desires the body itself is sanctified, and therefore, when
purity insists in its unshaken resolution to resist those desires, the
body's holiness is not lost, because the will to employ the body
endures . . . Therefore when a woman has been ravished without
her consenting, and forced by another's sin, she has no reason to
punish herself by a voluntary death. Still less should she do so before the event lest she should commit murder while the offence,
and another's offence at that, still remains uncertain . . .[2]

Augustine goes on to commend Christian women, in contrast to noble pagan ones, who have not added 'crime to crime' by adding suicide to the rape inflicted on them:

> They have the glory of chastity within them, the testimony of their conscience. They have this in the sight of God, and they ask for nothing more.[3]

Yet it would be mistaken to conclude that Augustine's concern for purity of motive implies that any action, given the appropriate circumstances, carries the possibility of justification. With regard to suicide Augustine considers a variety of circumstances in which taking one's life might be considered legitimate and concludes that it is always wrong. He took a similarly rigorous stance on the question of lying. He recognised that lies sometimes have good consequences, but even then regarded them as sinful. The fact that lies may be told to save others from exposure, or from a motive of kindness, certainly makes them less heinous; yet though the motive can be praised, the action cannot. Elsewhere Augustine says that in evaluating moral actions 'The act, the agent, and the authority for the action are all of great importance',[4] so clearly right motive (presumably subsumed here under the label of agent) was not only or not consistently the decisive consideration for him. Augustine displays a sharp eye for detail in analysing the nature of different acts, whether this be sexual intercourse in one area or military service in another.[5] He is more than capable of holding his own in rational argument. Yet he is also unembarrassed about calling upon divine authorisation: certain actions are deemed right or wrong because God commands or prohibits them. He assumes the Bible to be a totally reliable aid to discerning the will of God. And when God is depicted as commanding a particular individual in the Bible to do something contrary to his normal instructions, Augustine is content to accept both that these were authentic commands and that such exceptional behaviour is justified only because God approved it. Thus:

For Abraham to sacrifice his son of his own accord is shocking madness. His doing so at the command of God proves him faithful and submissive.[6]

Augustine even finds in the Bible an apparent exception to the general prohibition of suicide which he deduces from it:

And when Samson destroyed himself, with his enemies, by the demolition of the building, this can only be excused on the ground that the Spirit, which performed miracles through him, secretly ordered him to do so.[7]

Augustine therefore is prepared to conceive of exceptions to generally valid prohibitions such as that against committing suicide, but only on express orders from God; he appears to find the reason why God might provide such authorisation quite unfathomable and is unwilling to concede that human beings could ever justify such action on their own authority. But with regard to the broader issue of killing in general, Augustine is prepared to argue that certain types of killing are justified and others are not, and to offer reasons why this is so. He observed that in the Old Testament killing in war and killing as a capital punishment are commanded by God; and these are examples not of singular, unfathomable divine commands but prescriptions which have a general application and which can be defended in terms of bringing judgment on guilty parties. As Augustine saw it, they are expressions of a 'just law'.[8] Any other sort of killing is illegitimate; in short, it is murder.

The Just War

Augustine's defence of killing in war is important because it helped to cement the Church in an effective volte-face on this issue. For the first three centuries and more of the Church's existence Christians were generally united in taking a pacifist position. It is not difficult to understand why: the teaching and example of Jesus, their wish to distance their life style from that of their pagan neighbours, and their unwillingness to provide active support for an imperial regime which demanded unswerving loyalty and submitted them to periodic persecution, were all significant factors. But times changed. By the fourth century AD Christians were no longer a minority group on the fringes of society. Their faith had become widespread, and after Constantine's conversion it was adopted as the official religion of the Empire. Christians then had to face up to their responsibility as rulers: what ought they to do if the people for whom they were responsible were attacked? Not surprisingly, some Christian thinkers became less pacifist in inclination; they began to draw parallels between preserving the Empire from disorder within and defending it from attack from outside; and they started to read the Bible with a rather different pair of spectacles and discovered there a number of possible lines of justification for participating in war.

The first important church leader to defend Christian participation in war was St Ambrose, Bishop of Milan from 374 to 397. Ambrose's argument relied heavily on Old Testament heroes who brought glory to God and themselves in war, but he also drew on the notion of the 'just war' which was already popular in Stoic circles. Roland Bainton has commented that 'What Ambrose thus sketched, Augustine amplified.'[9]

In adopting the just war tradition, Ambrose and Augustine did not close their eyes to the fact that much of what happens in war *is* morally unacceptable. They recognised that many wars are fought for the unworthiest of reasons and are conducted in a gratuitously cruel manner. But they came to the conclusion that sometimes *not* to fight is an abdication of responsibility, and is liable to produce consequences more evil than would result through fighting a war. The just war tradition attempts to lay down certain guidelines for determining whether a particular war is just or unjust, and for setting limits as to how war should be fought. Augustine emphasised the following aspects.

For a war to be just it must be waged by the proper state authority. It must be fought for a just cause (e.g., to punish another country's wrongdoing, or to restore land which has been wrongfully seized). It should be waged only if absolutely necessary – a criterion later theorists called *last resort* – and with the restoration of peace as a constant goal. It should be fought with the minimum of violence possible:

> The real evils in war are love of violence, revengeful cruelty, fierce and implacable enmity, wild resistance, and the lust of power, and such like . . .[10]

Later just-war theorists amplified the tradition at various points. The limitation on means employed came to focus on two particular aspects: the immunity of non-combatants (including prisoners), and the exercise of a sense of *proportion* in the degree of force used. Clearly these restrictions are very difficult to observe in the complexities and highly charged atmosphere of warfare, and they have been ignored on countless occasions. But in its attempt to set boundaries – even when in the very business of shedding blood – beyond which man should not go, the limitation on means represents a decidedly deontological feature within just-war theory. The lives of non-combatants among the enemy are to be respected, *even if* it is militarily inconvenient to do this. However, another condition which became a significant part of the tradition is unashamedly consequential in character. This is that war must be fought in the reasonable expectation that the good which it produces at the end will outweigh the evil also caused by the war. An essential part of this expectation is that there is a reasonable hope of victory. Here the theory lays on one an *obligation* to estimate likely consequences. The just-war criteria therefore appear as a mixture of principled and more pragmatic considerations. Nevertheless, there is a principle of sorts contained within the pragmatism: for if no hope of victory exists, fighting involves the sacrifice of lives to no useful purpose. (However, there are occasions when *apparently* hopeless causes can be rescued, so like all the other criteria, this is not a straightforward one to apply.)

Augustine sought to provide Biblical warrant for participation in war. He drew comparisons between 'just wars' and 'holy wars' of Old Testament times. The fact that Jesus and John the Baptist did not challenge the vocation of soldiers with whom they came into contact (Matt. 8:5–13; Luke 3:14), Paul's teaching on the governing authorities who bear the sword on God's behalf (Rom. 13:1–7), and the interpretation of Jesus's non-resistance sayings in the Sermon on the Mount as a call for peaceful disposition rather than requiring literal obedience: all these play a part in his argument. But it is clear that his delineation of the idea of a just war also owes much to the classical tradition for which Cicero had been a notable spokesman. There the theory's claim to authority was essentially a claim to be *reasonable*, accepting that wars are going to happen, arguing that some may be fought from a worthy motive but seeking to reduce their number and the damage caused by them. There is a link between the notion of a just war, ideas of natural justice, and the concept of *natural law*, which also finds eloquent expression in Cicero.

It is natural law which lies at the heart of the ethical system propounded by the next great moral theologian in the Church's history, St Thomas Aquinas. Through him, natural law has tended to dominate the ethical approach of one of the major churches (in its own eyes the one true church!), the Roman Catholic. And it is the concept of natural law which has been linked with much of the allegedly inflexible stance adopted by the Catholic Church on many issues. To this key ethical concept I now turn.

Aquinas

Aquinas expounded his understanding of natural law in his massive *Summa Theologica*. He argues that God has instilled into nature a pattern of behaviour by which living creatures are able to fulfil his intended purposes for them. Animals do this in a purely instinctive way: presumably Aquinas had in mind the way that they provide for their needs, seeking food and shelter, finding a mate, and caring for their young. Human beings, in contrast, are able to *ponder* their needs and aspirations:

. . . rational creatures are subject to divine Providence in a very special way, being themselves made participators in Providence itself, in that they control their own actions and the actions of others. So they have a certain share in the divine reason itself, deriving therefrom a natural inclination to such actions and ends as are fitting. This participation in the Eternal Law by rational creatures is called the Natural Law.[11]

Aquinas clearly thought that by observing his own nature and the world of nature in which he lived, he was able to discern 'the pattern and conduct by which man will attain to his true end'.[12] Unlike animals, man has a rational knowledge of the eternal law, Aquinas's cipher for God's will for his creation; and Aquinas gives this law the name natural law insofar as it relates to humanity.

What then does observation of nature lead man to think that he should do? According to Aquinas, the first and most fundamental principle is 'that good is to be sought and done, and evil is to be avoided', but he goes on to define good in terms of following certain 'natural' inclinations. These are the instincts for self-preservation, the procreation of offspring, and the education of offspring, and the desires 'to know the truth about God', 'to live in society', 'to avoid ignorance', and to refrain from offending those among whom one has to live.[13] Aquinas calls these the *primary principles* of natural law. The *secondary precepts* of natural law, on the other hand, are the outworking of these principles in detail. When we come to consider how people can be helped to fulfil their inclinations, certain rules are an obvious aid. Decalogue-type prohibitions of such activities as murder, adultery and theft are examples of secondary precepts. Everybody can recognise the necessity of these if people are to avoid offending each other and live together in society contentedly. The affirmation of these rules in Scripture is essentially a *re*affirmation of obligations of which human beings are already aware. Nevertheless, the reminder is important, because Aquinas recognised that precepts could sometimes be blotted out from the human heart by 'wrong persuasions', 'perverse customs' and 'corrupt habits'.[14] Because 'lust or some other passion' can prevent reason from applying a primary principle correctly, it is possible for individuals to lose sight of these secondary precepts or no longer experience a compelling obligation to abide by them. In contrast, Aquinas thought that the first principles of natural law could never be blotted out. He was confident that humanity is not totally corrupted by sin and that a basic moral consensus among humanity exists.

Aquinas also thought that secondary precepts can be changed in some 'particular cases of rare occurrence'. He seems to have felt obliged to concede this to explain some Biblical stories of apparently dubious morality:

> the killing of the innocent is against natural law, and so is adultery and theft. Yet you find God changing these rules, as when he commanded Abraham to put his son to death, the people of Israel to spoil the Egyptians, and Hosea to take a wife of harlotry.[15]

In fact, it is very doubtful whether these three examples constitute the clear-cut exceptions which Aquinas considered them to be. Nevertheless, I have already argued that the Old Testament does recognise the validity of making exceptions to some rules at least; the general point is a fair one. And Aquinas does not seem to regard making exceptions as something that need necessarily be confined to occasions where God gives special authorisation. Thus he discusses the question of whether goods held in trust should be restored to their owners:

> This is true in the majority of cases, yet a case can crop up when to return the deposit would be injurious, and consequently un-reasonable, as for instance were it to be required in order to attack one's country. The more you descend into the detail the more it appears how the general rule admits of exceptions, so that you have to hedge it with cautions and qualifications. The greater the number of conditions accumulated the greater the number of ways in which the principle is seen to fall short, so that all by itself it cannot tell you whether it be right to return a deposit or not.[16]

St Thomas's tenor of thought here is clearly flexible and consequentialist. The prospect of one's country being under attack is an undesirable consequence sufficiently grave to justify setting aside the general obligation to return borrowed property. Aquinas is usually far from being dogmatic when he makes moral claims on the basis of natural law. It might therefore seem surprising that natural law has often been associated with an *absolutist* stance on moral issues. The reason it has is principally because Roman Catholic theologians who take their lead from Aquinas have traditionally adopted absolutist positions on a number of contentious *sexual* issues, notably contraception, abortion and homosexuality. On many other issues, a readiness to make exceptions is far more evident in the natural-law tradition.

Contraception

Contraception provides an interesting example of the natural-law tradition in operation. Aquinas certainly harboured no hesitations in rejecting the practice outright. To him it was 'unnatural' and an extremely grave sin, second only to murder. The fact that procreation is the natural physical outcome of sexual intercourse is sufficient to establish it as the act's end or 'purpose'.[17] Procreation is vital to the perpetuation of the race; while some individuals, the celibate clergy, have a special vocation which excludes the possibility of contributing to this (interestingly Aquinas was prepared to make this sort of exception), it is the task of married couples to get on with producing offspring unimpaired. Apart from the fact that the Reformation churches attacked the necessity of clerical celibacy, such a view held sway throughout the Christian church until the present century. It was not till 1930 that the Anglican Lambeth Conference made its first, very qualified, acceptance of the legitimacy of using artificial means of birth control. And in 1947 a notable Anglican moral theologian in the natural-law tradition, R. C. Mortimer, was still arguing that the use of contraceptives, quite apart from encouraging fornication and being unreliable, is unnatural because it is directly opposed to the end for which the sexual act is intended. To every human faculty God has ordained its proper end and means. The end of the sexual act is quite clear – it tends naturally and of itself to one thing only – the procreation of children. To use it in such a way as to frustrate that end is therefore 'unnatural'.[18]

While such a negative attitude to contraception has come to seem increasingly anachronistic in the Church of England, it has continued to receive official papal backing in the Roman Catholic Church. Yet even there two significant modifications of the traditional position have occurred, and these could be seen as opening the door (and providing the justification) for a more radical shift. First, papal statements have shown increasing – and belated! – recognition of the fact that sexual intercourse is not solely concerned with procreation but also with the expression and growth of love between two married partners. In short, intercourse has two natural 'goals' or ends, not one. Second, since 1951 the Catholic Church has provided official backing for use of the *rhythm* method, i.e., the exercise of birth control through making love only during the infertile phases of a woman's reproductive cycle. Here, according to the 1968 papal encyclical *Humanae Vitae*, couples may rightly use a facility provided by nature, whereas with artificial contraceptives they obstruct the natural development of the procreative process.[19]

Many Catholics, among others, have questioned the logic of the reasoning employed at this point. That natural-law arguments can be used to arrive at rather different conclusions on this issue is evident from one of the lines of argument in the Anglican Report, *The Family in Contemporary Society*, which helped shift the Church of England more decisively in the direction of accepting the legitimacy of contraception at the 1958 Lambeth Conference.[20] After arguing that sexual intercourse has a twofold end, *generative* (producing life) and *relational* (enriching a relationship), it points out that for various physical reasons (the menstrual cycle, the age of the wife, physical defects on either side) the first end cannot always be achieved, yet in such cases the act's potential for realising a proper end, the second one, still exists. Nature already provides the possibility – indeed a strong statistical probability – that many acts of sexual intercourse will not achieve a procreative end. To use an artificial means to prevent the likelihood of procreation in the case of other acts is therefore simply an extension, and a rather more trustworthy refinement, of a phenomenon already found in nature. The Report saw no decisive moral difference between using the rhythm method and using other, more artificial means to prevent conception.

So though the concept of natural law has been applied to the issue in terms of a hard-and-fast prohibition by the Catholic Church, it is possible to come to different conclusions while still working from the same premises, namely, seeking to derive guidance from the evidence provided by nature. Both the Catholic and the Anglican lines of argument are, in a sense, consequentialist: they look to the end results of sexual intercourse to evaluate the way in which it should be practised. I would argue that the Anglican approach assesses these consequences more accurately, and that a more open attitude to contraception is an appropriate reflection of this. However, 'more open' should not be taken as meaning *unlimitedly* open. Although analysis of natural processes need not lead to the conclusion that the use of artificial means of birth control is always wrong, it may be that the concept of natural law properly applied should lead one to the conclusion that *always* to use methods of birth control *is* wrong. Such a conclusion would be based on the observation that having children is, looked at from most points of view, a 'good thing': it is a supreme expression of human creativity, it usually brings joy, fulfilment and satisfaction to couples involved and it appears to be one of those profound experiences that it is God's will that most people should enjoy. If a couple who are fertile set themselves for the whole of their married lives against the possibility of bearing children, there seems something perverse about the decision; they appear to be spurning one of the great goods in life. Thus there may be validity in applying the adjectives 'natural' and 'unnatural' not to the use of contraceptives over each particular sexual

act, but to the use of contraceptives over the sexual relationship as a whole. Yet even then, I believe, one would have
to allow for couples in exceptional circumstances where
childbearing might appear not to be a responsible option
(e.g., where they marry in early middle age, or have a
hereditary condition, substantially increasing the chances of
giving birth to a handicapped child). One does not want to
encourage a hasty judgmentalism which adds to the social
pressure on those who, as likely through physical impairment
as personal choice, do not have any children.

Divorce

Another issue on which the Roman Catholic Church has
traditionally taken an inflexible stance is that of divorce. This
follows from its understanding of marriage as an indissoluble
bond, which cannot be broken whatever the degree of deterioration in an actual marriage relationship. The marriage
union is seen as one that persists on an *ontological* level, at the
level of very being, even if the union between the two
individuals is no longer felt on an *experiential* level. Jesus's
words: 'What therefore God had joined together, let not man
put asunder' (Mark 10:9) are seen not just as a statement that
marriages *ought* not to be dissolved but that they *cannot* be
dissolved. Of course, Christians who do not take an indissolu-
bilist view (which includes most members of the Protestant
and Orthodox churches) would certainly agree that a major
wrong is committed when solemnly-made marriage vows are
broken, and two partners go their separate ways. Nevertheless, they are prepared to concede that a marriage relationship has then come to an end. They might also see divorce
in some cases as a merciful response to 'human hard-
heartedness', the sort of disposition which can make a
marriage a living hell – in the same way that Jesus seems to
have interpreted the divorce provision allowed by Moses.
Clearly this is a more consequential line of approach than the
rigorously deontological position maintained by Roman
Catholicism.

However, the Catholic Church has discovered a different way to cope with the undoubted reality of marriage breakdown. It has not been prepared to accept the legitimacy of divorce, but it has taken on board the concept of *nullity*. Thus the Church is prepared to annul, i.e., declare as null and void, those marriages where, in retrospect, there appears to have been something seriously amiss in the circumstances in which the original decision to marry was made. For example, someone who did not seriously consider all that was involved in getting married, did not know the other person well, or was suffering from a mental disorder at the time, stands a fair chance of getting his or her marriage annulled on the grounds of *defective consent*. What is one to make of this idea?

It obviously contains an important insight, inasmuch as many marriages *do* run into difficulties because the original decision was unduly hasty, perhaps undertaken when one (or both) of the partners was very young, or perhaps undertaken too much under the influence of erotic and romantic feelings which are an important part of married love, but very much more than which are needed for the sustaining of a marriage. However, a significant proportion of – to the outside eye – inadvisedly undertaken marriages can, given time, patience and hard work on the two partners' behalf, develop into happy and successful marriages. And conversely, marriages undertaken in the most auspicious of circumstances, with all the desirable forethought from the couple concerned, can still break down – because circumstances change, and so do people. It therefore seems simplistic to locate the cause of a marriage breakdown *invariably* in problems at outset, which is what the advocates of annulment procedures effectively do. A marriage which has turned out badly and was probably a mistake is still a marriage, and needs to be recognised as such. A system which recognises divorce, rather than nullity, is surely truer to the very varied facts of what actually happens in marriage relationships.

Casuistry and Double Effect

Many Protestant Christians would see the system of nullity as symptomatic of the more unacceptable face of Catholic moral thinking: an aspect which combines harsh inflexibility with devious machinations to get round that inflexibility. There was a period during the seventeenth century when Catholic manuals of moral theology appeared to be principally concerned with appeasing troubled consciences, the argument being that one need not feel bound to do what one thought only to be *probably* right.[21] A lax approach to moral issues has alternated with a much more rigorous one. Where the latter approach has been the dominant one, Catholic moral theology has been criticised as legalistic, too pernickety, over-confident of ascribing sin of varying degrees of seriousness to different actions. The moral theologians who followed in the wake of Aquinas sought to make a science out of *casuistry* – the detailed application of moral principles to particular cases. For many outsiders to this tradition the very detail of the application feels like a betrayal of the freedom of the Gospel.

Yet it would be foolish to write off this branch of the Christian tradition too quickly. For in analysing dilemma situations in such detail, the casuists developed some general principles which deserve our serious attention and respect. One particular principle which they frequently put to use in problematical situations is the notion of *double effect*. Double effect really means side effect. In essence, the principle says that one is justified in permitting incidental evil effects from one's good actions if there is a proportionate reason for doing so. It is presumed that if there were any less harmful ways of achieving the desired good one would use them.

The sort of situations to which double effect has been applied are as follows. Within the context of a 'just' war, can attacks on crucial military targets be justified even though they involve the risk of harm to a relatively small number of non-combatants who live close to the targets? When a patient who is terminally ill with cancer is suffering excruciating pain, is one justified in using considerable quantities of drugs to remove that pain, even though these drugs may have a suppressive side effect on the patient's respiratory system, possibly shortening his or her life thereby? When a pregnant woman is suffering from a cancerous womb which threatens her life, are doctors justified in removing her womb, even though such an action will result in the death of the fetus contained within it?

By applying the doctrine of double effect Catholic moral theologians have usually justified each of these actions. The 'evil' caused as one goes about doing good has been viewed as justified or tolerable if it meets the following four conditions:

> (1) The action which has the two effects is itself morally good or morally neutral; it is not morally evil. (2) The intention of the agent is upright; the direct effect of the action is good, and the indirect evil effect, though foreseen, is undesired. (3) The good and the evil must take effect at the same time; the evil is not a means to a good end lying some time in the future. (4) The good effect must be sufficiently desirable to compensate for allowing the evil effect; there must be a proportionately grave reason for allowing the evil to occur.

If we apply these conditions to one of the above examples, that of the pregnant mother, we could say that the action of removing the womb is morally neutral (though not of course a matter of psychological indifference); the intention of saving the mother's life (the only life that can be saved) is a pure one; relief to the mother, the good effect, occurs at the same time as death of the fetus, the evil effect; and the life-or-death situation is surely grave enough to satisfy the criterion of proportion. The Roman Catholic Church is well known for its official disapproval of all methods of direct abortion; it is less well known that through use of this principle of double effect it has seen fit to allow cases which it would describe as *indirect* abortion.

It is interesting to note that though the principle of double effect clearly takes consequences into account, it does not submit to a thoroughgoing consequentialism. It does not say that 'the end justifies the means' because it insists that the action itself should not be evil. Furthermore, in emphasising that good and evil effects should take place at the same time (or thereabouts), it guards against the persistent human tendency to justify morally dubious actions in terms of some uncertain long-term good. There is a major difference between removing a womb (and indirectly killing a fetus) to save a mother faced with an imminent threat to her life and directly killing a fetus to protect a woman faced with a possible reduction in life expectancy if her pregnancy is allowed to continue. If we are looking for a rule of thumb which avoids both deontological and consequentialist extremes, the principle of double effect has the virtue of retaining a strict rule (e.g., against the direct taking of innocent life) while allowing action which increases the prospect of favourable consequences in a conflict situation (i.e., by saving one life, the mother's, when failure to act would result in the loss of two lives). I shall return to double effect later.[22]

Barth

In the writings of Karl Barth (1886–1968), perhaps the greatest of twentieth-century theologians, we discover a way of thinking about moral issues which resolutely sets itself against the Catholic casuistical tradition based around the concept of natural law. Insisting on the primacy of God's revelation in Jesus Christ and in Scripture, Barth had as profound a distrust for 'natural' morality as he did for natural theology. In his massive *Church Dogmatics*, he argued that Christian ethics must not be ashamed to regard itself as the final word on the subject. It should not be forever forging links with a general or 'natural' ethics:

> . . Theological ethics on its part will cease to be what it is, if it dares to free itself from this offensiveness, if it does submit to a general principle, to let itself be measured by it and adjust to it.[23]

For Barth, the essence of Christian ethics is obedience to the divine command, and a person who obediently listens to the divine command is not in any position to consider why he should obey it. The grace which reconciles man to God is a commanding grace; paradoxically, it is in obedience to what God commands that human beings discover their true freedom.

Barth emphasises that the divine command has a definite content. The Bible consists more of specific commands than general rules, and these are still applicable to the Christian. Barth acknowledges that God speaks to us individually, but his command

> cannot either formally or materially differ from that which was given to them [the men of the Bible] or heard by them . . . The divine command has eternal and valid content for us precisely in its temporary expression, and demands that we should hear and respect it in our very different time and situation.[24]

What Barth appears to be expounding here is a Bible-centred ethic which allows little scope for human beings to use critical discernment in applying it.

However, in the second major ethical section of *Church Dogmatics*, III: 4, Barth interprets the nature of the divine command rather differently. Turning his attention to specific moral questions, he now rejects the idea that 'special ethics' means 'the understanding of the command of God as a prescribed text'.[25] He applies the word casuistry in a pejorative way to such an approach, and says that it is unsatisfactory for three reasons. First, the moralist is wishing to set himself on God's throne: 'Casuistry is a violation of the divine mystery in the ethical event'.[26] Second, it involves the untenable assumption that the command of God is 'a universal rule, an empty form, or rather a tissue of such rules and forms'.[27] Third, casuistry involves the destruction of Christian freedom, without which a good action does not exist. Here Barth, mindful that the Bible cannot always be applied in a straightforward manner to people living in very different times and situations, seems to be according the divine command which comes to an individual in a problematical situation priority over divine commands found in the Bible. It sounds as if he is advocating the Christian's total dependence on what he or she understands to be the voice of God: what Nowell-Smith would certainly consider to be an infantile form of morality, and one which could – where a person is subject to delusions about what God is telling him – prove extremely dangerous.

However, having moved in the direction of this extreme position, Barth then draws back from it. His own treatment of different 'spheres' of human activity makes clear that he is not averse to rational *evaluation* of what God's will might be in any particular situation. An exploration of these spheres does not lead to the ethical 'answer itself', but to 'a definite lead in the direction of the answer', 'a directive, or rather a series of directives, which give guidance to the individual in the form of an approximation to the knowledge of the divine command and right human action'.[28]

Barth's discussion of issues such as work, marriage, parenthood and nation is extremely perceptive. It is characterised not only by a desire to be faithful to what Barth sees as biblical insights but also by an informed analysis of the particular issues. The language of divine command is still present. Marriage, he says, should be seen as a special vocation:

> It is a matter of the Holy Ghost freeing man for this in no sense ordinary but highly extraordinary fulfilment of the relation between man and woman.[29]

He says that the New Testament thinks only of the permanence and indissolubility of marriage, not from the standpoint of a terribly sharpened law but from that of a gloriously powerful Gospel. However,

> we cannot sufficiently seriously realise that by no means every human striving, coming and being together of two partners in love and marriage automatically implies that God has joined them together and that permanence and indissolubility attach to their union.[30]

In exceptional circumstances, marriages may therefore be dissolved in recognition of the fact that marrying in the first place did not represent obedience to the divine command. This basis for dissolution clearly bears comparison with

Catholic grounds for annulment, although Barth is prepared to use the language of divorce rather than that of nullity.

On the whole, however, talk of obedience to God's command is less dominant in Barth's discussion of practical issues than when he is speaking of ethics in the abstract. Moreover, his absorption in the detail of particular issues is often such as to make his method not dissimilar to the casuistry which he regards in such a jaundiced light. Thus in the section 'Freedom for Life' Barth considers a series of issues all involving, in some way, a threat to life. He regards life as a loan from God and as such worthy of honour and respect. In almost all circumstances life must be affirmed and preserved, but Barth persistently brings to attention the situation which might constitute an exception. On the questions of suicide, abortion, euthanasia, killing in self-defence, capital punishment and war, all of them issues which Barth surveys with no little insight, his attitude is basically similar. Normally these things are quite wrong, the divine command will clearly be against killing except . . . and in each case Barth finds an exception where the loss of life involved is counterbalanced by some more important consideration. For instance, in normal circumstances Barth is totally opposed to the death penalty: it is quite improper for sinful man to pass the ultimate judgment on his fellow-man. But where the actions of a traitor threaten a state and its stability in such a way that a choice has to be made between the existence of one or the other, Barth is prepared to concede that capital punishment may be justified.[31] The prospect of consenting to the dissolution of one's own state is a thought he finds intolerable; strongly though he stresses the principle of respect for life, there are limits beyond which he is not prepared to take it. Barth's exceptions take seriously the likelihood of unwelcome consequences.

Findings

At this stage it may be helpful to recall Nowell-Smith's criticisms of Christian morality. He argued that it has been dominated by rules, rules which derive their obligatory power from an authority that cannot be questioned, and rules which are regarded as absolute. This description may well be true of the way large portions of the Church have gone about their moral thinking down the centuries. But if we take Barth, Aquinas and Augustine as spokesmen for three major traditions in Christian ethics (the Protestant, the Catholic, and the Church Father to whom both Protestants and Catholics have looked for support), it is interesting to reflect how they stand up in the face of such criticism. Despite the considerable differences between them, certain generalisations can be ventured. Clearly they are prepared to place reliance on sacred authorities: the Bible, natural law or the Word of God understood as a more private revelation. Clearly they do too regard certain activities as *always* sinful, e.g., lying in the case of Augustine, contraception in the case of Aquinas. On the other hand, they still find a very crucial place for human reason in the decision-making process: explicitly in the theory which underlies natural law, and implicitly in the way that the Bible is interpreted and applied. Moreover, in most areas of human activity they do not adhere rigorously to absolute rules. They recognise the possibility of exceptions, and attempt (even Barth, for all his anti-casuistical rhetoric) to define what constitutes a legitimate exception. Whatever their blind spots, whatever the deficiencies in their logic at certain points, they defy simplistic categorisation as moral thinkers and certainly cannot be described as infantile. They, too, feel the pull of the tension between the rule-based and consequence-based approaches to ethics; and so our search for a distinctively Christian position in this debate continues.

Notes

1   'Homilies on 1 John', *Augustine: Later Works*, Library of Christian Classics, vol. VIII, SCM, 1955, p. 316.
2   St Augustine, *The City of God*, Penguin, 1984, Bk 1, ch. 18, pp. 27–8.
3   *Op. cit.*, ch. 19, p. 30.

4 St Augustine, 'Reply to Faustus the Manichaean', *The Nicene and Post-Nicene Fathers*, vol. IV, Eerdmans, 1956, Bk XXII, par. 73.
5 In saying this I am not denying that he has his blind spots with regard to e.g., sex.
6 'Reply to Faustus the Manichaean', par. 73.
7 *The City of God*, Bk 1, ch. 21, p. 32.
8 *Ibid.*
9 Roland H. Bainton, *Christian Attitudes to War and Peace*, Hodder and Stoughton, 1961, p. 91.
10 'Reply to Faustus the Manichaean', par. 74.
11 St Thomas Aquinas, *Summa Theologica*, II. 2, Qu. 91, Art. 2. As translated in *Aquinas: Selected Political Writings* (ed. A. P. D'Entrèves), Blackwell, Oxford, 1959, p. 115.
12 This phrase occurs in R. C. Mortimer's classical presentation of the natural law concept in *The Elements of Moral Theology*, A. & C. Black, 1947, p. 8.
13 *Summa Theologica*, II. 2, Qu. 94, Art. 2. As in *Aquinas: Selected Political Writings*, p. 123.
14 *Op. cit.*, Qu. 94, Art. 6. 1966 Blackfriars translation of *Summa*, vol. xxviii, p. 97.
15 *Op. cit.*, Qu. 94, Art. 5. Blackfriars translation, p. 93.
16 *Op. cit.*, Qu. 94, Art. 3. Blackfriars translation, p. 89.
17 St Thomas Aquinas, *Summa Contra Gentiles*, University of Notre Dame Press and Doubleday, New York, 1975, 3. II, ch. 122.
18 R. C. Mortimer, *The Elements of Moral Theology*, pp. 178–9.
19 See *Humanae Vitae*, Catholic Truth Society, 1968, par. 16.
20 The Report was published by SPCK in 1958, but may be more conveniently found in Ian T. Ramsey (ed.), *Christian Ethics and Contemporary Philosophy*, SCM, 1966, pp. 340–81.
21 The school of thought which argued this was known as Probabilism. It prompted a rival school of thought which urged stricter allegiance to what one honestly believed (probably) to be right: this was known as Probabiliorism.
22 See my discussion on p. 189–91.
23 Karl Barth, *Church Dogmatics*, vol. II: 2, T. & T. Clark, Edinburgh, 1957, p. 521.
24 *Op. cit.*, pp. 706–7.
25 *Church Dogmatics*, vol. III: 4, Clark, 1961, p. 6.
26 *Op cit.*, p. 11.
27 *Ibid.*
28 *Op. cit.*, pp. 30–1.
29 *Op. cit.*, p. 184.
30 *Op. cit.*, p. 208.
31 *Op. cit.*, pp. 446–8.

5

PRIVATE AND PUBLIC MORALITY

In the course of discussing the dilemma situations outlined in Chapter 1, I noted the common tendency to adopt less exacting standards in the social sphere than the personal one. Compromise seems to be part and parcel of the world of politics and economics. Things which an individual would never conceive of doing in a private capacity suddenly become thinkable – even obligatory – when one assumes official responsibility. Can there be any theological justification for this? Although the present theological fashion is to decry such thinking as dualistic, and to insist that the Christian faith has as many implications for the way society is run as the way we live our 'inner' lives, the possibility of a legitimate distinction between different spheres of activity should not be discounted too easily. Certainly it has been central to the ethical approach of one particular Christian tradition, that stemming from the Reformer Martin Luther (1483–1546).

Luther and the Two Kingdoms

According to Luther, Christians belong to two kingdoms, the Kingdom of Christ and the kingdom of the world. As people who have been saved through faith in the cross of Christ they are called to fulfil his radical commands to love in the power and inspiration of the Holy Spirit. Those who belong to the Kingdom of Christ properly

> need no secular sword or law. And if everyone in the world was a true Christian, that is a true believer, there would be no need or

use for prince, king, lord, sword or law. For what purpose would it serve, as long as they had the Holy Spirit in their hearts to teach them and ensure that they never did wrong, loved everyone, and gladly and joyfully suffered wrong from everyone, even death?[1]

The last phrase is a little illogical, because if everyone was guided by the Holy Spirit presumably they would not be in the business of inflicting wrong; but the fact is, of course, that Christians do have to suffer wrong, illustrating the fact that the world is *not* inhabited only by Christians. Few believe, and fewer still, according to Luther, behave in a Christian way. Because the forces of sin and evil are rampant in the world, human beings cannot be expected to live in peace and brotherhood with their neighbours without the threat of physical coercion. This God has ordained and provided for them in the form of political authority and the rule of law. The function and honour of government are 'to make men out of wild beasts and to prevent men from becoming wild beasts.'[2] Men are subjected to the threat of the sword, so that

> even if they desire to do evil they cannot, and even if they do it, they may not do it without fear or with joy and success, just as a fierce wild animal is bound with chains and bonds, so that it cannot bite and tear in the way it would like.[3]

Luther is therefore quite prepared to approve the use of force – by those in positions of official authority. To kings, princes, magistrates and soldiers apply Paul's words in Romans 13, about the divinely ordained use of the sword to punish evil-doers. To citizens in their private capacity, above all Christians with their vocation to be like Jesus in following the way of the cross, apply the radical commands in Matthew 5 and Romans 12 about turning the other cheek, not resisting evil and practising love of a thoroughly long-suffering kind. While Luther's concept of the two kingdoms owed something to Augustine's not dissimilar notion of the heavenly and earthly cities, and to a well-developed medieval concept distinguishing between spiritual and secular power, it was *essentially* an attempt to be faithful to two very different strands which Luther discovered in the Bible. As Helmut Thielicke, a leading twentieth-century Lutheran theologian, has commented:

> In theme and intention at least, the doctrine of the two kingdoms is simply a conceptual scheme whereby various key statements of the Bible are brought into systematic relationship, not just equilibrium.[4]

Luther emphasised that the kingdom of the world whose symbol is the sword is still God's Kingdom – God works out his purposes through it – and that the motive of love should inform all activity, even that of a coercive and superficially unloving character. For this to happen, it is important that Christians take their share of worldly responsibilities; Luther encourages Christians to volunteer for such roles as lord, judge, constable and hangman (!). On one occasion he wrote:

> Since the beginning of the world a wise prince is a mighty rare bird, and an upright prince even rarer . . . If a prince should happen to be wise, upright, or a Christian, that is one of the great miracles, the most precious token of divine grace upon that land.[5]

There are thus places in Luther's writings where he emphasises the distinctive element which the Christian can bring to the performance of his public duties, an element which seems to diminish the gulf between the two kingdoms and points to an underlying unity between them. On the other hand, there is an equally significant strand in his writing which emphasises the intrinsic legitimacy of political authority, whoever wields it, and which argues that *reason* is the basic all-important requirement for the business of ruling. That the emperor possess a healthy dose of reason was a more vital qualification for his office than his being a saint or a Christian. A wise non-Christian prince was preferable as a ruler to a foolish Christian one, who might be tempted to confuse the two kingdoms and try to rule with kid gloves.

> God made the secular government subordinate and subject to reason, because it is to have no jurisdiction over the welfare of

souls or things of eternal value, but only over physical and temporal goods, which God places under man's dominion.[6]

Here the self-sufficiency of man (even unbelieving man) for the tasks of government is stressed, and the focus is upon the separation, not the underlying unity between the two kingdoms.

In Luther's view, the kingdom of the world did not only include the political sphere, much though he had to say about this. It comprised what later Lutheran theologians came to call the *orders of creation*. Individuals also bear positions of official responsibility in the orders or areas of business, work, marriage and the family. They have God-given stations within these various orders, e.g., those of magistrate, farmer, husband and father. Such stations provide an opportunity to serve God and exercise love towards one's neighbour right at the heart of worldly existence; Luther emphasised the vocational element in ordinary activities in contrast to what he saw as the false vocation represented by the monastic life. And what one should do in discharging one's worldly responsibilities is usually evident to human reason. Luther thought that analysis of the costs of business should be competent to establish a just price; he believed that consideration of the physical constitution of men and women indicates the appropriateness of traditional masculine and feminine roles.[7] He brings in biblical material to support his advice, but the Bible is not here the determinative authority as it is where faith, salvation and the Gospel are concerned. Although many Lutheran theologians (not Luther himself) have objected to the notion of natural law, in the concept of orders of creation we find a process of reasoning from the evidence of natural phenomena not unlike that evident in the Catholic natural-law tradition. Such reasoning is often starkly consequentialist in character. If the state fails to punish evil-doers and restrain violent men, anarchy and chaos are the results. If the economy does not offer incentives to diligence and productivity, people are no longer motivated to work, and similar consequences ensue. In a modern-day Lutheran theologian such as Thielicke as much as in Luther himself, the emphasis is on viewing the orders as orders of *preservation* to protect humanity from the calamitous consequences of its indelibly sinful nature.

The Lutheran approach to social ethics has been subject to fierce criticism in the present century. The American theologian Reinhold Niebuhr (1892–1971) stands as one of the sharpest and most representative of its critics, even though he acknowledges a considerable debt to Luther in other areas, e.g., in Luther's theology of the cross. Niebuhr had three main criticisms. First, he criticised what he saw as a very stark dualism in Luther's notion of the two kingdoms. As Niebuhr put it, Luther lacked a necessary sense of the dialectical interrelationship between the 'realm of grace', and the 'realm of law'. For instance, he failed to see that forgiving love had a place in tempering the demands of justice. Second, Niebuhr accused Luther of being indifferent to most of the social and political questions of his day. A theology of the orders represents an essentially defeatist attitude, i.e., one of simply leaving the world of political and economic relations to take the course which natural impulse prompts, immune from any prophetic Christian critique. Third, Niebuhr criticised Luther's uncritical affirmation of state authority. Luther was hypersensitive to the dangers of anarchy in the egotism of citizens, but insufficiently sensitive to the dangers of tyranny in the selfishness of rulers. This is evident in his reaction to the Peasants' Revolt in Germany in 1525, where he urged the rulers to suppress the rebellion with great severity.[8] These three failings, dualism, social indifference, and uncritical support for state authority, can be traced throughout subsequent German history, heavily influenced by Lutheranism; indeed, they go part of the way to explaining the fairly negligible resistance of the German Church to Hitler.

Clearly Niebuhr's criticisms contain some substance: there are passages in Luther which substantiate these changes. Yet Niebuhr, along with other critics, appears to be blind to those strands in Luther's highly unsystematic body of writing which counteract these tendencies to some extent. As I have shown, elements in his writing unite the two kingdoms rather than separate them; love *should* still be operative in the kingdom of the world, even if it is hidden behind a sterner guise. Although he was certainly not a social revolutionary, it is unfair to describe Luther as indifferent to social and economic questions; his writings are chock-full of proposals as to how things could be run better! Furthermore, though the language with which he exhorted German princes to 'hit, stab and kill' the rebellious peasants was certainly extreme, he was not uncritical of the rulers of his day:

> . . . generally the biggest fools or the worst scoundrels on earth . . . the majority of the princes and lords are godless tyrants and enemies of God . . . We have no one on earth to thank for this disastrous rebellion, except you princes and lords.[9]

Luther was more even-handed in his criticisms than Niebuhr alleges.

Whatever reservations one may harbour about Luther's distinctive emphases, his central line of argument is difficult to dismiss wholesale. Some level of distinction between behaviour in personal and official spheres of life appears to be impossible to avoid. Assumption of an official role involves acceptance of a zone of responsibility, and if public expectations of that role are not to be hopelessly confused, acceptance of a code of behaviour which is to some extent 'given' is necessary. A treasurer of an organisation who gave money to literally all who begged from him would be guilty of mishandling the funds of that organisation. A policeman who 'turned the other cheek' as a response to the outbreak of public disturbance could hardly be said to be discharging his duties. He provides a public service by performing the duty of restraining violent individuals. Even pacifists, generally (Tolstoy being a notable exception), have supported retention of a police force. It is then plausible to argue that a government which fails to maintain any forces to defend its people from *external* attack, as well as internal attack, is abdicating a fundamental responsibility of government. However, this does not mean that it is justified in going to any lengths or using *any* means to defend its people. Luther's writing on the use of force is disturbing, not because he fails to distinguish between just and unjust pretexts for its use (this he does) but because he appears to give licence to excessive and uncontrolled use of force.[10] And in our own nuclear age, with conventional as well as nuclear weapons becoming ever more devastating in their effects, there is no doubt that the case for resort to armed force is becoming ever more problematical. Nevertheless, the possibility of using force in a controlled and disciplined way still exists.

In a way it is ironic that Niebuhr should accuse Luther of dualism, because he himself has been seen as advocating a sharp dualism between individual and social ethics. But in distinguishing between the two areas Niebuhr did not use the language of the two kingdoms; instead, he wrote extensively about love and justice. For twentieth-century minds, this may well be more helpful phraseology to use when distinguishing between different spheres of activity. I shall now examine Niebuhr's treatment of love and justice as a source of illumination on these, perhaps the two most fundamental concepts in Christian ethics.

Niebuhr: Love and Justice

Niebuhr described love in two different ways. One was in terms of *harmony*. Where people are motivated by love in their relations with each other, there harmony among them will be evident. Ideally, love will promote a spirit of brotherhood which will find expression in socially just relationships. The other way in which Niebuhr interpreted love was in terms of *self-sacrifice*. Self-sacrificial love is the type that Jesus taught and practised. It plays an essential role in enabling one to identify imaginatively with the needs and interests of other persons and groups. However, Niebuhr's personal experience of industrial life (he was a pastor in Detroit for many years, and knew of the harsh conditions under which workers toiled in the Ford factory) drove him to the 'realistic' conclusion that a love which seeketh not its own is not able to maintain itself in historical society. Not only may it fall victim to excessive forms of the self-assertion of others; but even the most perfectly balanced system of justice in history is a balance of competing wills and interests, and must therefore worst anyone who does not participate in the balance.[11]

Niebuhr's analysis of social life is therefore that self-sacrificial love generally does not work. The powerful do not identify sympathetically with the less powerful, so the latter are apt to suffer oppression and exploitation. This is true both of relations on the industrial scene, between management and unions, and of relations on the international scene, between stronger and weaker countries. Although individuals among the more powerful group might be willing to identify with the other group, as a whole it is extremely rare for a group to set aside a collective desire to promote its own concerns. As Niebuhr put it, individuals and groups have different possibilities of moral transcendence, though the title of his most famous book, *Moral Man and Immoral Society*, actually overstates his thesis: a more accurate, if less snappy, summary of the book's contents would have been 'The Not So Moral Man in His Less Moral Communities.'[12]

In the fallen world in which we live, a relatively just society is therefore less likely to be the result of human goodwill (which is all too often not reciprocated) as of an even balance of competing interests and powers, with those who start from weaker positions vigorously asserting their rights. If a group of workers is going to get a deserved pay rise, they will almost certainly have to *demand* that pay rise, and threaten industrial action if the rise is not forthcoming.

Society must strive for justice even if it is forced to use means, such as self-assertion, resistance, coercion and even resentment, which cannot gain the moral sanction of the most sensitive moral spirit.[13]

Here justice, conceived essentially if rather imprecisely as a principle of equality, appears to be demanding means far removed from the characteristics of self-sacrificial love. One may well wonder whether love still has any obligatory force in the sphere of social ethics. Yet Niebuhr insists that it has. He sees love as an absolute norm or ideal which reveals the inadequacies and the sinful elements in every programme of social justice. It is an 'impossible possibility' which cannot be fully achieved in this world, at least not in a complete or direct way, but which still has an inspirational value. Moreover,

> Individuals, even when involved in their communities, will always have the opportunity of loyalty to the highest canons of personal morality. Sometimes, when their group is obviously bent on evil, they may have to express their individual ideals by disassociating themselves from their group.[14]

Alternatively, a leader who has the opportunity to use his position of power for personal gain may display self-sacrificial love in not doing so, instead subordinating his own interests to promoting the concerns of the group he represents.

On the whole, Niebuhr is content to allow love and justice to stand in tension. The individual is encouraged to feel the pull of both, and his actions may properly reflect either one principle or the other, justice being the norm which is more likely to receive practical application in the sphere of social ethics. How then does Niebuhr proceed when handling a concrete ethical issue? Let us consider his treatment of the subject of war.

Niebuhr moved from a position of pacifism, in his early years, to become a forceful critic of pacifism, especially in the debate surrounding American involvement in the Second World War. He believed that there could be a place for non-violent resistance (for instance, he thought that the type practised by Gandhi was ideally suited to dealing with British imperial power), but on the whole he thought that pacifist tactics were doomed to failure: the side prepared to use force triumphs. The pragmatic orientation of his criticism is thereby evident. He was not ashamed of this, claiming that 'When viewing a historic situation all moralists become pragmatists and utilitarians.'[15] His moral assessment of wars and their conduct appears to hinge on the principle of proportionality:

the requirement to produce the best possible balance of desirable over undesirable consequences. This in turn requires that the cause be just, and the violence used not excessive. Niebuhr implicitly presupposes the validity of most of the traditional just-war criteria, but as James Gustafson has remarked, he 'does not attend to and use the principles of the just war tradition in any highly developed way'.[16] Niebuhr's writing is notable for its frequent mention of the primary principles of love and justice, along with others such as order, liberty and equality, but he prefers to maintain a dialectical tension between them rather than spell out any second-order principles which might follow from them.

In my view, this lack of second-order principles helps to account for the strongly consequentialist thrust of Niebuhr's ethics. With regard to the bombing of enemy cities in the Second World War, Niebuhr wrote in the summer of 1943:

> It is not possible to defeat a foe without causing innocent people to suffer with the guilty. It is not possible to engage in any act of collective opposition to collective evil without involving the innocent with the guilty. It is not possible to move in history without becoming tainted with guilt. Once bombing has been developed as an instrument of warfare, it is not possible to disavow its use without capitulating to the foe who refuses to disavow it.[17]

Niebuhr therefore regarded the bombing policies as 'tragic necessities', emphasising that 'no man has the moral freedom to escape from these hard and cruel necessities of history.'[18] Although in 1944 he complained that the military necessity of 'obliteration' bombing had not been satisfactorily explained by the Allied governments, he was clearly open in principle to the use of indiscriminate means in warfare:

> . . . once the instruments of a total war are unloosed they will guarantee defeat for the side that *fails to use* them, whether from want of resolution, or failure of organisation, or moral scruple.[19]

This is consequentialism taken to disturbing limits. Niebuhr is supporting a war fought in the name of justice, but in pursuing it he is prepared to tolerate the injustice of directly killing innocent non-combatants. He is ready to set aside his moral scruples because victory in war is regarded as absolutely essential. Yet the fact that Niebuhr retained his moral scruples is evident from his talk of actions which are *tainted with guilt*, and which require repentance even though they may be militarily necessary. Similarly, Niebuhr's rejection of the use (though not the possession) of nuclear weapons is largely based on the prospect of a heavy burden of moral guilt which would plague a nation which had used them.[20] It appears that the use of certain weapons does have something intrinsically objectionable about it, even when such use might be justified on purely consequential grounds. The yardstick by which moral guilt is being measured is presumably a non-consequential one.

Niebuhr's ethical methodology therefore appears rather confused; there are inconsistencies in his conceptual framework of which he does not seem to have been fully aware. He is still an enlightening writer. I think that James Gustafson has put his finger on why this is:

> he was a very learned 'moral virtuoso' whose brilliance achieved more intuitively what less talented minds have to strive toward more methodically . . . his effectiveness rested heavily on the persuasiveness of his interpretation of historic events and movements.[21]

Niebuhr's distinction between the nature of individual and social morality remains important. Nevertheless, he allows industrial groups, societies and governments a disturbing amount of licence; he is little less discriminating than Luther, whom he criticises, about the means which may be employed to achieve a desired end. Love and justice are left *too* much in dialectical tension, and not interrelated sufficiently clearly; for instance, the just-war tradition could be interpreted (and is by a fellow-American ethicist Paul Ramsey) as an 'in-principled' application of Christian *agape*.[22] A just war may be seen as an expression of love for one's neighbours who are under attack. Similarly, the principle of double effect (used by Ramsey but not by Niebuhr) can be defended as an attempt to ensure that justice is done to individuals when love for one's neighbour seems to demand drastic measures. Without second-order principles of this type, principles like love and justice appear capable of limitless variety of application. But Niebuhr is certainly correct to highlight the centrality of love and justice for Christian ethical thinking. I shall return to the question of what can be deduced from these fundamental ethical principles in Chapter 9.

Notes

1 'Temporal Authority: To What Extent It Should Be Obeyed', *Luther's Works*, vol. 45, Muhlenberg, Philadelphia, 1962, p. 88.
2 'A Sermon on Keeping Children in School', *Luther's Works*, vol. 46, Fortress, Philadelphia, 1967, p. 237.
3 'Temporal Authority: To What Extent It Should Be Obeyed', p. 90.
4 Helmut Thielicke, *Theological Ethics*, vol. II, A. & C. Black, 1969, p. 324.
5 'Temporal Authority: To What Extent It Should Be Obeyed', p. 113.
6 'Psalm 101', *Luther's Works*, vol. 13, Concordia, St Louis, 1956, p. 198.
7 'Trade and Usury', *Luther's Works*, vol. 45, pp. 247–52; 'Table Talk Recorded by Veit Dietrich, 1531–1533', *Luther's Works*, vol. 54, Fortress, 1967, p. 8. It is worth adding that Luther's exercise of reason in these areas reveals a certain amount of naïvety and prejudice!
8 'Against the Robbing and Murdering Hordes of Peasants', *Luther's Works*, vol. 46, pp. 49–55.
9 These quotations are taken from 'Temporal Authority: To What Extent It Should Be Obeyed', p. 113; 'Whether Soldiers, Too, Can Be Saved', *Luther's Works*, vol. 46, p. 115; 'Admonition to Peace, A Reply to the Twelve Articles of the Peasants in Swabia, 1525', *Luther's Works*, vol. 46, p. 19.
10 'Against the Robbing and Murdering Hordes of Peasants' and 'Whether Soldiers, Too, Can Be Saved', cited above.
11 Reinhold Niebuhr, *The Nature and Destiny of Man*, vol. II, Nisbet, 1943, p. 75.
12 Niebuhr himself acknowledged this in his *Man's Nature and his Communities*, Charles Scribner's, New York, 1965, p. 22.
13 Reinhold Niebuhr, *Moral Man and Immoral Society*, SCM, 1963 (first British edition; original Charles Scribner's 1932), p. 257.

14 *Op. cit.*, p. 273.
15 *Op. cit.*, p. 170.
16 James Gustafson, 'Theology in the Service of Ethics', *Reinhold Niebuhr and the issues of our time* (ed. Richard Harries), Mowbray, 1986, p. 33.
17 Reinhold Niebuhr, 'The Bombing of Germany', *Love and Justice* (ed., D. B. Robertson), Meridian Books, Cleveland, 1967, p. 222.
18 *Ibid.*
19 Reinhold Niebuhr, 'Airplanes Are Not Enough' (1944), *Love and Justice*, p. 90.
20 Reinhold Niebuhr, 'The Nuclear Dilemma – A Discussion', *Christianity and Crisis* 21, no. 19 (November 13, 1961), p. 202.
21 James Gustafson, 'Theology in the Service of Ethics', pp. 35 and 36.
22 See Paul Ramsey, *War and the Christian Conscience*, Duke University Press, 1961, and my further discussion in chapter 9.

6

THE PRIMACY OF VIRTUE

There are some writers who would object in a fundamental
way to the dominant framework of this book. They would say
that a concentration on the deontological and consequentialist ways of thinking, and the search for a *via media* which
partakes of the best and avoids the worst in both extremes,
represent serious mistakes in ethical thought. I do not believe
that they are right, but it is wholly appropriate that at this
stage of my argument I should stand back for a while and
consider three very significant types of challenge to it. Two
of these alternatives claim that there is a way to approach
moral problems which is orientated neither by rules nor by
consequences. The third alternative certainly takes rules and
consequences into account, but is pessimistic about the
chances of ever finding an ethically 'correct' answer.

Personal Relationships

First, there is the type of ethical thinker who argues that both
the deontological and consequentialist approaches err because they are essentially *abstract*. They forget that moral
dilemmas involve people, and what is really at stake in such
situations is the quality and depth of personal relationships.
Am I treating someone else with the honour, respect and
seriousness which he or she deserves? That, the *personalist*
would say, is the fundamental question, not whether I am
adhering to a time-honoured rule or whether my actions lead
to the most desirable consequences. The focus should be on

the other person or people, not on an abstract principle which may be irrelevant to their deepest needs and desires. Ethics should be person-oriented. And if one asks what is the quality which should characterise everything which goes on in the sphere of personal relationships, the answer usually given is the simple word 'love'.

Some humanist writers have voiced this sort of challenge. But it has also been made in the name of Christian ethics. This is not really surprising. Concern and respect for persons is a fundamental Christian principle. Jesus summed up the Old Testament law in the twofold command to love, and Paul clearly places love at the head of his lists of virtues. At first sight the person-centred approach appears far closer to the spirit of New Testament ethics than either the rule-based or the consequence-based approaches.

Nor is it surprising that the primacy of personal relationships and the emphasis on love have been particularly evident in recent writing on the morality of sexual relationships. Traditionally, Christian thinkers had tended to focus on the morality or immorality of different sexual acts, whether the subject in view was masturbation, intercourse or the use of contraceptives. Often the concentration upon the act (and in particular the question of whether human potential for procreation was or wasn't being frustrated) directed attention away from the subject-matter of a personal, loving relationship. There has been a decisive shift of perspective among virtually all recent Christian writers. The many writings of Jack Dominian, a Roman Catholic psychiatrist who has specialised in the area of sex and marriage, are a vivid illustration of this trend. Sexual actions are evaluated in terms of what builds up a capacity for loving, lasting relationships between two people. For instance, in contrast to the traditional hostile approach to masturbation, Dominian writes thus:

> Masturbation is an event to be neither encouraged nor associated with dire warnings. It is a transient activity in the life of the adolescent on the way to reaching and achieving sexual intercourse in marriage . . . Whatever its form, it should be associated with affirmative feelings about sex and seen as nature's and God's

way to reveal by stages the full plan of sexual activity. Insofar as it introduces young people to the mystery of sex, masturbation should not be surrounded by negativity, inhibition and/or guilt. Rather it should be treated as a means to an end, the end being adult sexuality situated in love.[1]

Dominian's approach to sexual ethics (and, one presumes, ethics in general) can be summarised in his statement that 'What really matters is the encounter of persons and the presence of love'.[2]

Although such things unquestionably do matter, it is not the case that morally controversial issues can be settled through a simple appeal to them. This is shown by the fact that equally person-centred, love-motivated thinkers can come to different conclusions on particular issues. Dominian, for all his departure from traditional stances on issues such as masturbation and his sympathetic treatment of those who diverge from sexual norms, still believes firmly that a marital relationship is *the* appropriate context for sexual intercourse. Joseph Fletcher, whose book *Situation Ethics*, published in 1966, is probably the most famous exposition of a personalist approach to ethics, is far more open to the possibility of intercourse being right in non-marital settings. For Fletcher love – understood as 'willing the good of one's neighbour' – is the only norm which requires unconditional obedience and any rule or law may be broken if it comes into conflict with what love demands in a particular situation. Although Fletcher concedes that traditional rules may contain moral wisdom which we do well to heed, the crucial test of: 'Am I hereby acting lovingly?' can, for him, justify all manner of surprising actions – such as a woman seducing a man in order to cure his predilection for little girls or a prostitute removing a sailor's doubts about his virility.[3]

In an earlier chapter, when emphasising the importance of treating persons as ends, I wrote that if one's intention in the act of sexual intercourse is 'to express love to that person, considering her interests and welfare as well as my own', the act assumes a 'morally defensible' character.[4] The words 'morally defensible' are somewhat question-begging and they were meant to be, because it is in fact debatable whether an intention of expressing love to a person represents a sufficient ground for entering into sexual relations with her. Many thinkers would argue that love is only present in the truest and deepest sense of the word when the act of sexual intercourse occurs in the context of a long-term relationship, where two people are committed to each other at every level of their existence (i.e., marriage, or something strongly resembling it). They would say that consideration of a girl's interests and welfare would necessarily lead one to establish such a relationship before embarking on full sexual relations. This would seem to be in line with the view of sex found in the Bible, where the act of becoming 'one flesh' is associated with a permanent 'cleaving' of husband and wife. Others would argue that such a view overestimates the significance of the act of intercourse and that the loving, personal nature of an encounter can make intercourse appropriate in a more short-term relationship as well as a long-term one. In short, some see love as linked to a particular way of structuring relationships, in which rules and prohibitions have their place; others see love as something far more flexible, transcending the structures and relativising the rules.

Writers who affirm the primacy of love, then, invariably end up veering either in a deontological or consequentialist direction. Fletcher ultimately emerges as an out-and-out consequentialist. He raises the question: 'If the end does not justify the means, what does?' and asserts that 'The answer is, obviously, "Nothing!"'.[5] He seeks a coalition between his love ethic and Utilitarianism:

> Our situation ethics frankly joins forces with Mill; no rivalry here. We choose what is most 'useful' for the most people.[6]

Fletcher is therefore fully prepared to approve actions which neglect, betray and sacrifice individuals (including innocent persons) if by so doing there is a reasonable chance of helping a greater number of people. What this signifies for the individuals who (unluckily) happen to be in the minority is a question I shall return to in Chapter 8; it is sufficient for the moment merely to note the statistical nature of his calculation. Significantly, Fletcher cannot accept that Jesus really approved the act of the woman who poured the costly oint-ment over him. He says that the choice lies between 'impetuous, uncalculating, unenlightened sentimental love', as represented by the woman, and 'a calculating, enlightened love'. Fletcher explicitly commends the disciples who saw that 'love must work in coalition with utilitarian distribution, spreading the benefits as widely as possible'.[7]

In contrast Paul Ramsey, who also makes love the corner-stone of his ethical thinking, inclines much more to a deon-tological standpoint. He thinks that there are certain rules which actually embody Christian love, *agape* (i.e., they are an accurate description of what love means in practice), and once one has accepted these rules it is one's moral duty to abide by them. Faithfulness in marriage is an example of this. The rule not to commit adultery so clearly embodies the principle of marital love that it would be quite wrong ever to violate it. (This is not, of course, to say that one fulfils one's obligations of love *simply* by refraining from adultery.) Ramsey's point is that to be of use in specific situations the guiding principle of love needs to be spelt out in terms of more detailed rules. And if there are some actions which appear by very definition to be unloving, there is surely nothing objec-tionable about a rule which forbids them absolutely. Ramsey is therefore quite prepared to talk of some moral rules being *exceptionless*.[8]

There is another question begged by the statement which I cited from Chapter 2. The personal pronoun 'her' clearly indicated that, as a heterosexual male, I was considering the morality of sexual relations with a member of the opposite sex. But many in today's world would argue that homosexual and lesbian partnerships can involve just as profound a quality of relationship and just as meaningful an expression of love as what goes on between men and women. Indeed, some of the strongest defences of a personalist approach to ethics have occurred in the context of controversy about the moral-ity of homosexual relationships. The plea has been made that homosexual relationships be judged by the same or similar criteria as heterosexual ones; in other words, where the homosexual encounter is one of committed, self-giving love between two freely consenting individuals, full physical relations are wholly appropriate.[9]

Although this argument has won an increasing level of acceptance, there are still many who are not persuaded by it, both in Christian and secular circles. This is doubtless due partly to social prejudice and differences in sexual taste, but these are insufficient explanations. The conviction persists that for all the depth of love which may exist across a wide range of relationships, sexual intercourse is *not* an appropriate expression of love in some of them. This is clearly true of the relationship between a parent and a child.[10] A relationship between two members of the same sex could also come into the same category. Arguments from natural law (found in an implicit form in the Bible in Romans 1:23–6) appear to have an enduring relevance here. Two important facts about heterosexual intercourse, the fact that men and women are physically complementary and that through their union procreation is potentially realisable, seem to suggest that it is this mode of sexuality which is fitting and beneficial for humanity. Men and women were created for each other, sexually speaking; where someone now feels principally attracted to individuals of his or her own sex, that person may be said to be at odds (though in very few cases deliberately at odds) with God's creative intentions. Such, at any rate, is the counter-argument which might be lodged against the personalist thinker who puts homosexual relationships on a par with heterosexual ones. What can be said with confidence is that the Bible does not put the two on the same level.

The claim that the quality of a personal relationship is *the* all-decisive ethical criterion is therefore open to dispute. The defender of a more traditional stance on homosexuality would argue that analysis of the sexual act and its appropriateness to different types of relationship is still in order. Of course, the quality of love is relevant to all types of relationship, but that love can be expressed in very different ways, depending on whether it is love between husband and wife, parent and child, two friends of the same sex, and so on. We come back to the question of the rightness or wrongness of the structures within which these relationships are lived out. Structures may inhibit and imprison; they may also provide an invaluable framework without which we flounder. Either way, the personalist approach is misguided if it chooses to ignore them.

Character and Virtue

The second sort of challenge to the analysis of moral dilemmas which I have outlined is, I believe, rather more substantial. Single-minded concentration on the quality of love now seems rather a dated approach. What has characterised a number of important books written in the last decade is concern with the virtues as a whole, and with the formation of individual character nurtured by immersion in a community dedicated to the same goals and ideals. This approach has found able advocates both in philosophical and theological circles. Alasdair MacIntyre, author of the brilliant work *After Virtue*, is its most important exponent among philosophers; and Stanley Hauerwas, an American ethicist who has been influenced by a number of different Christian traditions, has pioneered this approach in a prolific way among theologians.[11]

In *After Virtue*, MacIntyre laments various aspects of Western ethical thinking since the Enlightenment. Ethical thought has been conceived as a task done by morally autonomous individuals, whereas MacIntyre insists on the relevance of the community within which individuals find themselves. It has been mainly concerned with what we as individuals should *do*, with insufficient attention, in MacIntyre's view, to the question: What sort of person am I to become? He believes that in current moral debates the apparent assertion of principles usually functions as a mask for the expression of personal preferences – and yet the reductionist claim that moral statements are *merely* expressions of personal preference scarcely does justice to the force with which convictions are held. MacIntyre thinks that it is possible to make a rational defence of an objective standard of morality, but only by drawing afresh upon a tradition of thought which was prematurely abandoned:

. . . it was because a moral tradition of which Aristotle's thought was the intellectual core was repudiated during the transitions of the fifteenth to seventeenth centuries that the Enlightenment project of discovering new rational secular foundations for morality had to be undertaken.[12]

The second half of *After Virtue* is a sustained, subtly argued attempt to vindicate the Aristotelian approach to ethics.

Aristotle's ethics is of the type known as *teleological*. This word derives from the Greek word *telos*, meaning 'end' or 'goal'. Because moral behaviour is evaluated in terms of what it leads to, such a way of thinking has obvious affinities with the consequentialist viewpoint. Some would therefore equate teleological and consequentialist ways of doing ethics, and describe teleology as the opposite pole to deontology.[13] But there is a difference. The teleologist believes that human beings have a true end, a 'given' state; and though the shorthand description for this is the utilitarians' key-word happiness, it is happiness understood as being in accord with what by nature one is designed to be. MacIntyre sums up the Greek word used by Aristotle, *eudaimonia*, as 'the state of being well and doing well in being well, of a man's being well-favoured himself and in relation to the divine'.[14] The virtues are

> precisely those qualities the possession of which will enable an individual to achieve *eudaimonia* and the lack of which will frustrate his movement toward that *telos*.[15]

They are qualities such as justice, prudence, moderation and courage. These virtues are interrelated, and the good man cultivates them together. Virtues are dispositions not only to act in particular ways, but to feel in particular ways:

> To act virtuously is not, as Kant was later to think, to act against inclination; it is to act from inclination formed by the cultivation of the virtues.[16]

The outcome of the exercise of these virtues will be a choice which issues in right action.

MacIntyre emphasises that making choices in this way will not consist in 'a routinizable application of rules'.[17] There is actually little mention of rules in Aristotle's *Ethics*. Aristotle conceives of rules mostly in terms of laws enacted by the city-state, laws which prohibit certain types of action in absolute terms. He readily grants that such actions feature among those which a virtuous person would refrain from doing. Actions such as the taking of innocent life, theft, perjury and betrayal are offensive because they destroy the bonds of community in such a way as to render the achievement of a state of well-being extremely difficult.

However, even within a community where individuals are dedicated to a common goal, conflicts of interest may occur, situations not easily resolved by rule or law. Here the cultivation and application of wisdom should come into its own: what Aristotle calls judging 'according to right reason'. MacIntyre cites the following scenario as requiring just such a judgment:

> There is at the time at which I am writing a lawsuit in progress between the Wampanoag Indian tribe and the town of Mashpee, Massachusetts. The Wampanoag Indians claim that their tribal lands in the township were illegally and unconstitutionally appropriated and they are suing for their return . . . The claim has been quite some time coming to court and the hearings themselves will not be over soon. The party who loses in the lower court will almost certainly appeal and the process of appeal is extended. During this long period property values in Mashpee have fallen drastically and it is for the moment almost impossible to sell certain types of property at all. This creates hardship generally for homeowners and more especially for certain classes of homeowners, for example, retired people who had legitimately expected to be able to sell their property and move elsewhere, relying on the proceeds of the sale to reestablish their lives, perhaps nearer their children. What in this type of situation does justice demand?[18]

MacIntyre favours a 'just' solution which, he reveals, has now been devised by the tribal claimants. This is that all properties of one acre or less on which a dwelling-house stands shall be exempted from the suit. MacIntyre comments:

It would be difficult to represent this as in any way the application of a rule; indeed it had to be devised because no application of the rules could afford small homeowners justice. The solution is the result of rough and ready reasoning involving such considerations as the proportion of the land claimed which comprises such properties and the number of people affected if the size of property exempted were fixed at one acre rather than more or less.[19]

A prudential judgment such as this is typically Aristotelian in that it embodies the concept of a mean avoiding two undesirable extremes. All the virtues are described in terms of a mean avoiding excess on the one hand and deficiency on the other: for instance, courage is the middle way which lies between rashness and cowardice. Moderation is the virtue which steers human beings along this middle path.

The example which MacIntyre uses calls to mind a comparative study of the American and Japanese legal systems. At the time of the study, in the mid-1970s, the United States' population of 215 million was served by an estimated 350,000 lawyers; while Japan, with 115 million, had fewer than 10,000. The reason why so few are needed in Japan is that there is strong social pressure to achieve an out-of-court settlement which will almost always entail a compromise between two antagonists. Frank Bray Gibney, the author of the study, gives the example of a squatter suing a farmer for possession of ten acres which he would like to claim.

In the West a court would probably rule up or down on the squatter's rights. An approved solution in Japan would be to concede the squatter two acres even if he has been shown to have no rights to any land. The goal is not so much to determine narrowly the presence or absence of a right as it is to restore harmony to the society. Beyond the question of rights, harmony has been disturbed, and the restoration of peace is the supreme goal.[20]

Two other features of MacIntyre's book are noteworthy at this stage. One is the stress he puts on telling stories as a means of moral education. In pre-Enlightenment societies where an Aristotelian type of ethic still flourished, virtues were inculcated and encouraged by the telling of narrative sagas whose heroes and heroines displayed these virtues in exemplary form. MacIntyre cites Homeric poems in sixth-century Athens, stories of Ulster heroes related in twelfth-century Irish monasteries, and Icelandic sagas about events of the century after 930 AD as three notable examples of this. To give a flavour of what he means:

> In the Icelandic sagas a wry sense of humour is closely bound up with courage. In the saga account of the battle of Clontarf in 1014, where Brian Boru defeated a Viking army, one of the norsemen, Thorstein, did not flee when the rest of the army broke and ran, but remained where he was, tying his shoe-string. An Irish leader, Kerthialfad, asked him why he was not running. 'I couldn't get home tonight', said Thorstein. 'I live in Iceland.' Because of the joke, Kerthialfad spared his life.[21]

Second, an important feature of these societies was that social roles were not disputed, and each individual's *telos* could be seen as conforming to a particular social role or roles. MacIntyre observes: 'A man who tried to withdraw himself from his given position in heroic society would be engaged in the enterprise of trying to make himself disappear.'[22]

Particular virtues are therefore seen as especially important for people in certain positions, or as relevant to particular types of relationship. For instance, fidelity is often regarded as the key virtue in women, and courage as an all-important ingredient in friendship. The realisation of individual well-being is inseparable from playing an accepted and respected part in one's community. What is lacking in Aristotle's thought, and surprisingly unmentioned in MacIntyre's commentary, is a recognition of the fact that being expected to conform to a social role can be a restrictive and repressive experience: as for instance if one was confined to a role of slave, whom Aristotle wrote off as incapable of virtues and the good life. Nevertheless, the modern fault is to assume that fitting in with social expectations is *necessarily* an experience of being oppressed. The truth is that one does not have to be a rebel to be a fulfilled person. Some non-Western cultures (the

Masai in East Africa, for example) still hold fast to the view that identity can be found in being part of the community, rather than standing out within it or from it. MacIntyre's book then ends with a call for the construction of local forms of community within which 'civility and the intellectual and moral life can be sustained', and – implicitly – true individual fulfilment can take place.[23]

Many of the same themes appear in the work of Stanley Hauerwas. But they are recast in a theological, specifically Christian form. Hauerwas, too, stresses *narrative* as a key medium for learning about God and the moral life. He believes that Christian ethics should be rooted in a story, the story of what God has done in the history of Israel and the person of Jesus. Christian ethics 'begins in a community that carries the story of the God who wills us to participate in a kingdom established in and through Jesus of Nazareth'.[24] The community he has in mind is none other than the church, which is called to make God's story more and more *its* story. Christians are called to be like Jesus, and that means becoming part of a community which practises the virtues he practised. Above all, Hauerwas sees the characteristics of peace, forgiveness and non-violence as hallmarks of the life of Jesus. A Christian disciple comes to cultivate these qualities by 'growing into' the story of Jesus; only then

> do I learn how much violence I have stored in my soul, a violence which is not about to vanish overnight, but which I must continuously work to recognise and lay down.[25]

In Hauerwas's view, what we *are* is then ultimately determinative of what we *do*. He rejects the widespread modern preoccupation in ethical debate with difficult moral decisions. He thinks that both deontological and consequentialist alternatives give too primary a status to rules or principles.

> The concentration on obligations and rules as morally primary ignores the fact that action descriptions gain their intelligibility from the role they play in a community's history and therefore for individuals in that community.[26]

Hauerwas acknowledges that communities, including Christian communities, have their prohibitions, but this is because the nature of the activities prohibited is in fundamental contradiction to the type of character being promoted in those communities. He believes that if we are genuinely non-violent then it should be quite unthinkable that we use violence, even though an exceptional situation might *seem* to justify it. The decision against such an option has already been made by the type of people that we are. To take a pacifist stance is therefore not really a decision at all; it simply follows from the fact that one is a peaceable character dedicated to the establishment of a more peaceable world. Sometimes, however, conscious reflection may be needed to determine an appropriate ethical stance; Hauerwas redefines casuistry as 'the reflection by a community on its experience to test imaginatively the often unnoticed and unacknowledged implications of its narrative commitments.'[27]

In many ways I welcome the fresh breath of air which MacIntyre and Hauerwas have brought to ethical discussion. As I have already argued in Chapter 3, the moral teaching of the Bible (especially the New Testament, and more particularly Jesus) is very much concerned with the questions of character and virtue. Problematical moral decisions fade into the background before God's fundamental concern with what we are as people, with our motivation, our integrity and our faithfulness. MacIntyre has reminded modern readers of a moral tradition which has some affinities with this, a tradition whose valuable resources have too readily been discounted. Hauerwas has developed similar concerns from a specifically Christian perspective. In doing so he has been influenced in part by his openness to a Roman Catholic tradition which has emphasised the themes of character and virtue far more than the Protestant churches.

Nevertheless, it remains debatable whether MacIntyre and Hauerwas are as radically different in their approach as they think they are! Once their work is digested, questions about the place and status of rules still remain, and so do moral quandaries. They rightly emphasise that rules are subordinate to the ideals and purposes of a community; but many a moral

thinker happy to be classed either as a deontologist or a
consequentialist would concede that. It is still a matter of
interest, and it is not necessarily self-evident from a community's tradition, which actions should be prescribed and
prohibited; or, to pursue the question of prohibitions further,
which actions are absolutely forbidden and which might allow
of some exceptions. Both men would presumably seek to
settle such questions by affirming the primacy of a particular
virtue; but the choice of which virtue will clearly be crucial,
and almost certainly controversial. Here there would appear
to be some divergence between MacIntyre and Hauerwas.

In his use of the example of the Wampanoag Indians,
MacIntyre appears to suggest that prudence will usually point
in the direction of a compromise-type solution. I noted the
same concern to keep all parties reasonably happy in the
Japanese system of justice. This surely represents a utilitarian
or consequentialist way of looking at things. As such it is open
to some objections. I do not mean to suggest that compromise-type solutions are always wrong; I strongly suspect that
Americans resort to lawsuits far too readily; but where justice
does lie clearly with one side rather than the other, a one-
sided solution is quite appropriate. In other words, moderation can be a good thing, but not always. It all depends on
what one is moderating *between*.

Significantly, though the Christian tradition absorbed
much of Aristotle's teaching about the virtues, it had trouble
with his doctrine of the mean. In Jesus's ethic there is
obviously an element of the *extreme*: giving up one's life even
unto death, forgiving not seven times but seventy times seven.
Not surprisingly, then, Hauerwas, as an explicitly Christian
writer, accepts the possibility of Christian character and
virtue exhibiting an extreme response – as a totally non-
violent reaction to aggression might be taken to be. Here, the
exaltation of peace (or peaceableness) as the all-important
virtue points in a strongly deontological direction, viz., an
absolute prohibition of violence. But this too is open to
objections. Granted that peace is important, and a warlike
spirit totally to be rejected, what has become of the concern
for justice? Clearly this, too, is an important concern in the

story of God's dealings with his people as unfolded in the Bible, a story in which battles play their part. If a particular war could satisfy the criteria of being 'just', but is still rejected, this appears to reflect a prior decision to rank peace as a condition rating higher in importance than justice. I am sure that Hauerwas could mount a plausible justification of such a decision; my quibble is that he does not provide this. He assumes the moral priority of preserving peace, without arguing for this from the evidence of the biblical material.

For myself, when I take seriously the dilemmas that those in positions of government face and the responsibilities of defending a people which they bear, non-violence in all circumstances no longer looks so obviously right. At the very least, one has to face up to the fact that there can be serious dilemmas here, with the moral imperatives to preserve peace and to seek justice pointing in different directions. It is interesting to find MacIntyre acknowledging that there may be tragic situations in which

> *both* of the alternative courses of action which confront the individual have to be recognised as leading to some authentic and substantial good. By choosing one I do nothing to diminish or derogate from the claim upon me of the other; and therefore, whatever I do, I shall have left undone what I ought to have done.[28]

He then refutes any attempt to map the logic of different 'ought' assertions on to some 'modal calculus'.[29] But if different obligations are not given some order of priority, how does one decide between them? In an earlier chapter, MacIntyre suggests that tragic choices are best resolved by reference to the *telos* which constitutes the good of a whole human life. True though this may be, I do not see why reflection on life's ultimate context and meaning might not lead to some provisional, potentially helpful judgments about which are the greater and which are the lesser goods.

Notes

1 Jack Dominian, *The Growth of Love and Sex*, Darton, Longman &
   Todd, 1982, p. 43.
2 Jack Dominian, *Proposals for a New Sexual Ethic*, Darton, Longman
   & Todd, 1977, p. 58.
3 Joseph Fletcher, *Situation Ethics*, SCM, 1966, pp. 14 and 126–7.
4 See p. 45.
5 *Situation Ethics*, p. 120.
6 *Op. cit.*, p. 115.
7 *Op. cit.*, p. 97.
8 Paul Ramsey, 'The Case of the Curious Exception', *Norm and Context
   in Christian Ethics* (eds Gene H. Outka and Paul Ramsey), SCM,
   1969, pp. 67–135.
9 See e.g., Norman Pittenger, *Time for Consent*, SCM, 1976.
10 This is not to deny that incest is a widespread phenomenon which is
   increasingly coming to the fore. But those who practise it seem to do so
   with a good deal of shame.
11 See in particular Hauerwas's *Character and the Christian Life*, Trinity
   University Press, San Antonio, 1975, *Vision and Virtue*, University of
   Notre Dame Press, Indiana, 1981, and *The Peaceable Kingdom*, SCM,
   1984.
12 Alasdair MacIntyre, *After Virtue*, Duckworth, 1981, p. 117.
13 See e.g., the article by Nowell-Smith, cited on p. 55.
14 *After Virtue*, p. 148.
15 *Ibid.*
16 *Op. cit.*, p. 149.
17 *Op. cit.*, p. 150.
18 *Op. cit.*, p. 153.
19 *Op. cit.*, pp. 153–4.
20 This excerpt is from a summary of Gibney's study in Daniel Maguire,
   The Moral Choice, p. 324.
21 *After Virtue*, p. 123.
22 *Op. cit.*, p. 126.
23 *Op. cit.*, p. 263.
24 *The Peaceable Kingdom*, p. 62.
25 *Op. cit.*, p. 94.
26 *Op. cit.*, p. 21.
27 *Op. cit.*, p. 120.
28 *After Virtue*, p. 224.
29 *Ibid.*

7

THE LESSER OF TWO EVILS?

In 1981 a charge of murder was brought against the paediatrician Leonard Arthur for inflicting a three-day-old baby suffering from Down's Syndrome with a fatal dose of a powerful drug. During the course of his trial and the accompanying public debate, much reference was made to the 'grey area' in which doctors who treat handicapped babies have to make difficult decisions. The term 'grey area' has become quite a common one: it is used to indicate situations which are not clear-cut choices between good and evil, 'black' and 'white', but where everything appears shady and where each individual just has to decide as best he or she can. In such a situation, where a number of different choices is possible and defensible, it ill becomes outsiders to make definitive (especially condemnatory) moral judgments. This was the line pursued by many of Dr Arthur's medical colleagues, and it may well have proved persuasive to the jury, for he was acquitted. I should not argue with the view that many decisions, particularly in medical practice, are extremely difficult; but it is interesting to note that what seems to emerge from this talk of 'grey areas' is a relative indifference to the obligation to work out the morally best solution.

Sinning Boldly

There are theological counterparts to this talk of grey areas. In this chapter I shall draw attention to the work of Helmut Thielicke (1908–86), Professor of Theology for many years at

Hamburg, and author (between 1945 and 1964) of a vast *Theological Ethics*.[1] Fundamental to his ethical thought is his understanding of the *borderline situation*; and borderline situations, for Thielicke, are essentially problematical situations where the Christian has freedom to choose, but only between different alternatives all of which are marked by sin.

In viewing ethical decision-making in this way, Thielicke reveals some characteristically Lutheran presuppositions; Luther's theology is of central importance to him. The first presupposition is the Christian's *freedom*. Luther insisted that faith sets a Christian free, free to live and work with joy and confidence that God is pleased with him, secure in the knowledge that salvation does not depend on his own efforts.[2] In a similar vein, Thielicke writes:

> The Christian stands not under the dictatorship of a legalistic 'You ought', but in the magnetic field of Christian freedom, under the empowering of the 'You may'.[3]

The second, somewhat contrasting presupposition is the pervasiveness of human sin. The Christian is *simul justus et peccator* (at the same time a righteous man and a sinner). For Lutherans, this phrase operates on various different levels of meaning.

On one level, *simul justus et peccator* expresses the very heart of Christian existence: man is a sinner, through and through, but at the same time he is deemed righteous, and therefore made righteous, in the sight of God. In this context, with reference to God, man seems to be considered totally sinful and totally righteous simultaneously. *Simul justus et peccator* means something different to the regenerate man in his own observation of himself. Subjectively he sees himself as partially sinful and partially righteous, as the alien righteousness ascribed to him by God begins to take effect in him. Here the phrase describes the coexistence within the Christian of an old and new nature. But *simul justus et peccator* also describes the situation of the Christian living in a fallen world where involvement in the God-given orders of existence invariably involves sin, and where there are often no pure alternatives available. Sometimes Luther expressed impatience with an attitude of undue scrupulosity towards sin. In a letter to his fellow-Reformer Philip Melanchthon, he wrote thus:

> If you are a preacher of grace, then preach a true and not a fictitious grace; if grace is true, you must bear a true and not a fictitious sin. God does not save people who are only fictitious sinners. Be a sinner and sin boldly, but believe and rejoice in Christ even more boldly, for he is victorious over sin, death and the world. As long as we are here (in this world) we have to sin. This life is not the dwelling-place of righteousness, but, as Peter says, we look for new heavens and a new earth in which righteousness dwells.[4]

The phrase 'sin boldly, but believe and rejoice in Christ even more boldly' is often quoted by Thielicke, and for him sums up what should be the Christian's attitude when faced by a difficult moral dilemma. The Christian should acknowledge the sinfulness which pertains to either option, but nevertheless feel emboldened to act, confessing his sin and secure in the promise of God's forgiveness.

The Borderline Situation

Thielicke defines the borderline situation both in a broad and a narrow sense. Sometimes he uses it simply to refer to human existence in a fallen world. We live in a world which has boundaries determined by God (creation and the last judgment) and we live on the borderline between God's good design in creation and the perversion of those designs which has taken place because of the fall. In view of the constraints caused by the latter, Thielicke sometimes speaks as if *all* human activity is marred by sinfulness. It is impossible not to compromise our ideals:

> The structure of the world in which we are enclosed . . . is something we cannot get away from, even though we belong not to the world, but to the Lord who has overcome the world.[5]

Conduct is never entirely righteous:

> Conduct is *de facto* a compromise between the divine require-
> ment and what is permitted by the form of this world, by the
> autonomy of the orders, and by the manifold conflicts of duty.[6]

The sort of compromise Thielicke has in mind here is the
necessity for political authority to threaten, and on occasion
use, force. Because man's egoistic traits threaten the eruption
of chaos and disorder, coercive measures are required to
restrain them. Nevertheless, it is vital that the Christian does
not consent too readily to the need for compromise. He or she
must recognise that the world falls short of its divine intention
and that there is sin to be confessed in this falling short. Our
consciences are disquieted through compromise but 'the
miracle of justification in the very midst of such disquietude of
conscience is that we are liberated precisely for this questionable world.'[7] The disquietude of conscience should also help
us not to compromise God-given ideals more than is necessary. An example of this would be that we ought not to
sanction excessive use of government force.

More often, however, Thielicke uses the phrase 'borderline
situation' to refer to the moral-quandary type of situation.
These are situations where it appears impossible to obey one
of God's commandments without at the same time breaking
another; or where one is involved in a struggle with an
opponent who represents the forces of injustice and evil, and
who can only be opposed effectively by following his own evil
methods to some extent. Thielicke cites many vivid examples
from the Nazi period, when he was a member of the Confessing Church which offered some resistance to Hitler. He
points out how in the attempt to mitigate the worst effects of
Nazism, resort to devious means was often necessary. For
instance, complicated webs of forgery and deceit were often
constructed to save the lives of individual Jews. Thielicke
believes that such action was right: those who helped the Jews
to escape actually 'found their true existence'.[8] Yet because
of the illegality and deception involved, Thielicke thinks that
this assistance was not devoid of guilt.

Co-operating with an Evil Regime

Another, especially agonising situation which Thielicke describes is that which occurred in Nazi concentration camps, when the SS demanded that political prisoners should swiftly determine which of their fellow-prisoners were 'unfit', in order that they might be executed immediately. Any delay in making a selection only resulted in executions being carried out on a wider and more indiscriminate scale. Eugen Kogon, author of a work on the SS-State, has criticised Christians who were not prepared to 'shoulder guilt' in such circumstances. He thought that such decisions were best made by 'the less sensitive spirits, lest all should become martyrs and none be left to bear witness.'[9] In a similar situation, a doctor in a mental institution listed a portion of his patients for extermination in order to ensure that the SS doctor who would otherwise replace him would not condemn all his patients to death. The rationale behind such actions is that the sacrifice of a limited number of admittedly innocent people is justified if the alternative is the slaughter of a much greater number.

Here Thielicke admits the force of Kogon's argument, but remains unconvinced by it. He thinks that in this situation personal confession, together with the readiness to sacrifice oneself and all the rest rather than to share in doing wrong, is 'a genuine ethical possibility, in some cases even a binding command'.[10]

> Readiness to do wrong in order to 'prevent something worse' is a very dubious principle, because it implies that the end justifies the means, and because it reposes no confidence in one's confession and its creative power really to prevent that 'something worse' or to bring it under condemnation.[11]

Thielicke detects not so much 'softness' (Kogon's charge) as an incomparably powerful testimony to the sanctity of human life in the refusal of Christian prisoners to collaborate in their comrades' extermination. Similarly, in the case of the doctor, a position of strict obedience to medical ethics (which demands the saving of human life rather than its destruction) could have had the form of a demonstration which might have encouraged other doctors to make similar resolves, even

though the result in the short term might have been the
ruthless bloodletting of an SS doctor. Thielicke thinks that in
the long term bravery and steadfastness are the most prudent
forms of action, because they serve to combat the spirit of
inhumanity and demonstrate the fact that one really believes
in one's cause.

Having delivered what looks like a clear-cut judgment
against a course of action defended on pragmatic, short-term
consequentialist grounds, Thielicke then qualifies the force of
it. He acknowledges that the pressures prevailing in the
concentration camps were so intense as to make it quite
impossible to 'pass any simple judgment on this matter in
terms of theological theory'.[12] Both the attempt to save lives
in the short term and the concern to safeguard the sanctity of
life in the long term have their ethical justification. Thielicke
thinks that understanding is needed, 'not only of the
courageous symbolic protest of the conscientious objector,
but also of the conscientious determination to "sin boldly"'.[13]

Likewise, in his discussion of resistance in his volume on
politics, Thielicke suggests that there are two justifiable
courses of action open to an office-holder in a state which
experiences takeover by a totalitarian regime. One is to
proclaim one's resistance openly by resigning office. The
other is to feign co-operation, remain in office, and work to
overthrow the regime, or at least to mitigate its worst features, from within. Thielicke does not see either response as
clearly better than the other. Withdrawal from a problematical situation can signify an abandonment of responsibility and
an exchange of 'personal and direct guilt' for 'a suprapersonal
and indirect guilt'.[14] On the other hand, feigned co-operation
can involve an intolerable measure of participation in evil
practices, e.g., in preparation for war, mass executions or
persecution of minorities. It may thus run the risk of helping
to validate and perpetuate a disreputable system. Decision
here must be left to the individual conscience, and individuals
will doubtless decide differently. It may even make sense for
two persons working side by side to respond differently, one
making the outward demonstration of opposition and the
other working to save the situation from within.

An interesting biblical episode which shows two God-fearing men pursuing contrasting strategies in the face of an evil regime is the Elijah-Ahab saga in 1 Kings 17–19. Elijah's bold defiance of King Ahab and his syncretistic religious policies is well known. His response was one of outspoken criticism ('I have not troubled Israel; but you have, and your father's house . . .' (1 Kgs. 18:18)) and direct confrontation (challenging the prophets of Baal to a trial of strength which Elijah's God won conclusively). But another, intriguing character in the story is Obadiah. He is described as a devout God-fearer, but one who still held authority under Ahab 'over the household'. He was then able to use the advantage of his position to conceal and feed a hundred loyal prophets when Ahab's wife Jezebel was trying to root them out systematically (1 Kgs. 18:3–4).

Obadiah's position is clearly one that comes under moral question. A certain timidity is evident in his reluctance to do as Elijah asks and tell Ahab that Elijah wants to meet him. Some commentators have given him a harsh press, arguing that he had no business remaining in Ahab's household at all.[15] Yet his response to an evil regime can be defended, not as an alternative to Elijah's prophetic stance, but as a complement. He chose to pursue resistance not by resigning office but by feigning co-operation, remaining in office and working to overthrow the regime, or at any rate mitigate its worst features, from within. This seems to me a legitimate option, though it is easy to see that it is one which might be impossible to pursue indefinitely, as, e.g., if Ahab had insisted on Obadiah's actually participating in the execution of the prophets of the Lord. To be true to the God whom he revered, Obadiah would then have been obliged to declare his opposition to the king's policy openly. Obadiah-like discretion has its place, but there are moments when the conflict of loyalties becomes such that it needs to give way to the valour of an Elijah.

A Lutheran theologian who worked from inside the Nazi system actually to overthrow the regime was, of course, Dietrich Bonhoeffer; and in him – as with Thielicke – we see a readiness to confess sin even about what he regarded as a justified course of action. Involvement in the plan to kill Hitler grew out of the responsibility he felt towards the people both of Germany and of Europe, but it was still for him a matter of getting his hands *dirty*. In place both of 'an irresponsible lack of scruple' and a 'self-tormenting punctiliousness' which never leads to action, Bonhoeffer spoke of the discovery of free responsibility which is the mark of civil courage:

> It depends on a God who demands responsible action in a bold venture of faith, and who promises forgiveness and consolation to the man who becomes a sinner in that venture.[16]

This is very much the spirit of Luther's 'sin boldly, but believe even more boldly and rejoice in Christ.'

Appraisal

There are a number of things to be said in favour of this approach to moral dilemmas. First, the readiness to acknowledge sin corresponds to how people of sensitive conscience actually feel about such situations. They often feel that they cannot help but sin whatever course of action they take. Even though such a judgment may actually ensue from an *over*-sensitive conscience, it may well be more helpful and healthy for them to confess what they believe to be sin than to try to persuade themselves against their deepest convictions that there is really nothing wrong with what they are doing. In short, the 'sin boldly' advice works well – up to a point – on a pastoral and spiritual level; it gives an individual courage to act, while preserving the strength of his or her moral convictions.

Second, the uncertainty of our moral judgments may be the result of not having all the relevant information at our fingertips to help us in coming to a decision. Thielicke rightly points out the many factors which make judgment about the justice of a war extremely obscure. The obscurity is caused partly because those making the judgment are 'clouded in intellect, blinded by passions, and radically deceived as far as their information is concerned'.[17] But it belongs also to the very nature of war that there should be an endless changing of opponents, that there should be concealment and deceit, and that there should be a deep involvement in a historical guilt which recedes further and further into the distance the more we pursue it.[18]

If this is true, as it would seem to be, about the majority of wars, any judgment that a particular war is just, and can be supported, assumes a provisional character. It may be that facts which emerge later will lead one to revise one's judgment. The effects of official propaganda can give one a very one-sided view of events, but one is only dimly aware of this at the time. Nevertheless, because one is aware that one's judgment may be mistaken, that one may indeed be making a terrible mistake (for that is what fighting on the 'wrong' side surely is), confession of sin and living through the comfort of God's forgiveness is a right and fitting course of action.

Third, the Lutheran approach correctly discerns that whatever decision is taken in many quandary-type situations, something happens which is less than good. There is a falling short; there is a stark and vivid reminder of the tragic fact that the world is indeed *fallen*; in short, there is evil. It is very important that the Christian remains aware of this. In order to preserve one's moral integrity and one's faithfulness to a Lord who challenges even those very natural impulses of anger and lust,[19] it is crucial that one retains one's moral vision, and does not pretend that good is evil or that evil is good. Peter Hinchliff, an Anglican who has written in a similar vein to Thielicke and Bonhoeffer, makes some wise remarks in this context:

> The fact that one has not been truthful does not mean that a lie is as good as the truth. And one ought to acknowledge that fact by admitting that one's action has not been wholly right, wholly ideal. One is still a sinner in need of forgiveness because the untruth, if willingly embraced, might make one a kind of person other than the ideal to which one is committed. It is only because one acknowledges that the lie is an exception, which itself is accepted on moral rather than merely expedient grounds, that one is able to maintain the ideal of what is good.[20]

This readiness to face up to the pervasive reality of evil is certainly preferable to the approach taken by thinkers who argue that conflicts of duties can always be resolved eventually in terms of a straightforward decision between good and evil, i.e., that the choice between two evils is only an apparent one. If only our judgment was sounder, or we were more in tune with the mind of God, it would be quite obvious what we should do. The dilemma with which we *seem* to be confronted may then be resolved in one of two different ways. The first is to adhere to an unbending absolutism, as Kant did, refusing to take any responsibility for harmful consequences which are likely to ensue (such as the refusal of Kant's householder to tell a lie almost certainly leading to the committal of a murder).[21] The second is to go to tortuous lengths to explain that an action normally viewed in an ethically negative light (such as lying) does not really constitute that type of action at all. An example of the latter approach is found in a stalwart American evangelical writer, John Murray.[22] In his discussion of the Elisha incident cited earlier, Murray insists that Elisha did not lie. If, as is likely, the Syrian soldiers were standing just outside the city gates, Elisha could with perfect impunity have pointed to the ground on which they were standing and said, 'This is not the city that you seek.' Further, he kept his promise to bring them to the man they sought, though only after he had first brought them to their enemy. Elisha told the truth, practising the art of mental reservation – *sic* Murray.

I do not find either way of resolving dilemmas convincing. If one takes the Kantian approach, one is simply blinding oneself to one's real (if reluctant) contribution to an evil state of affairs; one *could* have taken a course of action which was likely to prevent the murder. As for the second approach, Murray surely ignores the fact that the essence (and the generally objectionable character) of lying is deception, and there is no doubt that Elisha deceived the soldiers in a thoroughgoing way. His doing so was doubtless justified in the context of their threat to his life; but let us not gloss over the fact that he lied, and that lying is in the vast majority of circumstances wrong. The necessity to lie is symptomatic of the evil cloak which shrouds our world, a world in which human beings periodically harbour hostile designs against each other.

Where I would take issue with Hinchliff and the Lutherans' approach, however, is in their making too ready an equation between evil and sin. If a tragic situation is not of one's creation and certainly not one's intention, yet one is inescapably bound up in it, why should one feel guilty about taking drastic measures to extricate oneself from it or mitigate its worst features? If one chooses the better of two morally questionable alternatives, it is appropriate to call that choice the lesser of two evils; but if one has made a well-informed, conscientious decision and believes that it *is* clearly the better alternative, I do not see why one ought to feel sinful about it. One has done the best one can, and should be able to rejoice in the presence of a kindly disposed God with a clear conscience – while naturally feeling regret that the action to which one has consented is in some respect 'evil'. Regret will certainly be fitting, but repentance (though understandable as an accompanying response) is not necessarily what God demands or desires. Indeed, it is conceivable that in some situations *clarity* of conscience might be a prime requisite if one was to have the necessary courage to act boldly.

Another telling consideration is this. Christians have traditionally believed in the sinlessness of Jesus, a conviction which originated with the first generation of Christians who actually knew him, and was soon linked with a theology of the atonement: the fact that he had lived a sinless life made him the one perfect sacrifice for sin.[23] But if, as Thielicke says, human conduct is '*de facto* a compromise between the divine requirement and what is permitted by the form of this world', and such compromise involves participation in the suprapersonal guilt of this world, how did the gracious accommodation of God to man in the person of Christ avoid this compromise? While it is difficult to find unambiguous examples in the Gospels, could Jesus *really* have lived thirty-three years on earth without at some stage being involved in a situation involving a conflict of duties? Did he never, for instance, promise to see someone at a certain time and then find himself forced to delay fulfilment of that promise by encounter with someone in more desperate need? If Jesus was miraculously preserved from such dilemmas, he can hardly be said to have experienced humanity and to have been tempted in every respect as we have. But if, as is surely the case, he did experience such situations, and because of the perfect harmony which existed between his will and the Father's was always enabled to make the right decision, this gives us hope. If we can attain a similar relationship with God, we may be able to discern his will more accurately, and in the process we, like Jesus, do not have to be troubled by a consciousness of sin.

There are, then, important qualifications to be made about the 'sinning boldly' approach. It identifies important features about dilemma-type situations, but it detects, imputes and confesses sin in too all-embracing a fashion. It does not make some important distinctions. In particular, it fails to identify a crucial distinction between sin which pertains to actions in the past and sin which pertains to actions in the present. The reason why individuals often experience consciousness of sin in these situations is that they may bear some responsibility for the fact that a difficult conflict of loyalties has arisen. There *is* guilt to be acknowledged, but it is guilt which attaches to a wrong turning or neglect of obligations in the past rather than the course of action which is chosen to resolve the situation now. Thielicke comes close to recognising this, but does not do so explicitly. When he argues that it is the Church's duty to 'confess' the guilt of individuals in giving illegal aid to the Jews, much of the guilt he has in mind actually applies to the Church's failure to speak out boldly enough in defence of the Jews at the onset of Nazi persecution. I should be inclined to say that in this case all the guilt pertained to failure in the past; the Church thus having neglected its duties, and persecution of the Jews being in full swing, *no* attribution of sin is appropriate to measures taken to offset that past failure, i.e., to hide the Jews and help them to escape.

A similar judgment might be made about Bonhoeffer's involvement in the plot to remove Hitler. Although it is obviously much easier to make these criticisms with hindsight, Christians in Germany were at fault in allowing Hitler to come to power, in failing to recognise him at an early stage for the evil man that he was, in 'baptising' elements of Nazi ideology with a veneer of Christian theology and in confining their belated opposition to Hitler largely to the matter of wrongful State interference in the Church rather than voicing a strong protest against Nazi treatment of minorities like the Jews and the mentally handicapped.[24] However, recognition of the sin which was involved on all these scores should surely have strengthened the conviction that replacement of Hitler's regime by another was eminently justified. It was not itself a sinful act. Of course, there are perfectly understandable reasons why Bonhoeffer and some of his fellow-conspirators felt they were assuming a burden of guilt in acting in this way. Traditionally German Lutheranism had placed a very strong emphasis on the duty of Christians to obey the existing government, and this conviction was reinforced by the fact that many of the conspirators, being men in positions of official authority, had sworn oaths of allegiance to Hitler.[25] They were able to persuade themselves that breaking these oaths was justified, but only on the understanding that in doing so they were assuming a vicarious mantle of guilt. In my view, the rightness of the assassination attempt was such that they had no need to labour under these scruples. It can be defended convincingly either on deontological or consequential grounds. On the one hand, the manner of Hitler's life made ending it in this way appropriate. It was an act of righteous (if non-juridical) judgment on a terrible tyrant. Interestingly, Barth names tyrannicide in extreme circumstances as one of his two exceptions to a negative verdict on the rightness of capital punishment; it is as a form of capital punishment that he sees it.[26] On the other hand, the attempt to kill Hitler can be defended in the light of all the terrible events it was intended to prevent. It represented the best hope of rescuing the morally twisted and physically devastated state of Germany, and for saving the lives of innumerable people engaged in the maelstrom of the Second World War – because the government planned to succeed Hitler would have brought the war to an end.

There is one section in his discussion of borderline situations where Thielicke seems to depart from his dominant theme that any possible course of action in these situations partakes of sin to some extent. This is where he is discussing lies told in the process of offering resistance to an oppressive totalitarian regime. Here he speaks of individuals who have 'forfeited the claim to truth'.[27] The officials of an unjust totalitarian regime come into this category. They are pledged to a system in which truth is repeatedly desecrated because it is made to serve particular goals and special interests. In a confrontation between representatives of a system of falsehood and representatives of a system of truth, the latter sometimes feel that they are forced to depart from the truth in detail in order to protect their cause. An interrogator may apply pressure by making his opponent swear an oath to tell the truth, but he uses this simply as a moral weapon in a power struggle. Thielicke thinks that an individual can exert a claim to have the truth told to him only when he subjects himself to the same claim, and when two people speak with each other on the same level. Where this is missing a white lie told under hostile interrogation 'can no more be called lying in the strict sense than killing in self-defence can be called murder'.[28] As will be evident from my earlier discussion of Murray, I am doubtful about how constructive it is to dispense with the word 'lying' in such circumstances, but I agree with the thrust of Thielicke's remark, viz., to exonerate lying of this kind from any sort of blame at all. What is strange is that he does not pursue a similar line when discussing the question of deception in the cause of helping the Jews.

If Thielicke's talk of the all-pervasiveness of sin has its limits, so too does the freedom which he believes may legitimately be claimed by the Christian in certain conflict situations. In other words, there are some sins which the Christian should never commit; they are not excused by the notion of 'sinning boldly'. A deontological stand in Thielicke's writing here becomes evident. Thielicke says that sometimes an individual is confronted by a situation entailing two possibilities, one of which is 'transcendence itself'.[29] He gives two examples of this. One is where pressure is exerted on an individual to deny Christ or blaspheme God. The other is where what is imperilled is the personhood of one's fellow-human, as it is, in Thielicke's view, when individuals are subjected to torture in order to extract vital information from them. To choose either of these two options (denying one's faith or approving torture) brings one into a direct confrontation with 'transcendence', i.e., the transcendent God or the human person who has been made in the image of God. I shall not go into the detail or the validity of Thielicke's arguments here. It is simply interesting to note that a writer who emphasises to a high degree both the complexity of dilemma situations and the freedom which is available to the Christian in these situations still regards certain things as completely unacceptable. They should not even be countenanced as *possible* courses of action by the Christian. Thielicke says that,

> While this is not to admit casuistry, it is to admit a kind of 'casuistical minimum'. There are not casuistical norms but there are casuistically demonstrable limits.[30]

However, Thielicke reveals here a curious perverseness in logic, one which stems partly from his distaste for the word *casuistry* – an aversion shared by many Continental Protestant theologians of his generation (including, as we have seen, Barth).[31] If he is prepared to admit casuistical limits, it must be on the basis of some overriding casuistical norms, like the notion of divine transcendence. He does make use of norms or principles; but the question raised by many borderline situations is: Which principle takes precedence? Thielicke's characteristically Lutheran emphases deter him from shedding much light on that question. His exploration of quandary-type situations is fascinating in many respects; he certainly helps to remind us of the *agony* which is experienced by someone caught on the horns of a painful dilemma; but he does not provide a very *systematic* approach to the ethical issues involved.

Sustained Analysis

In conclusion, I believe that we should resist the current tendency to reduce the various options posed by moral dilemmas to an undifferentiated mass of greyness. Just because we cannot choose between a clear-cut black and a clear-cut white, it does not follow that everything in between is exactly the same shade of grey. Making distinctions and placing one obligation above another is certainly no easy matter; it demands close attention and careful analysis. But if we opt out of the hard work which it involves, we are all too apt to end up rationalising the decision which is most convenient to us personally. Of course, this *might* be the right decision, but labelling all the possible alternatives as equally sinful and therefore equally excusable prejudices us in that direction prematurely. I believe that this sort of mentality was at work in the doctors who defended their colleague at the Arthur trial; but I will reserve further discussion of the particular issue of the care of severely handicapped children for Chapter 9. Here I shall present a different, imaginary – but, I believe, plausible – scenario which may serve to highlight the dangers I mean.

A Western university, suffering from government cutbacks, is about to launch a major appeal to improve and expand its facilities. To help raise money it has enlisted the aid of some leading financiers and businessmen. Just before the appeal is launched, a large group of students (with the support of a few members of staff) request that the institution cease banking with a particular bank on account of the latter's strong South African connections. The issue is debated by the university's governing body, and the arguments for and against continuing with the bank are keenly debated. The bank has written to the governing body emphasising its good record of treating black employees in South Africa and its aim of constructive involvement to try to bring about change in that country. On the other hand, representatives of the student viewpoint argue that the bank still provides financial help for many companies which do discriminate against blacks (as well as the South African government itself) and that anti-apartheid groups are strongly in favour of boycotting this particular bank. Then other considerations which affect the well-being of the university are raised. It might be difficult for the university to change banks just before the launch of the appeal; and some of the financiers whose help has been enlisted are saying that they would no longer be willing to support the appeal if the university took a step which they believe to be ill-judged and financially naïve.

In the stalemate which ensues from the clash of opposing arguments, the vice-chancellor suddenly starts talking about 'there being no right way forward in this situation. Whatever we do, it's wrong in some respect, it's hurting a particular group'. A clergyman on the governing body weighs in with a remark about 'sin sometimes being inescapable'. Because the arguments for disinvestment from the bank are not felt to be conclusive, the weight of opinion then shifts towards preserving the status quo. Better to stay as we are, it is felt (and not jeopardise the university appeal, incidentally), than rush ahead with some controversial change. In the end the governing body votes not unanimously, but decisively, in favour of keeping its accounts with the same bank.

What has happened in this situation? Effectively the attempt to find the right way forward has been abandoned. Disinvestment in South Africa *is* a complex issue, and there are arguments of substance on either side. But seeing wrongdoing and sin in whichever decision one makes renders it all too easy to opt for the course of action which poses least inconvenience to those who make it. It would have been better to scrutinise the policy of the bank (and other banks, for that matter) more closely, in the hope that the truth about whether they do more to prop up or break down apartheid would ultimately emerge. We must not so stress moral ambiguity that it becomes a cloak for self-interest.

Notes

1   Considerable parts of this have appeared in English: *Theological Ethics*, vol. I: *Foundations*, A. & C. Black, 1966; *Theological Ethics*,

vol. II; *Politics*, Black, 1969; *The Ethics of Sex*, James Clarke, Cambridge, 1964. Eerdmans republished these three volumes together in 1979.

2   See e.g., his 'Treatise on Good Works', *Luther's Works*, vol. 44, Fortress, Philadelphia, 1966.

3   Helmut Thielicke, *Theological Ethics*, I, p. xii.

4   'Letter to Philip Melanchthon, August 1, 1521', *Luther's Works*, vol. 48, Fortress, 1963, pp. 281–2.

5   *Theological Ethics*, I, p. 567.

6   *Op. cit.*, p. 499.

7   *Op. cit.*, p. 500.

8   *Op. cit.*, p. 588.

9   Kogon made these comments in his book *Der SS-Staat*, translated in abridged form as *The Theory and Practice of Hell: The German Concentration Camps and the System Behind Them*, Farrar, Straus & Co., New York, 1950, p. 278.

10 *Theological Ethics* I, p. 591.

11 *Op. cit.*, p. 590.

12 *Op. cit.*, p. 621.

13 *Op. cit.*, p. 622.

14 *Theological Ethics* II, p. 355.

15 See e.g., F. B. Meyer, *Elijah and the Secret of his Power*, Marshall, Morgan & Scott, 1954.

16 Dietrich Bonhoeffer, *Letters and Papers from Prison*, SCM, 1971 (enlarged edn), p. 6.

17 *Theological Ethics*, I, p. 414.

18 *Ibid.*

19 Matthew 5:21–30.

20 Peter Hinchliff, *Holiness and Politics*, Darton, Longman & Todd, 1982, pp. 111–12.

21 See my earlier discussion on p. 50.

22 John Murray, *Principles of Conduct*, IVP, 1957, pp. 142–3.

23 See e.g., 1 Peter 2:22–4.

24 For fascinating reading on this period see J. S. Conway, *The Nazi Persecution of the Churches*, Weidenfeld & Nicolson, 1968, and the biographies, Eberhard Busch, *Karl Barth*, SCM, 1976, and Eberhard Bethge, *Dietrich Bonhoeffer*, William Collins, 1970.

25 Thielicke has an interesting discussion of this in *Theological Ethics* II, ch. 21.

26 Karl Barth, *Church Dogmatics*, III:4, pp. 448–50.

27 *Theological Ethics*, I, p. 533.

28 *Op. cit.*, p. 531.

29 *Op. cit.*, p. 644.

30 *Op. cit.*, p. 643.

31 See my earlier discussion on p. 94.

8

BETWEEN RULES AND CONSEQUENCES

In the last two chapters, I have considered some of the alternatives to the deontological and consequentialist approaches to moral decision-making. I have acknowledged that each of these alternatives has something important to contribute to our understanding of how we should behave. A loving concern for people and the quality of personal relationships are clearly matters of fundamental importance. An integrated view of the person as a whole, and of the virtuous person as an agent who comes to moral dilemmas with certain predispositions already well established, appear to be well grounded Biblical emphases. The language of evil, sin, forgiveness and grace helps to put difficult moral dilemmas in an appropriate theological context. Nevertheless, my argument has been that none of these alternative approaches absolves us from the responsibility of doing some hard thinking about the actual dilemmas themselves. We still need to pay close attention to what is involved in a particular act, or a particular choice of acts. And in analysing alternatives, the contrast between a rule-based approach and a consequence-based approach is one which repeatedly emerges as significant.

In this chapter, I shall take comparison and evaluation of these two approaches rather further than I did in Chapter 2. I shall try to identify their strengths and weaknesses, and thereby clear the ground for outlining an approach which hopefully draws on the best (and avoids the worst) in both approaches.

Consequentialism For and Against

What are the strengths of the consequentialist view? First of all, it contains a hard core of *realism*. Actions (and, equally true, lack of actions) do have their consequences; it is an ostrich-like trait *not* to face up to what they are. Most of us are guided by a prudential, results-orientated mentality for much of the time. There again, when the reasons for a particularly well-established rule or law are elucidated, appeal to good or bad consequences usually plays a major part in the argument. In that case, why not frankly acknowledge consequences to be *the* decisive criterion in moral decision-making?

Second, the advocate of consequentialism displays a certain amount of courage in his readiness to assume *responsibility* for the effects which follow from human actions. The underlying assumption is that consequences are (to a reasonable extent) predictable, and if harmful results ensue – even if the harm only flows indirectly from one's own action – one bears a partial responsibility. The believer who sticks to the rules at all costs, even in situations where the consequences look likely to be dire, may justify this attitude as an outworking of his faith in the providence of God. In other words, he trusts that if he is obedient to God, God will so direct events that calamitous consequences do not ensue from his action. In contrast, the consequentialist – even the consequentialist who is a believer – objects to such an attitude as embodying an abdication of responsibility. God may intervene to prevent a catastrophe, but the fact is that in the past he has permitted many catastrophes (Auschwitz, for example), and it is entirely conceivable that if responsible political leaders act in an *ir*responsible way he will allow the ultimate catastrophe (nuclear devastation of the world). God expects us to face up honestly and deliberately to the likely consequences of what we do, and adjust our plans in the light of these reflections. And in weighing up alternative courses of action, what will benefit people who are affected by our actions is as important a consideration as maintaining our own moral purity. Dietrich Bonhoeffer has some interesting thoughts on this:

> Although it is certainly not true that success justifies an evil deed
> and shady means, it is impossible to regard *success* as something
> that is ethically quite neutral. The fact is that historical success
> creates a basis for the continuance of life . . . The ultimate
> question for a responsible man to ask is not how he is to extricate
> himself heroically from the affair, but how the coming generation
> is to live. It is only from this question, with its responsibility
> towards history, that fruitful solutions can come, even if for the
> time being they are very humiliating. In short, it is much easier to
> see a thing through from the point of view of abstract principle
> than from that of concrete responsibility. The rising generation
> will always instinctively discern which of these we make the basis
> of our own actions, for it is their own future that is at stake.[1]

These words were written in the context of Bonhoeffer's
covert struggle against the Nazi regime. But they are clearly
applicable to other issues today, notably that of survival in the
midst of a nuclear threat.

Third, the most common form of consequentialism is, as I
indicated in Chapter 2, Utilitarianism; and utilitarians' concern to increase the sum of human happiness and reduce the
lot of human suffering is certainly not something to be
sneered at. Of course, happiness narrowly defined in terms of
sensualistic pleasure cannot be a satisfactory ethical yardstick. Happiness with any depth to it is often the fruit of
loyalty in the face of testing; and there is no true joy, only a
lurking sense of dissatisfaction to be gained in taking the *easy*
way out of a dilemma situation. But if happiness is defined in
as broad and deep a way as possible, it *is* an important
consideration. It is worth reflecting how great a proportion of
Jesus's time seems to have been taken up with healing – with
ridding individuals of the physical and mental pain which had
dogged them, and replacing it with joy and wholeness. There
is a crucial place for sacrifice in the Christian life, but it is
self-sacrifice to which Jesus calls us, not a readiness to put
other individuals to avoidable inconvenience and suffering.
We need to think long and hard before we justify an action
which adds substantially to the quota of human suffering –
even though it may seem to be performed for the highest of
motives, from the purest of principles.

The weaknesses of consequentialist thinking, however, are almost as transparent as its strengths. Indeed, they are closely connected: because it is in over-emphasising all these virtues that the preoccupation with consequences can actually turn into a dangerous obsession and lead to a distorted view of reality.

First, it is *un*realistic to evaluate actions *only* in terms of the consequences which follow from them. If a father nobly chooses to spend time constructing a toy railway with his little boy rather than satisfying his own personal passion for watching Test cricket on TV,[2] the virtue of his action cannot be reduced to the good effects which are likely to follow from this. By acting in this way, he is doubtless helping to build up a good relationship with his son, setting him a good example as a father, preventing him from pestering his mother and so on; but there is value in the kindness of the act itself. Actions can radiate goodness. They have significance for the very moment in which they take place. They can also be a *witness*, the authenticity of which is not diminished by the fact that the prospects of a particular act of witness leading to more desirable consequences may be extremely slim. If a couple come to hold strong convictions about the value of animal life, and feel that the all-too-unthinking consumption of meat serves to *de*value the animal creation, taking up a vegetarian diet can be a meaningful moral gesture. Their change of diet is most unlikely to have any effects, directly or indirectly, on the meat trade; the number of animals slaughtered for food, and the amount of grain consumed in fattening them up, may still remain the same as if they had stuck to their previous eating habits; but they have shown integrity in being true to their new-found convictions. Conversely, actions stand condemned when they communicate the very opposite. In 1 Corinthians Paul deplores behaviour among Christians which blatantly contradicts their fundamental unity. Division into party-groups, or taking out lawsuits against fellow-Christians, is wrong largely because it is a failure to recognise truths about one's Christian state and in the process bears a bad witness. The thoroughgoing consequentialist tends to be blind to these dimensions of human behaviour. Actions take *some* of their meaning and value from the consequences which follow from them; but they also have their own intrinsic significance, which should not be ignored.

Second, it is all very well to stress responsibility, but this needs to be responsibility saddled with humility. It would indeed be irresponsible to omit the business of calculating consequences, when confronted by a hard dilemma; yet a feature of some of the trickiest moral quandaries is that prediction of the likely consequences is extremely hazardous. What will ensue from the different alternatives open to one cannot be forecast with any degree of certainty. An interesting example of this is provided by a bizarre case which has provoked a good deal of discussion among ethicists (though not usually for this reason). It is related by Joseph Fletcher. At the end of the Second World War, a German woman, Mrs Bergmeier, was taken into custody by Russian soldiers and transported to a prison camp in the Ukraine. Her three children were left to fend for themselves in Berlin. Eventually her husband made his way back from imprisonment in Britain and found the children, but the family felt desperate without the mother:

> She more than anything else was needed to reknit them as a family in that dire situation of hunger, chaos, and fear.[3]

Mrs Bergmeier heard of their situation from a sympathetic commandant. She knew that she could be released only on one of two grounds: illness necessitating medical facilities elsewhere, or pregnancy. She decided to ask a friendly Volga German camp guard to impregnate her, which he did. Her condition being medically verified, she was duly sent back to Berlin where she was joyfully reunited with her family. Fletcher clearly implies that these happy consequences justified her act of committing adultery.

Certainly, Mrs Bergmeier's action was not typical of most acts of adultery: it was intended to further her wish to express marital faithfulness to her husband through being present with him and providing practical, emotional support to him and the family in Berlin. But it is worth pondering how fortunate she was that the consequences worked out as favourably as they did. After having sex with the guard, she might not have become pregnant, or she might have had to indulge in intercourse repeatedly before that happened. When they found out the circumstances in which she had become pregnant, the camp authorities might have decided *not* to release her as a punitive measure. And when she had returned to Berlin and her husband discovered that she was expecting a child by another man, he might have found it difficult to accept what she had done or to love the child in the same way as his natural children. On the other hand, if Mrs Bergmeier had been prepared to wait a bit longer, she might have been released anyway – or there again she might have been kept in prison for years. All these uncertainties ought to have been taken into account; and it seems to me that when they are weighed seriously Mrs Bergmeier's well-meaning act of adultery is no longer so obviously right as Fletcher, in his unreflective and rather sentimental way, too readily assumes.

The same uncertainty applies to many dilemmas which occur rather more frequently. It is often unpredictable how an unmarried girl will respond if she is persuaded to go through with the birth of a child rather than have an abortion. Although the prospect of having a child can seem bleak, her feelings may change; she may discover a joyful vocation in motherhood and receive an unexpected amount of support from her family and friends, or the experience of childbirth and motherhood may lead to a complete abandonment of career prospects, to depression and to child battering. There again, the experience of having an abortion may have profound psychological repercussions, or it may provoke as little trauma as a routine visit to the dentist – and women are frequently surprised by the way in which they do react.

To take another example, workers are often confronted by a whole series of baffling unknowns when deciding whether or not it is right to take strike action. Will a strike have the sudden financial impact which will make management rethink its policy on pay or conditions, or will it simply make management dig its heels in harder? Will the damage done by a strike actually be so crippling that the workers themselves will ultimately suffer, when the firm is forced to cut its losses and make employees redundant? Will a strike cause serious, even life-endangering harm to ordinary citizens who have no involvement in the dispute? Will it lead to a split among the workforce, and a spirit of bitterness and resentment which could sour relationships in the industry for years to come? Or is it likely to be only a very brief episode which has the constructive effect of making management realise the workforce should be treated with dignity and respect? What, moreover, are the personal effects of going on strike likely to be: will a growing family be able to cope without any salary coming in, and how will involvement in strike action be regarded in the local community? It may be possible to answer some of these questions with a fair degree of assurance; others are likely to be much more problematical.

However, it is not only the uncertainty of future events which makes calculation of consequences difficult. It is also the fact that different sets of consequences do not always lend themselves to straightforward comparison. We are not necessarily comparing like with like. A decision about whether or not it is right to fight a particular war illustrates this aptly. Such a decision is not merely a matter of assessing as best one can how many lives are likely to be lost if one goes to war, and comparing that figure with the number of lives which might be lost if an oppressive totalitarian power was allowed to take over one's country without resistance, and then put into operation its policy of eliminating dissident groups. (Even if the calculation was simply a matter of head counting, there would still be a question over whether the soldiers used by an oppressive power 'count' equally with one's own fellow-citizens.) The fact is that the country which is under threat is concerned not just for life itself, but with the preservation of a certain quality of life. It is concerned about human freedom, national integrity, a people's right to determine their own form of government and conceptual values of this kind. These are not vague abstractions; they have very practical implications. But their value cannot be quantified in a way which makes the deprivation of individual freedom, dissolution of traditional national boundaries and so on easily comparable with the harm inflicted in taking people's lives. Some sorts of good and evil may be commensurable; of others, it is just not true.

Calculation of consequences is also affected in a crucial way by the depth of perspective with which one views the effects of an action. Some dilemma situations are quite closely defined: they affect a strictly limited number of people and little impact is made one way or another on the wider community by the way in which they are resolved. Other situations have no clear boundaries: the effects which decisions have are like ripples on a pond, the ferment caused diminishing with time and space but very real none the less. Actions which capture the public imagination, especially when performed by individuals who are already the focus of public attention, can have an influence which actually *increases* with the passage of time. For example, the theory of pacifism and the techniques of non-violent resistance are somewhat in vogue at present, partly because they have been championed with a significant degree of success earlier in the century by individuals who have been acclaimed as heroes of our time, Mahatma Gandhi and Martin Luther King.

Certainly, possible long-term consequences need to be taken into account as well as short-term ones. And, as I noted in Chapter 2, adopting this long-term view seems to increase the likelihood that one will stay loyal to an established rule rather than break it.[4] One will recognise that breaking a rule where exceptional circumstances seem to justify it may set a precedent which will lead to the rule being broken all too often, so that eventually the respect with which the rule is regarded evaporates completely. Because one wants to avoid this, one accepts the cost which comes with abiding by the rule in the exceptional situation. But as soon as one makes such a move, one is apt to be granting the rule a status sufficiently awe-inspiring that its psychological impact overrides the consequential considerations. For the rule to hold fast under conditions of stress, it needs to acquire a solemn aura of inviolability – thereby giving the individual the strength of will to resist the obvious temptation to break it. If Christians are inclined to stress rule-keeping more than most, it is probably because they take human weakness and vulnerability to temptation very seriously.

Third, admirable though it is to want to maximise levels of happiness, this by itself cannot be allowed to become the all-decisive ethical criterion. Human beings can become perverted and depraved about what makes them happy. As Alasdair MacIntyre has written:

> The concept of the public happiness has obvious legitimate application in a society where the consensus is that the public happiness consists in more and better hospitals and schools; but what application has it in a society where the public happiness is found by the public itself to consist in the mass murder of Jews?[5]

The danger of working by a purely utilitarian calculus is that it puts despised and unpopular minorities in society permanently at risk. Apart from racial and religious minorities, the very young (including the unborn), the very old, the seriously handicapped, the severely demented and the worst criminal offenders are the groups who are most likely to suffer thereby. Exploitation, cruelty and wholesale extermination may follow, if the majority finds itself feeling particularly threatened by such groups, or if recognition of the latter's basic rights stands in the way of what the majority conceives to be their entitlement to a trouble-free, happy existence.

Not surprisingly, utilitarians have a reply to this objection. They point out that 'the greatest happiness of the greatest number' does *not* mean that one should necessarily seek to please the majority. It may be that the intensity of pain felt by the minority in their experience of being persecuted outweighs the considerable but less intense pleasure felt by the majority in doing the persecuting (and enjoying the fruits of their privileged position). It is *overall* happiness rather than majority happiness which is the utilitarians' yardstick. But this defence will not suffice. First, inasmuch as pleasures and pains can be compared realistically, the intensity of the majority's pleasure *may* be greater than the intensity of the

minority's pain. The minority might consist of a solitary
individual. Sadistic pleasures may have completely got the
better of a group who are committing torture; and an element
of masochistic delight or a spirit of passive resignation may
have overtaken the victims – yet something very wrong is still
happening to them. Second, it is all too easy for a majority
group in such situations to regard the minority group as less
than human (as 'animals', in the case of notorious criminals,
or 'vegetables', in the case of those incapable of rational
thought), so their feelings of pain are viewed as unimportant
or even as non-existent. To guard against this temptation, it is
very important that societies build up a strong allegiance to
codes of rights which protect all members of the human
species against fundamental violations of their dignity. In
other words, there is a question of justice here, and justice
cannot be subsumed under the principle of utility. I shall
develop this theme further in Chapter 9.

Deontology For and Against

The merits of an ethical approach in which rules are seen as
having central significance are not difficult to identify. First of
all, rules may be said to provide invaluable signposts in the
maze which often characterises our moral life. They take
some of the pressure off the individual in the lonely business
of decision-making. Well-established rules reflect the tried
and tested wisdom of past generations; they are the distil-
lation of human experience, providing an authoritative testimony to what makes for human well-being and what doesn't.
The persistence of these rules points us to the need for
constancy and stability in our dealings with our fellow-men.
They certainly hold us in good stead for the vast majority of
situations which we are likely to encounter in everyday life.
Fletcher's repeated use of abnormal situations, as with Mrs
Bergmeier's 'sacrificial' adultery, builds up a quite misleading
picture of human existence. The adultery which most people
are aware of and may feel tempted by is behaviour of a quite
different kind: it really does represent unfaithfulness to a

partner to whom one has made solemn vows of allegiance. As such it is quite definitely wrong, though the perceived short-comings of one's partner and the contrasting attractions of another individual may give the prospect of an adulterous liaison a bogus justification. Because we are so prone to deceive ourselves in this way, it is all the more important that a rule like 'do not commit adultery' exerts a strong psychological hold over us. That grip is likely to be fatally weakened if we are preoccupied by the possibility of exceptional situations which almost never occur in real life.

Second, some rules do appear to hold good for every type of situation which is realistically conceivable. The prohibition of rape is a good example. By very definition, rape is an unloving act: it is forcing another person into the most intimate of physical behaviour against his or her will. It invariably humiliates, hurts and damages (mentally and physically) the person who is its victim. There is no need to hedge qualifications and possible exceptions round a rule against rape; there is everything to be said for forbidding it absolutely. Again, it is noteworthy that even an act which meets with universal opprobrium is apt to adopt a different guise when the victims are seen as belonging to a lower species of humanity: it is in this light that I would interpret the frequent practice of soldiers expending their lust and hostility on the womenfolk of the enemy. Even the few rules which genuinely deserve the description 'absolute' are broken all too often.

Third, when we look closely into most of the rules which are strong candidates for being accorded absolute status, they appear to have something important in common. Rape, bestiality, torture, framing an innocent person, performing potentially lethal experiments on someone without their consent . . . all are violations of that mysterious thing we call human dignity. They represent failures to respect the special value which is inherent in the human person. They are treating other people as playthings; in effect, as dirt.

Daniel Maguire has argued that the whole of ethics is organically linked to the sacred value of persons.

Ethics exists as an effort to see what does and does not befit persons in all of their marvellous and compelling valuableness and sacredness . . . Because persons are so valuable, we owe them fidelity and truth and justice. A moral ought is basically a specified utterance of awe before the phenomenon of person-hood. Because persons are persons, they may not be bought and sold like cattle, plucked like weeds, set aside and segregated like mere objects, misled, etc.[6]

In arguing this, Maguire does not pretend that all societies display this reverence to the same degree. Indeed, he mentions one African group who have been the focus of a famous anthropological study, the Ik, who delight in selfishness and cruelty and scorn any manifestation of generosity and concern, even among their own people.[7] Such societies, however, appear to be deviations from the norm. The Ik themselves seem to have become as they are partly because they were treated harshly in being deprived of their natural hunting grounds. Maguire also adduces examples of the way in which acts of heroic self-sacrifice are widely admired across a considerable variety of cultures. But self-sacrifice makes sense only if one believes that the people or person-related values on behalf of whom one is making the sacrifice are precious and valuable.

The widespread nature of this 'foundational moral experience' (Maguire's phrase) needs to be recognised; it is not a monopoly of Christians alone. Nevertheless, Christian convictions should serve to reinforce these feelings of reverence. The Christian believes that God created mankind in his image, and that he has gone on caring for mankind and loving him ever since. Although human beings have defaced the divine image within them through their sin, they remain the apple of God's eye. Psalm 8 describes man as 'little less than God', and as crowned 'with glory and honour'. Moreover, God loves men and women so much that he was willing to share their humanity, even going to the length of dying for them, and redeeming them with Christ's precious blood. All this emphasises the value which God puts on each individual human person. In the light of this, Christians ought surely to be in the vanguard of movements which seek to cherish and protect human dignity. They can certainly lend their support to those rules which are fundamentally concerned with preventing its abuse.

Nevertheless, a rule-centred approach also has its limitations. Again I shall suggest three important counter-arguments. First of all, too much emphasis on a rule can distract attention from the principle which the rule is designed to safeguard. Principles (such as the respect for human dignity discussed above) are more fundamental to our moral understanding than are rules. Whereas rules name certain types of action as obligatory, permissible or forbidden, principles describe certain qualities or attitudes which should be present across a whole range of different actions. Rules often follow from principles, but sometimes the outworkings of a principle cannot easily be summed up in a rule with regard to a particular situation. An example may serve to illustrate this point.

Jill is a housewife with a 3-year-old child and is looking after a neighbour's 3-year-old child while that neighbour, a single parent, goes into hospital for a minor operation. One afternoon the neighbour rings up from hospital to say that she is being let out unexpectedly early. She asks if Jill can collect her by car: she is too weak to come home on the bus. Jill says 'of course' and puts the phone down. Then she realises that she only has one child-seat in the car, and she will have to make a choice between putting her own child or her neighbour's child in that seat. Jill is very safety-conscious and hates the thought of a young child sitting unharnessed in the back of her car. What are the moral issues at stake in this dilemma? The dilemma *could* be expressed in terms of two conflicting rules: 'do not let children travel unharnessed' versus 'fulfil the promise undertaken to one's neighbour'. Also, alternative courses of action could be considered: Jill might be able to leave *her* child temporarily with another neighbour, or she might be able to ring the hospital and ask them to bring her friend home in an ambulance, or she might be able to get her husband to collect the neighbour on his way home from work (if he has a company car). But supposing all these possibilities are non-starters, what then? Jill will almost certainly feel that she cannot let her friend down, and that she must take the admittedly slight but potentially momentous risk of exposing one of the two children to a greater degree of danger. In deciding *which* child, rules are much less likely to be of help to her than principles. I can think of three principles which might be relevant:

(1) Loyalty to her own flesh and blood. Jill's first loyalty is to her own child – after all, the child-seat was purchased for that child! Her neighbour has placed *her* child into Jill's care, but she cannot reasonably expect that care to be at the possible *expense* of Jill's child. We have more responsibility to some people than to others.

(2) Self-sacrificial love of neighbour. Where there is a clash between one's own interests and those of another, the principle of heroic self-sacrifice says that the other person should come first. Jill's own child may be seen as an extension of her own self, so giving the other child preference is justified.

(3) Extending most care to the most vulnerable. It may be that despite their similar ages, one of the children is more mature, responsible and safety-conscious than the other. (In the light of Jill's own conscientiousness about this matter, it is quite probable that her own child would be.) That child can more likely be trusted to sit still while Jill is driving than the other child. Risk is thereby reduced. The child who is more likely to wriggle and be vulnerable if an accident occurred should be given the extra security of the seat-belt.

All three considerations appear eminently worthy. For a Christian, calling to mind the teaching and example of Jesus, (2) and (3) will probably rank more highly than (1). The dilemma is then sharpened if (2) and (3) point in opposite directions, as they doubtless would if the neighbour's child was a couple of years older than Jill's child. Principles too may come into a delicate balance of conflict; but they do seem to have more bearing on this sort of dilemma than any particular rule would.

In a similar way, the problem faced by the Council of Jerusalem which is described in Acts 15 is best understood as a dilemma where three different principles were at stake. The dispute was over what should be expected of Gentile converts by way of obedience to the Mosaic law. One principle which was articulated was the continuing relevance of the law, the appropriate expression of that being seen as Gentile complicity with Jewish customs. The second principle, which was backed by Paul, Barnabas and Peter, was that salvation comes by 'the grace of the Lord Jesus' (Acts 15:11), and that burdensome demands which obscured this should not be made of the converts. The third principle, which is implicit in the compromise solution proposed by James, is the preservation of Christian unity. Circumcision was not demanded of the Gentiles, but abstaining from 'the meat of strangled animals and from blood' (15:20 NIV) was. Some, but not all of the distinctively ceremonial aspects of the law were preserved. In time the food regulations, too, were dropped, indicating that the second principle is more fundamental than the first, as well as the fact that Christians came to be more discriminating about which parts of the law still applied to them; but in the meantime the crucial third principle had averted a potentially damaging split.

I noted in Chapter 3 how Jesus identified certain key principles as central to a proper understanding of Old Testament law. He criticised the scribes and Pharisees for neglecting 'the weightier matters of the law, justice and mercy and faith' (Matt. 23:23), and described love of God and love of neighbour as the two commandments on which 'depend all the law and the prophets' (22:40). One implication would seem to be that where rules and regulations do *not* give any unambiguous guidance, principles like love and justice will find a way. They are to be our guide; and because they are of such abiding relevance, the significance of specific rules is somewhat reduced.

A second limitation regarding rules concerns their cultural relativity. Rules whose validity seems obvious to one generation are often held in light regard by another. It may be that, judged by the objective moral standards which are God's, the customs of one society are more in accord with his will than another; yet the variedness of ethical codes also reflects the fact that certain rules 'fit' some cultures much better than others. Social, economic and demographic factors will all have a bearing here. For most peoples killing seals represents a cruel and unnecessary thing to do; but for certain Eskimo groups it may be the only means to an economic livelihood. A prohibition on usury (charging interest when lending money) makes far less sense in an age of rapid inflation than during a period when prices are remaining constant. Polygamy, which has been outlawed in Western countries, would doubtless appear in a far more attractive light if the male population was decimated by war or sex-linked disease and there was a vast surplus of women over men.

From a Christian perspective, polygamy is a particularly interesting example of a practice which falls short of a God-given ideal, but which cannot be said to warrant absolute prohibition. Monogamy and polygamy are not equally satisfactory forms of marriage; nevertheless, polygamy should not be ruled out *per se*. There are a number of reasons why monogamy may be said to conform more closely to the divine intention. The blueprint for marriage which is found in Genesis 2:24, and was reaffirmed by Jesus in criticising the practice of divorce, clearly visualises one man united to one woman as the ideal: '. . . a man leaves his father and his mother and cleaves to his wife, and they become one flesh.' Monogamous practice tallies much better with a monotheistic faith: as with one's attitude to God, where one's loyalty is divided, one's love tends to be diminished. Polygamy can provoke a spirit of jealousy between the different wives who share unequally in the husband's affections: several of the Old Testament stories of polygamous marriage show emotions strained in this way.[8] Moreover, because it is almost always polygynous (one husband having more than one wife) as opposed to polyandrous (one wife having more than one husband), it tends to reinforce men's position of social superiority over women. Where it is only the male sex which is entitled to choose more than one partner, and the male who is 'doing the round' of his entourage of females, equal relations between men and women can hardly be said to exist. Polygamous practice may also be a mark of social élitism: in any polygamous society it will only be a minority of men who have

more than one wife – the roughly equal ratio of men and
women being what it is – so the custom tends to be the
prerogative of the rich and powerful. In the light of all these
considerations, it is not surprising that the Christian Church
has tended to discourage the practice where it has evangelised
polygamous societies, and that many converts have been
willing to accept this change in marital custom as they have
come to understand the implications of the Gospel.

However, that is by no means the whole story. Despite the
dangers to which Leah and Hannah alert us, it is significant
that the Old Testament law never forbids polygamy. God
allowed it, even if he didn't approve of it. In fact, in the case of
levirate marriage he implicitly commanded it, because many
men who married their brothers' wives in order to raise up
offspring were presumably already married (Deut. 25:5).
Furthermore, the fact that one of the qualifications for being
an elder or deacon in New Testament times was that a man
should have 'one wife' (1 Tim. 3:2, 12; Titus 1:6)[9] – while
supporting the view that monogamy is a preferable state –
seems to imply that ordinary members of the congregation
were permitted the option of polygamy.

In African societies today, polygamy is often practised in a
tender and considerate way, women certainly being kept in
a subordinate position, but not necessarily the victims of
oppression or the objects of lust. Where the attempt is made
to uproot polygamy too quickly, problems undoubtedly
occur. Until recently, the official practice of the Anglican
Church in Africa has been that converts living in a polygamous state cannot be admitted to baptism, but that they must
either dissolve all their marriages but one *or* wait until all their
wives except one had died. If they did the former, this was
likely to result in considerable emotional and financial
hardship for the discarded wives, especially in societies where
unattached women are unusual. If they did the latter, they
might serve as loyal church members for a whole lifetime
without enjoying the status of being a baptised person. A
gradual approach to the question is surely far better: those
who are already in polygamous marriages should not be
discouraged from fulfilling the obligations they have to their

several wives, and they should be allowed all the normal privileges of church membership; but those who are baptised as Christians before getting married should do so on the understanding that their marriage is expected to be monogamous.[10] Even then we need to note that there are special features about African culture which make resort to a second wife understandable. A tremendous emphasis is attached to the importance of producing heirs, and the women of some East African tribes refuse to continue co-habiting after the menopause. Particular pressure is therefore felt by the husbands of barren or non-sexually-active wives.

We need to be very careful, therefore, before making too universal a claim for a particular moral rule. This does not necessitate a tolerance that fears ever to make a moral judgment about a culture other than its own – though it is important to 'get inside' and understand a culture before venturing any criticism of it. We can, in humility but with the help of God's revelation, be so bold as to say that some ways of behaving are better than others. But this does not mean that practices we find questionable (as opposed to blatantly immoral) should be prohibited altogether or that they can be eradicated overnight. A particular practice might not be as deeply embedded in the local culture as it is unless there is something good to be said for it. While polygamy does appear to be deficient in its failure to express the equal standing of the sexes, it still reflects a concern for order, structure and considerate behaviour in the realm of sexual relationships. Polygamy is a far cry from promiscuity or prostitution.

The third reason why rules do not always settle moral dilemmas conclusively is that even the most important and fundamental moral rules sometimes come into conflict. The disorder of our world is such that in extreme circumstances God's commandments come into competition. We have already noted some examples of this. Kant's hypothetical situation, the Hebrew midwives, Rahab and Elisha in the Old Testament, and a number of incidents in the Second World War confront us with an unavoidable clash between the duties to tell the truth and to preserve life.[11] Sometimes one's duty to obey the existing government (see Romans 13:1) is in direct opposition to one's personal loyalty to God. 'Render to Caesar what is Caesar's, and to God what is God's' is all very well when a government is humanitarian and respects religious liberties, but what if Caesar starts to usurp the place of God? Believers may find themselves forbidden to worship God in public, as Daniel was, or to seek to communicate their faith, as happened to Peter and John.[12] On other occasions, the Biblical command to love appears to run counter even to supposedly inviolable rules. 'No direct killing of innocent persons' is a good example of the latter; but what if shooting someone is a case of putting a person suffering a lingering death out of his misery when there is no prospect of medical aid becoming available? That is what colleagues have sometimes done to mortally wounded soldiers screaming in terrible agony.

Conflicts of fundamental duty do occur, most often in times of war or political upheaval, but sometimes in much more mundane situations as well. We are obliged to rank one duty higher than another, to disobey one rule in order to obey another. In doing so, we place a question-mark about the absolute status of the vast majority of rules. Any rule that might *one day* be set aside in favour of another can no longer, strictly speaking, be called an absolute. Because it retains its validity in virtually all situations, it still deserves high status, and is worthy of the description *universal*; but the fact that a rule is widely and rightly recognised does not mean that it is totally without exception. I shall look further at the question of how these duties should be ranked in Chapter 10.

A Middle Way?

Both the deontological and consequentialist approaches to ethics thus seem to have strengths and weaknesses in roughly equal proportions. In view of this, the obvious way forward would seem to be a middle way which avoids both extremes. As my earlier survey has indicated, neither the Bible nor Christian tradition seem to support one approach to the exclusion of the other. Both stress rules and consequences at different points. There has probably been more of a stress in a deontological direction, but not nearly as much as Christianity's secular utilitarian critics have frequently supposed. Should we simply conclude, then, that Christian ethics is a matter of keeping a balance between the two approaches, of showing respect for widely-held rules while retaining one's options about adhering to them in the light of difficult circumstances and the prospect of undesirable consequences? Is it just a case of falling back on a *via media*, of feeling the tug of both approaches while surrendering to neither, of preserving a proper *tension*?

In an essay in his book *The Working Faith*, John Habgood, the present Archbishop of York, seems to imply that this is what a Christian approach is about, at any rate with regard to the vexed area of medical ethics. He discusses the question of the lengths to which doctors should go in trying to prolong the lives of the deformed newborn (with particular reference to spina bifida children) and embarks on an interesting digression on ethical theory. He notes that behind the two traditional aims of medicine, the prevention of suffering and the preservation of life, lie 'two broad ethical theories both of which have been found necessary in practice to complement and correct each other'.[13] On the one hand, there is the theory which entails making an estimate of the balance of suffering and happiness for all those concerned in a contemplated action. This tries to draw up a balance-sheet of happiness for a family with a deformed baby and attempts some estimate of the baby's potential for enjoying itself or finding some minimum of fulfilment. On the other hand, there is the theory which asserts overriding moral principles, such as that of the sanctity of life. These principles *appear* to introduce an authoritarian note into the discussion, but actually reflect what most people believe to be the case about human beings, viz., that they are valuable and their lives ought to be respected. This is how Habgood sums up his discussion:

> To argue solely in terms of general happiness provides no safeguard against injustice towards individuals. A newborn child with severe spina bifida has little to put in the scales of a utilitarian

balance, unless the sheer fact of its humanity is respected. No doubt in many cases such respect for its life will be outweighed by the potential misery the child might suffer and cause. But unless there is seen to be a conflict of principles at stake, not just a single principle, the gradual assumption of powers over life and death could become too easy. And the converse is also true. To assert respect for human personality, and so to preserve life at any cost without considering what in general makes human beings happy may, and often has, led to unnecessary suffering for the sake of blind adherence to beliefs.[14]

There are a number of echoes here of things that I have said in this book. Essentially, it is a middle way that I am advocating, and so I have some sympathy for Habgood's position.[15] But a problem with middle ways is that they may fail to provide much by way of specific guidance. If one simply says 'avoid the two extremes', that scarcely spells out a definite line of approach. At their worst, middle ways are excuses for muddling along in an arbitrary and unprincipled manner. I believe that we can avoid this. A Christian ethic which is neither obsessed by rules nor subordinated to consequences *can* offer quite a lot in the way of constructive help. It is possible to formulate principles, both of a general and more detailed kind, which are true to this judicious mediatory approach *and* give it some sort of cash value. In the next chapter, I shall draw together many of the threads which have permeated the book thus far, and make some positive proposals.

Notes

1 Dietrich Bonhoeffer, *Letters and Papers from Prison*, SCM, 1971 (enlarged edn), pp. 6–7.
2 Of course, if there is a television in the toy room, it may be possible to combine these activities, though this is liable to lead to frustration on either son or father's part!
3 Joseph Fletcher, *Situation Ethics*, SCM, 1966 p. 165.
4 See my comments on p. 48–9.

5   Alasdair MacIntyre, *A Short History of Ethics*, Macmillan, 1966, p. 238.
6   Daniel Maguire, *The Moral Choice*, pp. 73 and 81.
7   The anthropologist Colin Turnbull has written about the Ik in *The Mountain People*, Simon & Schuster, New York, 1972.
8   See e.g., the stories of Rachel and Leah (Genesis 29 and 30), and Hannah and Peninnah (1 Samuel 1).
9   An alternative understanding of these verses is that they refer to the phenomenon of *re*marriage, but I favour the polygamous interpretation.
10 This is the policy which has now been adopted by the Church of the Province of Kenya.
11 See earlier discussion on p. 50 and 63–4.
12 See Daniel 6 and Acts 4.
13 John Habgood, *A Working Faith*, Darton, Longman & Todd, 1980, p. 170.
14 *Op. cit.*, p. 171.
15 But also important reservations: see my comments on p. 198.

9

FIRST- AND SECOND-ORDER
PRINCIPLES

The two pivotal principles which should lie at the heart of all Christian decision-making and action are those of justice and of love. There are, of course, many other virtuous qualities whose meaning cannot simply be subsumed under the notions of love and justice; nevertheless, they can all be related to them. For love and justice are the two themes to which the Biblical writers return again and again. Their central significance and universal relevance have often been noted by Christian writers, particularly recent ones. This is what Lewis Smedes, author of the valuable book *Mere Morality*, has written:

> Justice and love are absolute, unconditional, unequivocal. They are global, universal, all-embracing commands. They pin us down at every corner, grip us at the centre, allow us no qualifications or evasions. Justice and love cover every conceivable human situation. They are the be-all and end-all of the moral life.[1]

Love

However, it is important to define what is meant by these two words. I take love to be a disposition which delights in other persons and wills the best for them. Some readers may be surprised at the first part of that definition, because there is a common tendency in Christian circles to distinguish 'loving' sharply from 'liking' and to say that the former has nothing to do with warmth of feeling. According to this way of thinking, love is a resolute determination to seek the other's good, however objectionable one may feel that person to be. Clearly, there are occasions when people behave so offensively that that is the only way in which we can love them; and sometimes, when it is difficult to feel much affection for individuals whom we do not know personally, we can still *do* something loving to help them (e.g., by sending donations to charities which feed starving people in the Third World). But the distinction between loving and liking should not be carried too far. For one thing, it is difficult to make sense of the idea of loving God if love is seen only as a matter of seeking another's welfare. God both desires and deserves a response of joyful thanksgiving from us; it is right that we should take delight in him. Furthermore, if relations between ourselves and a person whom we are loving but not liking remain on a cold and clinical level, something is sadly missing from that relationship. It may be that an act of 'initiative-taking' love will help to transform the other person into someone more attractive, and real affection may then come into the relationship; but it is also possible, as Helen Oppenheimer has suggested, that liking can be a good way into loving.[2] Thus if we are prepared to look for good and attractive qualities in a person whom initially we find repellent, we may find that liking them is not as difficult as we thought, and loving them in terms of acting constructively on their behalf will then come rather more easily.

Warmth of relationship, then, is not something to be set aside as irrelevant to love. It is a mistake to drive a wedge between *agape* (often defined as self-giving love) and *eros* (love which meets one's own needs and leads to self-fulfilment).[3] A good marriage obviously draws on both types of love, and in the process integrates them. Nevertheless, there are practical limits to the number of people with whom we can relate intimately. We are still called to love those with whom we have much more passing relationships. Yet by thoughtful, considerate and constructive acts of will, we can add to their quality of life, or in some cases assist their struggle to stay alive at all. Practical care for other people is a mandatory part of discipleship. Would-be disciples of Jesus who were not prepared to face the cost entailed in this were sadly turned away.[4]

The fact that there is a cost leads to the next important aspect of love: its readiness for self-sacrifice. To promote another person's welfare, I agree (for the time being) to put considerations of my own welfare to one side. This is not the same as saying it is wrong to love oneself. Jesus's command to love your neighbour as yourself seems to imply that it is right to love ourselves; if we lack a basic self-esteem, we are failing to value ourselves as God does, and attending to one's own needs (e.g., through eating properly, or having a day off) is usually necessary in order to be able to care effectively for others. Nevertheless, where there is a choice between my welfare and another's, the needs of the other person should come first. This may mean that *sometimes* we have to give up that treasured day off! On two occasions in Mark's Gospel we read of Jesus's trying to get away from the crowds, in order to rest and recharge his batteries, but each time he abandoned this plan of action when confronted by the needs of desperate people who pursued him – the Galilean crowd, whom he saw as 'sheep without a shepherd' (Mark 6:30–44), and the Syrophoenician woman with the sick daughter (Mark 7:24–30). When the time came for his supreme act of self-sacrifice, Jesus recoiled from the horror of what lay ahead ('Father, all things are possible to thee; remove this cup from me'[5]) but was still prepared to accept a humiliating and excruciating death in order to fulfil God's plan for saving humanity.

Most of the time, thankfully, the cost demanded of us in loving self-sacrificially is less extreme. Even when heroic measures are called for, it is usually a matter of risking one's life rather than abandoning it. A passer-by who leaps into a stormy sea to try to rescue a drowning child hopes to preserve his own life as well as the child's; the threat to his life and health is a risk which may not in fact materialise. It is our neighbour's good which should be the focus of concern, not our own deprivation; there is a twisted sort of self-love entailed in an attitude of actively seeking one's own martyr-dom. Nevertheless, where other people (rather than the vagaries of sea, mountain and weather) are threatening to inflict death, self-sacrificial action can represent a very definite choosing of death in the place of others. There is an extremely vivid example of this in Ernest Gordon's book about life in the Japanese prisoner-of-war camps.[6] At the end of a day's work toiling over the construction of a railway bridge, a group of prisoners-of-war hand their shovels in to the Japanese guard. He counts them and one appears to be missing. In a mounting rage, the guard threatens to kill the whole group unless someone owns up to having stolen a shovel. His frenzied demeanour makes clear that he means what he says. A prisoner then steps forward, says, 'I did it', and is violently beaten to death by the guard. When the shovels are recounted later, it emerges that in fact none of them was missing.

In the light of inspiring stories like this, it is tempting to imagine that love is an all-sufficient ethical principle: what need can we possibly have of any other? The fact remains that we do. Partly because we are sinful and delude ourselves as to what love is, partly because some moral dilemmas are horribly complex, and partly because our horizon on who are the neighbours to be loved can become extremely limited, love by itself is not enough. Love requires *dir*ection (and in some cases this may mean *cor*rection) from the principle of justice.

Justice

What is justice? It was classically defined by Aristotle as *suum cuique*, 'to each his due', and this has been a highly influential definition ever since. I believe that it is a helpful one. Every person has his or her just deserts; and it is incumbent on other individuals either to grant those deserts, or to refrain from taking them away. Nevertheless, what one's 'due' is considered to be is obviously open to a variety of interpretations. There seem to be four main ones.

First, justice can be understood to mean absolute equality.

Because all human beings are fundamentally equal (in value, if not in ability) they should all be treated in the same way. If this concept of justice was put into practice by a prices and incomes board which had power to fix wages across the whole range of occupations, it would mean that everyone (from the Prime Minister to a lavatory attendant) would be paid at exactly the same rate. Indeed, if the concept was applied consistently, it would mean that unemployed people would be paid the same as those who are employed.

Second, justice can be understood to mean similar treatment for similar cases. Here it is recognised that not all human beings are in comparable situations. Justice differentiates between these situations, but insists that all those who are in a comparable situation should be treated equally. Therefore water workers, gas workers and electricity workers should have strictly comparable rates of pay, because they do very similar sorts of job – so I recall the water workers arguing during an industrial dispute a few years ago.

Third, justice may be understood as a matter of reward for meritorious achievement. Human beings differ in how hard they work and what they achieve, so they do not deserve the same rewards. In that case, those whose work involves the most demanding physical labour, or the most taxing brain-power, or the longest period of training, or the highest level of responsibility, ought to be paid the most.

Fourth, justice may be based on the criterion of need rather than merit. Again different treatment is allowed for, but on the principle that people's needs vary. Therefore the highest pay should be given to those who are in greatest financial need: probably those languishing at the bottom of the pay-structure, or those who are disadvantaged because of poor housing or expensive transport.

It will by now be clear that what one conceives to be a just pay-structure (or looking beyond that a just society) will vary quite widely depending on one's underlying perception of justice. The differing proposals of political parties regarding taxation and social-security systems are essentially linked to disputed notions of what are people's just deserts. However, though politicians and the public at large differ in their emphases, it is likely that few would opt for *one* of these definitions of justice to the complete exclusion of the others. In this connection, it is interesting to note how the co-existence in Britain of different types of state benefit reflects an unspoken desire to complement the differing concepts of justice: child benefit may be said to be based on the second notion (similar treatment for similar cases; all parents with children can claim it) while supplementary benefit is based on the fourth (to each according to his need; it involves means-testing). Consideration of special circumstances, needs and merit all appear to have a part to play in devising the conditions for a more just society. Very few people would justify a pay or social-security system which was completely egalitarian, as suggested by my first interpretation of justice. All the same, the fundamental equality of human beings *is* an important consideration to keep in mind, because it helps to correct our undoubted tendency to exaggerate the disparity in worth between different people's jobs. The huge gulf between what individuals at the top and bottom of the pay-structure earn, in this society and the world over, is utterly unjust. For example, there is no way that a top football manager deserves to be paid a salary *twenty times* the earnings of one of the club's groundsmen.

There are elements of Biblical teaching which suggest that all these nuances of interpretation have a proper part to play in our understanding of justice. It is fascinating that Jesus's command to love one's enemy is modelled on the first notion of justice, God's *egalitarian* treatment of humanity:

> . . . he makes his sun rise on the evil and on the good, and sends rain on the just and the unjust (Matt. 5:45).

The Old Testament commands impartiality in the administration of justice:

> you shall not be partial to the poor or defer to the great, but in righteousness shall you judge your neighbour (Lev. 19:15).

A *bias to the poor* has no biblical support if it is held to mean absolving the poor from responsibility for their misdeeds.[7]

But society's more recurrent temptation is a bias to the rich, as we see in the prophets' complaints about the administration of justice, and which James warns against in his advice to stewards ushering people to their places in church services![8]

Yet within the context of a general equality of treatment, different groups are repeatedly singled out as warranting particular *kinds* of treatment. Paul clearly believed that husbands *owe it* to their wives, parents to their children and masters to their slaves to treat the other party in a particular way.[9] The same also applies to the reciprocal relations. 'Similar treatment for similar cases' underlies the instruction of other biblical passages with regard to a wide range of groups, from widows on the one hand to strangers to the religious community on the other.[10]

The link between merit and reward is not missing from the Bible. In 1 Timothy 5:17 we read that elders who lead a church well are worthy of 'double honour'. Paul, in the middle of chiding the work-shy Thessalonians, asserts that 'If anyone will not work, let him not eat' (2 Thess. 3:10). But he also recognised need when he saw it, and regarded giving by those with plenty to those suffering the effects of famine as a just redistribution of resources – hence the earnestness with which he collected for the Christians in Judaea.[11] In the Old Testament, God is described as one who 'delivers the needy when he calls, the poor and him who has no helper' (Ps. 72:12). There is a right way to understand God's bias to the poor, namely, as a concern to redress our unjust way of arranging society in which the balances are loaded in favour of the privileged. The need of the under-privileged provokes partiality; but it is a partiality which survives only as long as the injustice does, and it should not be taken to imply that in the meantime God abandons his loving interest in the rich and powerful – rather that he desires them to become aware of their contribution to a state of injustice, and resolve to take measures to change this.

There is, then, a proper place for making distinctions in deciding what is and is not just; there are also times when we should make no distinctions. Another way of putting this is to say that there is scope within the scheme of justice for special treatment, but not for arbitrary treatment. To pay headmasters more than schoolteachers may be just (though I think it is questionable[12]); but it would definitely be *unjust* to pay headmasters something and schoolteachers nothing at all. On the basic matter of whether teachers (or any other employed persons) should receive remuneration, justice has an unequivocal answer: they should. Employees are alike recipients of a minimum notion of justice inasmuch as all of them are paid.

In Chapter 8 reference was made to codes of rights which protect all members of the human race against fundamental violations of their dignity. There are certain ways of treating people which cannot but be unjust, whichever particular human individual or group one is dealing with. The egalitarian concept of justice is central to the notion of human rights. 'Giving someone his due' can never mean torturing him or raping her.

I often meet Christian people who are suspicious of this talk about rights. A Christian, they say, has no rights; to assert one's rights is arrogant, to claim them is greedy, and the person who has 'died with Christ' should have nothing to do with such worldly notions. I believe that this way of thinking is dangerously mistaken. It is certainly true that the Christian should be willing, where appropriate, to forgo his or her rights: 'turning the other cheek' when struck would be an example of this. But this does not alter the fact that these rights exist. When Jesus himself was struck at his trial, he certainly didn't hit back but he *did* object to the fact that he'd been hit:

> If I have spoken wrongly, bear witness to the wrong; but if I have spoken rightly, why do you strike me? (John 18:23).

Implicitly, he was saying that he had a right or a just claim not to be treated in such a way. In essence, rights are the converse of duties. If I have a *duty* to treat someone in a particular way, that person has the *right* to expect it. Hopefully, where relationships between individuals are healthy, language about rights and duties can recede into the background. A marriage where two partners are always harping on about their respective rights and duties is likely to be in a very strained state. Nevertheless, thoughtless exploitation of the one by the other can make this language relevant even in that context. Assertion of a right can shock the offending party into realising that he or she is behaving in a presumptuous way.

The theological basis for an affirmation of human rights is the fact that they reflect man's God-given dignity. I have already spelt this out in a little detail on pp. 158–9. Additional support for the concept can be provided by dwelling on a prominent aspect of Jesus's ministry. Jesus repeatedly affirmed the value of groups who were regarded as outcasts or second-class members of humanity by respectable Jews. Women, little children, Romans, Samaritans, tax-collectors, lepers, prostitutes: all were held in decidedly low esteem by the religious leaders of Jesus's day. Jesus went out of his way to insist that they too were objects of God's loving care; they too had an important part to play in the Kingdom of God and the emerging family of the Church. Jesus affirmed the dignity of social outcasts as equal human beings through his practice of treating them with consideration and respect. This did not prevent him from challenging – where appropriate – their sinful way of life; but that itself is a mark of respect for someone, that one considers him or her a responsible agent who is worthy to be *called to account*.

In our day, we can rejoice that minority groups who encounter ostracism and discrimination may now claim the protection of certain generally accepted human rights. It is an encouraging sign of hope that the United Nations, representing countries from all over the world, were able to agree on a Universal Declaration of Human Rights in 1948; what is disappointing is the number of countries who subscribed to that Declaration who regularly violate some of those rights. Vigilance in the cause of justice – as demonstrated by the work of an organisation like Amnesty International – is an ever-pressing requirement.

The Interrelationship of Love and Justice

On p. 172 I wrote that awe-inspiring though love is as an ethical principle, it requires direction and in some cases correction from the principle of justice. There are three main reasons for this.

The first is that love, at least as it is customarily understood and practised, has a short-term consequentialist bias which is liable to lead us well-intentioned but sinful human beings astray. Because we are preoccupied with the immediate need of our neighbour, we take short-cuts. Consider this scenario. A grown-up daughter who lives away from home drives to a hospital to pay her sick father a surprise visit. When she arrives in the car park she finds that the only spaces left are two which are reserved for handicapped drivers. She parks her car in one of them – in the name of loving her father and with the comforting thought that 'it doesn't look as if they are going to be used this visiting time'. But is this just? It is hardly fair to a handicapped person who might come along later and find himself without a parking place. If everyone acted as the daughter did, handicapped drivers would definitely be getting a raw deal. Despite her highly commendable eagerness to see her father and cheer him up by her visit, it is surely better that she, rather than a handicapped person, should have to make the longer walk which will result from parking outside the hospital grounds. (It may even be that if she explains the circumstances, the ward sister will allow her to extend her bedside stay, so her father will not necessarily 'miss out'.) Love can tempt us to take short-cuts – but justice supplies a corrective.

Similar considerations apply to situations where the stakes are very much higher. Thielicke's example of the concentration camp, where prisoners were asked to determine which of their fellow-prisoners should be executed, is worth re-examination here.[13] It is easy to see how collaboration with the SS might be justified in the name of love. Surely it is better that some prisoners die than all – one might as well try to save what lives one can. Yet the fact remains that to 'name' one's fellow-prisoners in this way represents active (if reluctant) participation in a grossly unjust state of affairs. It is colluding with a system of evil. Co-operation by the oppressed in a process of selective murder also helps to perpetuate the oppressive system. Today's collaborator may well be tomorrow's victim. There are *long-term* consequentialist considerations, as well as the more straightforward question of justice, to be set against the short-term consequentialist factors whose standard-bearer may be love. It would appear that justice is the principle which actually accords more frequently with these long-term considerations. Interestingly, the Nazi policy of enlisting doctors in the process of eliminating the mentally ill and mentally handicapped did *not* continue indefinitely – partly because certain well-known heads of institutions for the handicapped, like Pastors Paul Braune and Friedrich von Bodelschwingh, refused to have anything to do with the policy (and publicised this widely).

It seems to me that doctors in Britain who disagree strongly with the 1967 Abortion Act (and even more so with the liberal way in which that Act is commonly interpreted) may have reached a parallel situation. If one holds the view that fetal life should be valued as fully human life, one may believe that abortion is morally justified in certain extremely rare circumstances (e.g., where the mother's life is at risk, the most serious type of fetal handicap which offers little prospect of life after birth, and possibly rape); but one cannot but be aghast at a situation where the legal ground of 'threat to the mother's health' is used as a catch-all for the overwhelming majority of abortions.[14] Of course, in some situations the threat to health is genuine, though even then it is difficult to justify a threat to health taking priority over a threat to life; in other cases, it is simply a cipher for personal inconvenience. Doctors who take a high view of fetal life, however, are divided in their response to the dilemma with which the Act confronts them. Some refuse to perform or approve any abortions at all, or do so only in a very limited category of cases such as those mentioned above. In the latter case, very few requests then come their way, because the medical system gets wise to the attitude of the doctor and steers patients towards colleagues with more liberal attitudes.

Partly because of this, a significant proportion of doctors (often Christian ones) with strong conscientious objections to most abortions remain in 'the system', and accede to a fair proportion of abortion requests (fewer than do their colleagues, but higher than they actually think are justified). For instance, I have heard a Christian gynaecologist talking in terms of performing about 30 per cent of abortion requests – the 'hardest' cases that come before him – and turning away 70 per cent. While about half of the latter figure might still get an abortion through resorting to another doctor, either on the National Health Service or privately, at least 35 per cent of the original quota of fetuses will have been saved. This figure might be considerably more than if the gynaecologist had opted out of the system altogether, and been replaced by a doctor with fewer scruples about abortion.

This approach is persuasive on short-term utilitarian grounds, but not on any other. If one performs even 30 per cent of abortion requests, one is still being a direct party to many acts of unjustified killing. That is a heavy burden to lay on one's conscience. The utilitarian sacrifice-some-to-save-others approach fails to appreciate the seriousness of involvement in taking even one innocent life. In my view, the best hope of society's waking up to the wrongness of the present law (or at least reopening serious debate about it) lies in large numbers of doctors taking a stand against the present law and practice by refusing to co-operate. At the moment the number of conscientious objectors is still small, and gynaecological medicine can bear the strain on the system which they impose, but if taking a stand was to become contagious, medicine and society might have to think again.

The second way in which love requires direction from justice is closely related. Not only does justice insist on *depth* of perspective; it also summons love to a *breadth* of perspective. Love tends to respond to the most eye-catching and desperate types of need, whereas justice demands that one spreads one's gaze rather more widely. For instance, in the distribution of limited financial resources in the health service it is tempting to spend a disproportionate amount of money on surgery making use of advanced medical technology, at the expense of rather more mundane treatment like care of the mentally ill or geriatric patients. Love is aroused by the critical state of the patient requiring a heart or kidney transplant; but justice may be required to insist on a proper deal for patients who often have to wait years for a hip operation. Of course, it is both just and loving that those whose lives are in danger should take precedence in the surgical pecking order over those whose lives are not threatened directly. Nevertheless, it is imperative that we do not lose sight of the very real suffering endured by those who experience long-term debilitating illness. A just ordering of medical resources is sensitive to the whole gamut of human need.

In a similar way, considerations of justice demand that we adopt a loving response to the needs of deprived people both in our own country and other countries. I suspect that our concern is liable to be narrowly focused in one direction or the other over different issues. Thus the problems of poverty and malnutrition are likely to strike us as a characteristically Third World issue, and we may become blind or indifferent to the existence of genuinely poor, ill-fed groups of people in this country. In contrast, the instinctive tendency on the issue of unemployment is to concentrate attention on Britain's situation (with a horrifying 1 in 8 of the workforce unemployed) and to forget that in some Third World countries the problem is very much worse – unemployment figures sometimes reaching as high as 35 per cent. An attempt to improve our own employment situation by adopting protectionist policies towards certain industries might then force even more workers in other countries out of jobs. There is no easy answer to these massive problems, and it may be right that individuals feel called to a particular concern over one group or another who are suffering deeply; but a passion for justice should keep us alive to the needs of groups which are not immediately obvious to us – the reason for this probably being that they are not a regular object of media attention.

The third way in which justice helps to direct how love operates is through exposing the structural flaws which may lie behind the phenomena of human need. It is not simply charity which the needy require, though charitable giving and charitable organisations certainly have their place. Without denying the fact that poor people, for instance, sometimes contribute to their own state of deprivation by squandering what resources they have, it is frequently true that they suffer from unjust social and economic systems. Economic relations between Western and Third World countries have often been a case of one exploiting and keeping the other in a state of dependence. Low prices have been paid for raw materials produced in the Third World; and manufacture of those primary products in the developing countries by local entre-preneurs has been discouraged both by the erection of tariff barriers and (more recently) by taking control of such a process through the expanding activity of multinational com-panies in those countries. Justice demands that any thorough-going attempt to improve the lot of people in the Third World attends to the practicalities of change on this structural econ-omic level, complex though it is. It desires not only that the bellies of hungry people should be fed, but that hungry people be given the chance to participate in the economic process on a free and equal basis.

However, there are also ways in which love provides an essential supplement to the principle of justice. Where justice makes life hard for someone, love remains attentive to the individual's needs, and seeks to mitigate the harshness of the verdict. If justice does dictate that long-term considerations take priority over short-term ones, love does its utmost to make those immediate consequences bearable. If society was ever to adopt a stricter abortion law, then it is vital that compassion be awakened for many thousands of unhappy women who will be expected to go through pregnancies against their will. They will require a great deal of emotional, pastoral and practical support. A stricter abortion law would actually constitute a call to *men* to display care, love and responsibility towards the women they have played a part in impregnating. It is because men often – in different ways – leave women in the lurch that abortion is so frequently requested, yet paradoxically the existence of a liberal abor-tion law *encourages* men to be irresponsible. But where support from a partner-cum-father is still not forthcoming, then clearly others in society (the duty being especially pressing on those who have campaigned against the present law) have a moral responsibility to fill some of the gap.[15]

Love also supplements justice in the way that it transcends the notions of right and duty. If justice consists essentially in giving someone his due, the hallmark of love is its willingness to give individuals *more than* their due. Just as God revealed his love to us in Christ even when we were locked in a state of sinful enmity with him (i.e., we did not deserve his love), so we are called to follow his example in loving those whom we regard as undeserving. Justice may demand that an employee who is guilty of a serious theft of company property be brought to book; but love seeks a way of showing care and concern for individuals at the very same time that they are being disciplined. One of Jesus's commands that is all too rarely heeded is his call to visit the prisoner.[16] Another way in which love goes beyond the dictates of justice is in its readiness for acts of spontaneous generosity. Although justice bids us to think widely, of *all* the neighbours we should love, there is certainly a place for warm-hearted gestures which shower affection and help on particular individuals. Jesus himself was both recipient and donor of this extravagant sort of love. He accepted the sinful woman's outpouring of expensive ointment, and he gave the hungry multitude twelve basketfuls more than they needed to eat!

It is also true that love may be the motivating factor which fuels a concern for social justice. Hearts which have been touched by the fly-pestered, pencil-thin bodies of starving Ethiopian children, may then lead minds to ask how at the same time EEC governments can justify disposing of surfeit food mountains. The motive of love can still be operative in those trying to bring about change at a structural level. In the final analysis, it is a mistake to see love simply as *supplementing* attempts to secure greater justice; ideally, love should inspire and penetrate such attempts. Where love and justice are motivating human beings as they should, it actually becomes very difficult to disentangle the two principles, to say exactly where the work of one ends and the work of the other one begins. Although, as a stylistic device, I have spoken of love and justice in quasi-personal terms (a technique with sound biblical precedents![17]), there is a measure of artificiality in this; what we encounter in life are individuals who act lovingly and justly in a much more piecemeal and less self-conscious sort of way. But sometimes we do meet instances of people whose love is flawed by a blindness to the claims of justice, or whose preoccupation with justice renders them singularly unloving: and this prompts analysis of the different nuances and emphases of the two words.

Both love and justice, then, are fundamental requirements in relation to moral decision-making. Yet there can still be problems in interpreting their demands in the context of a difficult dilemma. Are there no second-order principles which spell out these splendid abstractions in greater application of detail? I suggest that there are, and to these I now turn.

Respecting People Rather Than Using Them

The principle formulated by Kant, that we should never treat humanity only as a means but always also as an end, is a good example of a second-order principle which is true to the demands of love and of justice.[18] It is both just and loving to respect a person's intrinsic dignity; it is not just and loving to use them simply as a means to achieving an end unconnected with their welfare. The word 'simply' applies an important qualification. In some situations we can in a sense 'use' people at the same time as loving and respecting them. For instance, while I have been writing this book, a couple who are good friends asked to discuss with me a particular moral dilemma which is of great personal concern to them. In agreeing to their request, I feel there is a sense in which I have used my friends for the purposes of this book, because discussing their problem has given me additional insight into the complexities of that dilemma. But I can also honestly say that I have been motivated by concern for them and a desire that they resolve their dilemma as satisfactorily as possible. Nevertheless, writing is an area where using others merely as means must often be a severe temptation. One thinks of novelists who are tempted to put thinly-disguised accounts of acquaintances' marriage break-ups into their works of fiction, or newspapers which disclose saucy, sordid and flimsily researched revelations about well-known individuals in order to boost their flagging sales.

One much-discussed dilemma to which I have already alluded is worthy of fresh examination from this perspective. When Mrs Bergmeier persuaded the camp guard to have sexual intercourse with her, was she not guilty of using him simply as a means to her very worthy end? It would appear that she used him as a means of impregnation and nothing more. It will not suffice to say that he probably enjoyed the experience (though being human he probably did!) or that he and Mrs Bergmeier may have felt some genuine affection for each other. First, the fact that individuals often consent to and even derive enjoyment from being degraded does not render such action right. Second, the greater the level of affection which Mrs Bergmeier and the guard actually felt for each other, the more likely it was that the physical expression of that emotion through the act of intercourse might cause a bond to develop which could have serious implications for her marriage relationship. Thus Mrs Bergmeier *might* be treating the guard as an end in himself, but it would be an illegitimate end, because she would be putting him on a comparable level with her husband. It is also possible, of course, that the guard was married himself (Fletcher does not tell us); if so, the incident cannot have been devoid of implications for the relationship with *his* partner.

The ends-means principle (as I will abbreviate it for purposes of convenience) has possible relevance to a number of the new techniques in the realm of artificial fertilisation and embryology. The Warnock Committee, which inquired into them, noted its application to one technique, the practice of surrogate motherhood. A 'surrogate' mother is one who carries a child in her womb with the intention of handing it over after birth to a couple who have commissioned the child. Her help might be sought when a woman who wants a child is physically incapable of carrying a child through pregnancy, or when either she or her husband is infertile; the genetic father may therefore be either the husband or an anonymous donor, and the genetic mother may be either the wife or the surrogate (depending on the circumstances, artificial insemination and *in vitro* fertilisation can both be used in conjunction with surrogacy). Despite the very real hopes of circumventing infertility which are raised by the practice, the Warnock Report sees dangers of persons being 'used' on both sides. On the one hand the surrogate mother (and of course a commercial agency) may exploit the couple's need, and in the process demean her own body: '. . . it is inconsistent with human dignity that a woman should use her uterus for financial profit and treat it as an incubator for someone else's child.'[19] On the other hand the couple may exploit the woman: pregnancy involves risks, and 'That people should treat others as a means to their own ends, however desirable the consequences, must always be liable to moral objection.'[20] Considerations such as these led the Warnock Committee to recommend that surrogacy agreements and commercial agencies arranging these agreements should be made illegal.

What is perhaps surprising is that the Warnock Committee failed to note that the same ends-means principle can also be applied to some of the techniques which it was prepared to approve. Is a donor not being treated as a mere means (in a way comparable to Mrs Bergmeier's guard) when a couple use his sperm to bring about an artificial insemination? Are not embryos being treated as mere means when they are used for the purposes of research? Admittedly, how one evaluates the latter technique depends largely on what one considers to be the status of the embryo, a subject on which the Warnock Committee failed to make up its collective mind.[21] But throughout the whole range of issues which the Committee considered, there seems to be a persistent danger of people being used in a way which does not have their own welfare at heart, and is thus scarcely compatible with notions of human dignity.

Nevertheless, the statement that this is a danger means what it says and no more: these dangers will not necessarily be realised in every situation where such practices occur. It is possible to conceive of a surrogacy agreement where the couple and the surrogate respectively do not exploit each other; they may treat each other with consideration and care. The ends-means principle cannot always be applied to a category of action wholesale; what it may do is serve a warning note about attitudes which are all too liable to be in evidence. As far as surrogacy is concerned, there is another weighty consideration which makes the practice questionable. Even though surrogate mothers doubtless enter into agreements with every intention of handing over a child once born, it can be expected that during the course of a pregnancy a fair degree of bonding between the surrogate mother (who may also be the genetic mother) and the child will take place. Giving up the child could then be a very real emotional wrench for her. Is there not something perverse about an agreement which *obliges* a mother to go against that most natural of all instincts, to keep and to nurture the child to whom she has just given birth? For all its altruistic overtones, surrogacy is a singularly unnatural process. Here then is an example of a practice which is rendered dubious on more than one count: the ends-means principle raises doubts, but it is arguable that only alongside another important consideration does the objection become decisive.

Observation of the ends-means principle is a way of ensuring respect for individual rights in the midst of aiming for the common good. It is a mistake to regard this as a case of putting the interests of the individual ahead of the interests of the larger group, though adherence to the principle may sometimes look like that in the short run. The fact is that society ultimately stands to gain rather than to lose from this scrupulous respect for human dignity. Societies where individuals are habitually used rather than respected are apt to end up as societies with two classes of people, a master class and a slave class.

Never Directly Harming an Innocent Person

There is another way of expressing this concern for human dignity, and it may be that in some situations this second example of a second-order principle is the more helpful. I believe that it is consistent with the principles of both love and justice that we should never directly harm an innocent person. This statement contains three key words.

By *harm* I mean inflicting deprivation on a person so that he or she can no longer experience those positive aspects of human existence which we habitually call 'good'. It is difficult to make an exhaustive list of these basic goods, but they would certainly include human life itself, physical and mental health, freedom of movement and speech, and involvement in the political process, to name a few.[22] If we deliberately deprive an innocent person of any of these, we are inflicting a grave injury, one that fails to respect their human dignity and leaves them crippled to a greater or lesser extent.

The word *innocent*, of course, supplies an important qualification. It is not innocence in the sense of sinlessness which is meant by it, but innocence of any offence which warrants deprivation of a particular good. It is appropriate that perpetrators of serious crimes should suffer some such deprivation. In some emergency situations this might also involve innocent bystanders. Thus a nightly curfew might justifiably be imposed on a community which has shown a repeated tendency to riot. The rioters have brought the deprivation of a basic good, that of freedom of movement, upon themselves. Doubtless some individuals who have not been responsible for rioting might suffer thereby, but it may be temporarily impossible for the authorities to distinguish between rioters and non-rioters, and in any case the imposition of the curfew will probably make life for the latter group safer. Indeed, it is arguable that deprivation of a basic good actually redounds to the benefits of the wrong-doer also. It would be unloving to allow a murderer freedom to go on murdering; it would be unjust not to punish him (murderers nearly always are men!) in one way or another. There is substance in all the leading theories of punishment: it is important that the public be kept safe, *and* that they be deterred from performing similar crimes, *and* that wrong-doers get their just deserts, *and* that attempts be made to reform their anti-social attitudes.[23] Of course, prisons are always imperfect and prisoners often intractable, but where punishment *is* effective, it becomes questionable whether 'harm' is actually the right way to describe what a person has experienced. Nevertheless, my definition of harm would become unhelpfully convoluted if I wrote into it a qualifying clause which said that deprivation of these goods can be beneficent as far as *guilty* persons are concerned. The words 'harm' and 'innocent' need to be understood together.

The qualification implied by the word *directly* expresses the point that sometimes we can hardly avoid harming innocent persons, but to do so should never be our intention. The pilot of an airliner suffering from engine trouble decides to make an emergency landing on a piece of wasteland in a built-up area. There is a danger that the plane may cause serious or lethal harm to a couple walking along the edge of the wasteland. Obviously he will try to avoid them, because he does not wish them any harm, but he correctly discerns that his first duty is to his passengers. Their safety is his primary concern. If injury to the couple was the indirect effect of a safe landing of the airliner, no one could fairly blame the pilot.

Use of the words 'direct' and 'indirect' calls to mind the principle of double effect, which I have already commended because it steers a middle way between moralities dominated either by rules or consequences.[24] The action of the pilot would clearly satisfy all the principle's requirements: landing an aircraft safely is a morally good thing to do, the pilot's intention was upright, the evil and the good effects take place simultaneously, and there was a proportionately grave reason for doing what he did. It is possible to conceive of circumstances where the evil effects would have been such that the criterion of proportionality becomes more disputable. If the couple had been walking in the middle of the wasteland, or if there had been twenty-two schoolboys involved in a game of football on it, the pilot would probably have had second thoughts about landing there. Yet if there was no practical alternative landing-place, the pilot's action in aiming for the wasteland might still be strongly defended on proportionate grounds. The death of any individuals resulting from the landing would also remain indirect and undesired.

There are some situations, however, where the distinction between direct and indirect becomes forced and difficult to justify. If a soldier complies with his mortally wounded colleague's request to shoot him because he is suffering excruciating pain, there is no denying that the act of killing is direct. The wounded man is, moreover, (certainly from his colleague's perspective) innocent of any offence for which he deserves to die. But it is difficult to deny that killing is a right and merciful act in this case. Again, the principle of double effect applies neatly to cases of abortion to save the mother's life where it is a matter of removing her womb or Fallopian tubes, because there the death of the fetus is indirect, but what if her medical condition is such that the only way to relieve it is through a direct assault on the fetus? This would be true in rare cases where the mother has a misplaced, acute appendicitis, or where the wall of her aorta is so weakened that it balloons out behind the uterus. In each situation the doctor must first deal with the fetus (i.e., kill it) in order to take the action which will save the mother's life. It seems artificial, by a strict interpretation of the principle of double effect, to accept abortion in the first two cases but exclude it in the latter two. In all four cases the death of the fetus would be equally undesired, and in all four cases the fetus's existence is imperilled by the mother's condition. In each situation it makes sense to save the life which can be saved, i.e., the mother's, sadly accepting the fact that such action – directly or indirectly – involves the loss of the fetus's life.

Although these two examples suggest that, useful as it is, the principle of double effect has its limitations, I do not think that they invalidate my principle of never directly harming innocent persons. Again one needs to reconsider what harm means in these particular situations. In the absence of medical aid, it is surely a prolongation of his agony which would harm the soldier; he was destined to be deprived of the good of life in a short time anyway, and bringing forward the moment of loss would actually come as a merciful relief. Similarly, the fact that the fetus was doomed makes talk of it being *harmed* by the process of abortion misleading and inappropriate. There are some extreme situations where words do not carry their normal meaning. Usually we can unhesitatingly describe killing as an illustration – the most grave illustration – of what it means to harm someone, but there are rare occasions when this is no longer true.

The Just-War Criteria

There are other examples of second-order principles which are applications of the principles of love and justice to specific areas of ethical concern. The criteria which were laid down in the just-war tradition are an example of this.[25] Of course, Christian pacifists will argue that this tradition constitutes a major misapplication of these principles. They would ask how it is ever possible to love one's enemy in the process of killing him, dispute the possibility of making a sober judgment about the justice of a cause with which one is intimately involved, and question whether war can really lead to a more just state of affairs in view of the appalling suffering and havoc it entails. These are substantial objections which need to be taken seriously by the just-war theorist.

Certainly, that theory has often been applied in a partial, unrigorous or haphazard way – so that it may well have served the purpose of *excusing* war more frequently than it has *limited* it. Nevertheless, there are impressive examples of individuals invoking its principles. Vittoria, one of the Spaniards who gave the just-war theory coherent expression in the sixteenth century, bravely argued that the Spanish war against the South American Indians in the 1530s was unjust; and George Bell, the Bishop of Chichester, damaged his chances of ecclesiastical preferment by condemning Churchill's policy of bombing civilians in Dresden and other German cities during the Second World War.

Augustine certainly believed that taking up arms to fight could be an act of *love*, the point being that defending a people from external threat is a way of expressing love for one's neighbours. Luther similarly thought that it could be 'a work of Christian love to protect and defend a whole community with the sword and not to let the people be abused'.[26]

That Aquinas intended the issue of war to be set in the context
of love is shown by the fact that he approaches the question
from the perspective of whether war signifies a vice against
peace (a quality he regards as one of the effects of love). His
answer is that it isn't, necessarily. Unlike Augustine, who
believed, on the basis of his interpretation of Jesus's words in
the Sermon on the Mount, that killing in self-defence was
wrong, Aquinas argued that this, too, is legitimate. 'Love thy
neighbour as thyself' suggests that one's own life, too, is
worthy of defence, and it is repulse of the attack, not the
death of one's assailant, which is the intention of one's act. If
the latter does occur, that is an undesired secondary effect.[27]
The fact that Aquinas regarded the death of one's attacker as
undesirable (though effective defence may leave one little
option but to inflict it) also indicates that thoughts of loving
one's enemy have not been abandoned. It is difficult, but not
impossible, to go on loving one's enemies in the process of
fighting them. The Bible clearly sees love as underlying the
practice of *discipline*:

> It is for discipline that you have to endure. God is treating you as
> sons; for what son is there whom his father does not discipline?
> (Heb. 12:7).

A just war may be seen as an act of discipline on an aggressive
and unruly nation. Of course, in the maelstrom of war,
feelings of hatred and vengeance often blemish the motives of
the disciplinarians, but the history of war shows that acts of
goodwill do from time to time break through the atmosphere
of hostility. A prime duty of the church in wartime is to ensure
that the ultimate welfare of the enemy is not lost to view.

As I acknowledged in Chapter 7, it is difficult to make a
detached judgment about the justice of a war in which one's
own country is involved, but in all complex moral dilemmas
our perspective is liable to be distorted to some extent. We
must still act courageously on the basis of the most informed
judgment available to us. In some wars the claim of both sides
to have a just cause may seem equally plausible, or for that
matter implausible – either situation prompting a strong case

for refraining from active involvement. But in other wars retrospective judgments confirm that one side *was* clearly in the right and the other in the wrong. Many Germans alive today would agree that in the case of the Second World War it was the Allied cause, not that of their own country, which was basically just. Admittedly, even a war whose justice is relatively uncontroversial can be enormously expensive in terms of human lives. About 50 million people died in the Second World War. The likelihood that military action could lead to a worldwide conflagration is a consideration that may rightly deter political leaders from defending even what they see as just causes. Estimating the cost of a war is, however, an extremely difficult thing to do accurately in advance. At the outbreak of the Falklands War, it was widely predicted that the Islands would be very hard to retake from the Argentinians. This was one consideration, among others, which led me to think that this was not a war which Britain should be fighting. In actual fact, the Argentinian soldiers were poorly trained and capitulated quickly. As wars go it thus involved a relatively small loss of human life: about a thousand men, though that is not of course to deny the sorrow which each individual bereavement brings.

What I have just presented is only a very tentative and sketchy defence of the just-war tradition. The theory certainly has its limitations. But in the hands of its best exponents, it is an attempt to be faithful to the axiomatic principles of love and justice. The just-war criteria are examples of second-order principles applied to a particularly controversial area of human endeavour.

Only Caring for the Dying

Another area which has seen the development of some important second-order principles is that of medical ethics. With the advance of medical technology, doctors are often left with some agonising decisions about whether it is right to take all possible measures to save a patient's life. Are they justified in switching off artificial support machines when a comatose patient has lost all hope of recovering spontaneous activity of heart and lungs and his brain has been damaged to such an extent that there is little prospect of recovering consciousness? Are they justified in withholding a routine course of antibiotics for pneumonia from an old man who is in the last stages of dying from cancer? Are they justified in not performing an operation to remove an intestinal blockage on a newborn girl who has been diagnosed as suffering from Down's Syndrome? The conundrums become even more puzzling as one delves into the case-books of patients suffering from rare and grotesque types of handicap or illness.

'To save or let die: the dilemma of modern medicine'[28]: that is the choice with which we (patients, relatives and society, as well as doctors) are confronted on many occasions. A guideline which has often been used by Roman Catholic moral theologians, and which offers some hope of illumination, is the distinction between ordinary and extraordinary means of saving life. This has been typically defined as follows:

> *Ordinary* means of preserving life are all medicines, treatments and operations, which offer a reasonable hope of benefit for the patient and which can be obtained and used without excessive expense, pain, or other inconvenience . . . *Extraordinary* means of preserving life . . . mean all medicines, treatments and operations, which cannot be obtained without excessive expense, pain or other inconvenience, or which, if used, would not offer a reasonable hope of benefit.[29]

According to this line of argument a sick person is obliged, as are those who have the care of him, to employ all the obvious available means of preserving his life and restoring his health. If a woman is diagnosed as having a malignant lump in her breast, it denotes an irresponsible attitude to her body not to have the lump removed. But a patient need not feel bound to incur, or impose on his family, an impoverishing expense; nor is he bound to submit to treatment which would cause him great distress and of which the benefits are problematical. A man who is dying from acute leukaemia need not feel obliged to submit to chemotherapy, if that is likely to produce a remission of no more than a year and there is less than a 50 per cent chance of its doing that. He may accept such treatment if he wishes but others should not force him to do so.

This distinction between ordinary and extraordinary means is one which might be defended on theological grounds. It does seem to correspond in a rough-and-ready sort of way to the Christian attitude to life and death. This, I think, consists of a readiness to accept both life and death in a positive spirit. St Paul looked forward to life beyond the grave, but was determined to serve God as best he could all the days left to him on earth.[30] On the one hand, Christians regard life as a gift from God, a state of being which we should hold sacred and seek to preserve. On the other hand, death too can be a gift from God, a merciful release to a life beyond suffering, and so it should not be viewed as an enemy to be kept at bay at all costs. A balanced view of this sort points to the appropriateness of a medical policy which seeks to save life whenever the prognosis gives cause for hope, but is ready to accept death when the prospects are dire.

However, the distinction between ordinary and extraordinary means also has its limitations. First, the issue is complicated in some cases by the fact that patients are incapable of communicating whether they wish extraordinary means to be used to prolong their lives. Decisions have to be made for the comatose or mentally retarded. Second, the line between ordinary and extraordinary means is a sliding one which changes with the passage of time. At one time amputation of a limb was clearly an extraordinary medical procedure: it was unusual, dangerous and very painful. Anaesthetics, disinfectants and artificial limbs have surely moved it from one category to the other. Heart transplants are perhaps still classed as an extraordinary means, but they may not be for very much longer. Third, the distinction begs the question of whether the fact that death is diagnosed as imminent makes a difference. A course of antibiotics for pneumonia would generally be considered an ordinary means, yet from time immemorial pneumonia has been described as 'the old man's friend'.

I believe that a more helpful second-order principle is

provided by Paul Ramsey in his book, *The Patient as Person*.[31] He speaks, quizzically but persuasively, of caring only for the dying. 'Dying' here refers to someone in an irreversibly dying condition. It is not enough simply to say that a patient has cancer. If detected in its early stages cancer can be arrested, and even where it persists it may permit an individual several years of life. The fact that one has an incurable disease need not prevent one from doing and experiencing many worthwhile things. But where a patient is in the final stages of a terminal illness, and doctors know that they can now do nothing to arrest its progress, it is right that medical objectives switch from saving life to providing the best possible quality of care. This will probably include the administration of drugs to relieve the pain caused by the illness; it may also entail *not* administering remedial treatment for a secondary illness which brings a certain death closer. The emphasis should be on care, of filling the final days of a patient with as much companionship and as little suffering as is practical.

If failing to provide antibiotics sometimes hastens the moment of death by an act of omission, the administration of pain-killing drugs has been known to hasten it in a more active way. Large doses of drugs such as morphine tend to have a suppressive effect on the respiratory system, making breathing slow and shallow. Such action has been defended in the past by reference to the principle of double effect: if the intention of the doctor was to relieve pain, but the secondary and incidental effect was to cause death, the action was seen as permissible. Nowadays, the fact that drugs are more sophisticated and knowledge of their workings more precise means that the chances of inflicting a fatal dosage are much reduced. There are clearly recommended maximum dosages well below what is reckoned likely to have a lethal effect. In this and in other ways, the hospice movement has been instrumental in developing the art of caring for the dying into a fine one.

It is tempting to substitute the phrase 'seriously handicapped' for 'the dying' and regard a policy of not intervening to supply corrective treatment as equally appropriate in their situation. But to jump to that conclusion is a temptation which should be resisted. Admittedly, the extent of the handicap may sometimes be so severe that the patient's death can be predicted as imminent. It makes no sense to operate on a newly-born spina bifida baby if one can be reasonably certain that, notwithstanding the operation, the baby will die within a few days. But usually handicapped children are not in a situation analagous to that of the patient in the last throes of cancer. They have a condition with which they may – assuming that medical help is forthcoming – live several years, if not into adulthood. They should surely be given that medical assistance. I agree with the verdict of Paul Ramsey:

> If an operation to remove a bowel obstruction is indicated to save the life of a normal infant, it is also the indicated treatment of a mongoloid infant. The latter is certainly not dying because of Down's syndrome. Like any other child with an obstruction in its intestinal tract, it will starve to death unless an operation is performed to remove the obstruction to permit normal feeding.[32]

If some doctors (and, for that matter, parents) are reluctant to agree with that opinion, it is because they are swayed by considerations about the quality of life which will be experienced by the child in years to come. But speculating about somebody else's quality of life is an extremely hazardous venture. Who are we to judge whether another person's handicap is so severe as to make life not worth living? Many handicapped people have defied extreme odds and wrested a measure of satisfaction and fulfilment out of life. I know wheelchair-bound residents in a Shaftesbury Society home who paint marvellous pictures holding a paint-brush in their mouths, and play bar billiards to a high standard, manoeuvring their cues with hands which are deformed stumps. Admittedly, there are also handicapped people who appear extremely miserable with their lot, but the correlation between handicap and happiness is not straightforward.

Those who use utilitarian arguments in this context are actually liable to stress the suffering and burden caused to a handicapped person's family (or even society as a whole) as much as to the bearer of the handicap herself. Those who would justify depriving a Down's syndrome child of standard medical attention are obliged to adopt this line, because it is well known that Down's children are often happy and easily contented; the fact is that they seem to be spared some of life's anguish which accompanies the possession of greater intelligence. Bringing them up does involve pain, but parents' experience is often one of pain mingled with, or succeeded by, joy. One doctor has commented that 'The Mongoloid child who has broken his mother's heart will usually mend it again in 2–3 years.'[33] It is thus debatable whether non-treatment which thwarts their chances of survival can be justified even on purely utilitarian grounds. But we do better to avoid such dubious calculations and pursue the logic of love and justice. It cannot be just for a handicapped child's prospects for survival to be dependent on its initial capacity to evoke its parents' affections. Rather, the principle of justice demands that where they do have a chance of continued existence, severely handicapped children should be given the surgical treatment which will enable them to realise that opportunity. At the same time, the principle of love insists that we offer to parents saddled with the daunting task of caring for such children as much support and as many resources as can be summoned.

If I may now refer back to John Habgood's observations on spina bifida children, it will be clear that, though both of us avoid extreme positions, the middle way which I favour is rather different from his.[34] I do not believe that all such children should be operated on, but I believe that the criteria which should govern such decisions are purely medical (i.e., whether the child is likely to benefit significantly from the operation), rather than including doubtful speculation about the happiness likely to be experienced by the child and those closest to it. It is interesting that Habgood states a (provisional) agreement with the list of initial adverse criteria which was used by Dr John Lorber in a Sheffield hospital to select which spina bifida babies should receive active treatment.[35] Lorber's policy has been widely criticised since as writing off prematurely a fair proportion of children with reasonable chances of survival. He has also been accused of hastening the deaths of those children who were not selected for treatment by sedating them so that they demanded to be fed less often. Where this sort of practice occurs, it is a far cry from only caring for the dying. It is deliberate neglect which harks too much of playing God.

Notes

1   Lewis Smedes, *Mere Morality*, Eerdmans & Lion, 1983, p. 25.
2   Helen Oppenheimer, *The Hope of Happiness*, SCM, 1983, ch. 14.
3   An influential writer who did make a very sharp distinction was the Swedish theologian Anders Nygren in his *Agape and Eros*, SPCK, revised trans., 1953.
4   E.g., the rich young ruler, Mark 10:17–22.
5   Mark 14:36.
6   Ernest Gordon, *Miracle on the River Kwai*, Collins Fontana, 1965.
7   The phrase has become a controversial one in the wake of David Sheppard's book *Bias to the Poor*, Hodder & Stoughton, 1983.
8   See James 2:1–7, and for an example of the prophetic critique, Amos 2:6–7.
9   See his 'household tables' in Ephesians 5:21–6:9 and Colossians 3:18–4:1.
10 See e.g., Deuteronomy 24:17–22 and 1 Timothy 5:3–16.
11 See especially 2 Corinthians 8:1–15.
12 Headmasters may have more responsibility, but schoolteachers have a lot more contact with what can be very demanding children!
13 For earlier discussion see pp. 133–4.
14 This is not the place to develop an argument that fetal life should be valued in this way. I have argued this in 'The Foetus as a Person', a contribution to the Church of Scotland Board of Social Responsibility symposium *Abortion in Debate*, Quorum Press, Edinburgh, 1987.
15 To its credit, the anti-abortion organisation, Life, does provide a care and counselling service in many parts of the country at present.
16 See the mention of prisoners in Matthew 25:31–46.
17 See 1 Corinthians 13:4–8 for an example of love being used in this active sense. Proverbs uses the word wisdom in the same way, e.g., in Chapter 8.
18 For earlier discussion of Kant's principle see p. 45.
19 *Report of the Committee of Inquiry into Human Fertilisation and Embryology* (Warnock Report), HMSO, 1984, p. 45.
20 *Op. cit.*, p. 46.

21 I have expressed my view on this in *Reply to Warnock*, Grove Booklet on Ethics No. 63, Nottingham, 1986.
22 The right to exercise some of these goods is restricted, but not necessarily removed, by factors of age and maturity. A young child cannot vote, but he or she can still write to the newspaper or local MP.
23 The biblical material on punishment supports this many-sided view. Deuteronomy 19:19–21 speaks of social protection ('you shall purge the evil from the midst of you'), deterrence ('And the rest shall hear, and fear, and never again commit any such evil among you') and retribution ('it shall be life for life, eye for eye, tooth for tooth . . .'). Meanwhile the limitation on the extent of corporal punishment in Deuteronomy 25:1–3 reflects a humanitarian concern for the offender's dignity.
24 See my earlier discussion on pp. 92–4.
25 For a summary of these see my earlier discussion on pp. 82–3.
26 'Sermons on the First Epistle of St Peter', *Luther's Works*, vol. 30, Concordia, St Louis, 1967, p. 76.
27 St Thomas Aquinas, *Summa Theologica*, II. 2, Qu. 64, Art. 7.
28 This is the title of an article by the American Roman Catholic moral theologian Richard McCormick, in his *How Brave A New World?*, SCM, 1981.
29 Gerald Kelly, SJ, *Medico-Moral Problems*, The Catholic Hospital Association, St Louis, Missouri, 1958, p. 129.
30 This attitude was memorably summed up in Philippians 1:21: 'For me to live is Christ, and to die is gain'. See also 2 Corinthians 5:1–9.
31 Published by Yale University Press, New Haven & London, 1970. See also Ramsey's *Ethics at the Edges of Life*, Yale University Press, 1978.
32 *Ethics at the Edges of Life*, pp. 192–3.
33 Eugene F. Diamond, 'The Deformed Child's Right to Life', *Death, Dying and Euthanasia* (eds Dennis J. Horan and David Mall), University Publications of America, Inc., Frederick, Maryland, 1980, p. 130.
34 See earlier discussion on pp. 166–7. I have expressed my views in greater detail on this subject in 'Life, Death and the Handicapped New-Born: A Review of the Ethical Issues', *Ethics and Medicine*, 3:3, 1987.
35 Lorber decided not to operate on children with the symptoms ('adverse criteria') of severe paraplegia, gross enlargement of the head, kyphosis (a pronounced curvature of the spine), associated abnormalities or major birth injuries, and an open wound on the back.

10

A HIERARCHY OF DUTIES

It was not my intention in the preceding chapter to suggest that spelling out second-order principles *guarantees* the immediate solution of dilemmas. I have already cited situations where two or more relevant principles may be in tension.[1] The obligations which follow from these principles will point to contrasting courses of action. What is therefore demanded is a weighting of respective obligations. In this chapter, I shall complement my talk of first- and second-order principles with discussion of a *hierarchy of duties*.

Truth-telling

At various points in this book I have mentioned a particular category of moral dilemma which seems to involve a clear choice of one duty as having higher claims than another. This is the situation where the duty to tell the truth comes into conflict with the duty to preserve life. The latter duty overrides the former duty. Telling the truth is an excellent general rule, but it cannot be universalised to cover every situation, because it is not *the* fundamental duty above all others. The preservation of life comes higher up the hierarchical scale. If a person is not alive, he or she no longer has the capacity to be concerned about what is being done to their property, their spouse or their good reputation. King David did Uriah the Hittite a grave wrong when he committed adultery with Uriah's wife Bathsheba; but he committed an even greater offence when he connived at the death of Uriah in battle.[2]

If Uriah had still been alive when David repented of his adultery, David would have had the opportunity to make restitution to him. Both moral intuition and biblical examples (referred to earlier[3]) indicate that life itself is a good deal more fundamental than the many and varied things which commend themselves as good *in* life.

However, it is important to ask the question how a duty such as telling the truth can come into conflict with a duty such as preserving life. Normally these duties are not in conflict. If they are, there are two likely reasons why this is so. The first is that a certain individual or individuals are behaving in a way which unjustly threatens life. Pharaoh should not have been trying to massacre newborn male Hebrews; Kant's murderer should not be pursuing his intended foe; Nazi soldiers should not have been rounding up refugee Jews in occupied Holland. In each case, innocent life was in deadly peril. Because of their murderous intent, the would-be assailants no longer deserved that most basic mark of social respect, the right to have the truth told to them. Thielicke is quite right, in the context of discussing resistance to an oppressive totalitarian regime, to speak of individuals who have forfeited the claim to truth.[4] Thinking in this way is fully compatible with the underlying principles of justice and love. Concealing the persecuted Jews was an act of love towards them; it was also just *not* to co-operate with an anti-Semitic regime.

Nevertheless, the idea that other people can forfeit their usual rights is one that must be handled with care. We must beware of jumping to this conclusion overhastily. In today's world we see an all too prevalent tendency to write off those regarded as 'the enemy' as cruel, inhumane and individuals to whom we owe no duties whatsoever. The possibilities of conciliatory dialogue with the other side therefore tend to be discounted prematurely. The work of Terry Waite, the Archbishop of Canterbury's special envoy, has served as a valuable antidote to this attitude. The risks involved in Waite's approach, underlined by his sad disappearance in Lebanon, should not allow us to forget his achievements. When he sought to secure the release of British businessmen in Libya, Waite refused (in the style of mediamen or Western political leaders[5]) to pillory Colonel Gadaffi as a mad dog, but instead appealed to his better instincts, reminded him of the Muslim commitment to justice, and won the businessmen's release. There is surely a lesson here that we should appeal to the better instincts of aggressive and antisocial people for as long as possible. But if they show no response, if they persist in their evil ways, there comes a time when they forfeit the right to expect *us* to conform to standards which *they* have no intention of observing.

What I am envisioning here is a declaration of hostility by the perceived opponent which amounts, implicitly or explicitly, to a state of war. What we must avoid is the temptation to see everyday relations with an insurance company, tax office or tradesman in similarly dramatic terms.[6] Because we feel that such parties are doing us an injustice, we are tempted to conceal or misrepresent in order to even things out. But we delude ourselves about what is at stake in these situations. Insurance companies may be bungling in their bureaucracy or ungenerous in the strict interpretation of their policies, but they can scarcely be said to have hostile intent towards their clients. If we practise dishonesty towards these apparently anonymous agencies, we contribute to a diminution of trust which actually makes relations between these agencies and the public more warlike. We need to look to the long-term consequences. The more that people fiddle a system, the more likely it is that prices, premiums or taxes will have to increase. And in practising deceit on agents whom we regard in an impersonal light we increase the likelihood that we shall resort to deceit in other areas of life, in relation to persons whom we actually respect and love.

In affirming a limitation on our duty to tell the truth in exceptional situations, then, I am certainly not attempting to decry the importance of honesty in general. In general terms we need more honesty, not less. In relationships between husband and wife, parent and child, teacher and student, and clergyman and congregation, to name but a few, misunderstanding and mistrust are all too frequently caused because important things go unsaid or half-said. The concealing is often done in the name of love, because truth can hurt; but

how much more constructive it is to face the truth *together* and
nurse each other through the pain.

All the same, there is a second reason why the duty to tell
the truth *might* conflict with the duty to preserve life. It could
be the case that telling a patient who has been diagnosed as
having a potentially lethal illness the full truth about the
gravity of her illness might impair her chances of making a
recovery. If she is the sort of person who is much encouraged
by good news but easily deflated by bad, it may be that casting
the medical information about her condition in either a
positive or negative light could materially alter the outcome
of her illness by its effects on her will to live. The connections
between our mental and physical conditions are subtle but
well established. Thus deceit here is a hypothetical possibility, though the likelihood is that the patient will already
have got wind of the fact that something may be seriously
wrong. Concealing the gravity of her illness from her is then
more likely to make her suspicious about the trustworthiness
of doctor or relatives than to lead her to harness all her
positive resources to fight the illness. Protecting the patient
from uncomfortable facts is too often a patronising approach
devoid of positive effects. Nevertheless, the truth that a
patient may be dying is not something to be blurted out
insensitively nor, necessarily, as soon as it is known. People
need time to make the shift from thinking of death in abstract
and timeless terms (as something that happens to humanity,
or will happen on a remote 'one day') to thinking of it in
personal and historical terms (as something that will happen
to *me*, possibly quite soon). In other words, they may not yet
be *ready* for the truth: but that is an argument for its gradual
disclosure, not for overt denial of the truth.

Gradual disclosure also has its place in other situations
which do not involve the imminence of death. It will be
appropriate with individuals who share with the dying patient
the (temporary) capacity of limited understanding. It is therefore bound up with the question of maturity. An example
from the other end of life is the issue of what parents should
reply to the very young child's question: 'Where do babies
come from?' A detailed explanation of the act of intercourse

is an inappropriate answer, not because there is anything shameful about it, but because the idea that human genitalia can be put to such uses will be mind-boggling to the child, and the incorporation of the physical activity into the context of a loving relationship elusive. A suitable reply would seem to be along the lines of, 'God gives little children to two people when they love each other, and puts them in the mummy's tummy for protection until they are strong enough to come into the world.'[7] This tells the child all that he needs (and probably wants) to know, and – in contrast to silly legends about storks – does not contradict any further information about the mechanics of child-begetting which will be given to him at a later age. The content and style of the disclosure have been tailored to the child's particular stage of maturity.

Respecting Property

A duty which probably comes somewhere around the same level on the hierarchical scale is the obligation to respect other people's property. Owning property is an important aspect of individual identity and a contributor to social stability. Stealing possessions is therefore an assault both on the person and society. But to build a prohibition on stealing into an absolute which brooks no exceptions is to run the risk of giving property the status of an idol.

As with lying, stealing becomes a moral possibility when the alternative is a risk to life itself. It is conceivable that an individual or family might become so destitute and a society so heartless that they had no recourse but to steal in order to have food to live. Even in a society with no welfare system, however, the likelihood is that they will be able to find someone who will respond to their appeal to help. Inability to make such an appeal, for reasons of safety, is more likely to occur in the circumstances of wartime: a prisoner-of-war escaping through enemy country may have little option but to pilfer secretly. Another type of situation where stealing might avert a threat to life is where a particular person is known to harbour violent intent against others. If an armed bank robber carelessly left his ignition keys in his van while raiding a bank, an alert passer-by's act of stealing those keys (or driving off with the van) would surely be highly commendable. Any implement with which an individual is threatening murder may be rightly withheld from him, at least until he is reckoned no longer to be a threat. By his violent manner he has forfeited the right to possess such an implement. Obviously cases such as these are rare, but it is only honest to admit that stealing would then be a legitimate possibility.

There is another category of action which might technically count as stealing, but can be morally defended on the grounds that it constitutes a just restoration of what has been wrongfully taken. In most cases it should be possible to rely on the upholders of law and order (e.g., the police) to effect the restoration, but sometimes this may not be so. A couple may have good reason to believe that their young teenage daughter who is now with the Moonies was kidnapped and is being held against her will, or alternatively that she has been brainwashed by them. The police may prefer not to get involved in a case of this kind, arguing that there is no proof that the daughter has not joined the Moonies of her own free will. In the absence of help from official authority, the couple may well be justified in taking their own measures to remove the girl from the Moonies' hold. This might involve an act of kidnapping in return. Kidnapping effectively amounts to stealing a person, but in the parents' case it would be a matter of restoring to her own home someone who belongs there – though this is not to deny that at an appropriate age parents should give children freedom to make momentous decisions which may cut across the parents' wishes.[8]

Another situation where restoration of property is defensible, but possible only on a quasi-legal basis, is where a selfish dictator has taxed a people into a state of grinding poverty for the purposes of his own selfish aggrandisement. If the dictator is overthrown, the representatives of the people who replace him are justified in confiscating some of his wealth in order to reimburse – either through tax refunds or the provision of improved public services – the people who have been wronged. I say 'quasi-legal' because the new government may in fact pass a law confiscating the ex-dictator's property. Normally retrospective legal measures of this sort are an extremely dubious device, but sometimes they represent a genuine attempt to put apparently arbitrary (yet justified) actions on a publicly accountable footing.

No doubt there are other instances where perpetrators of theft might claim to be motivated by a desire to redistribute property on a just basis. The way that property is distributed so unequally in almost every society *is* unjust, there can be little doubt about that; but for private individuals to take the solution (which implies others' property) into their own hands can only lead to intolerable chaos. It is for society, through its appointed representatives, to decide how extensive the re-distribution of property should be and how best it may be carried out. The jubilee legislation in Leviticus 25 is a striking example of provision being made for periodic restoration of land to its original owners. Although there was opportunity for people to become rich and poor over a considerable span of time, every fifty years an attempt was made to redress the balance. The jubilee legislation offers a challenge, if hardly a precise blueprint, for societies of a later age. Society must find ways of correcting the imbalance which is all too evident in the vast discrepancies of property ownership; the prohibitory command not to steal needs to go hand in hand with this sort of active social concern.

Preserving Life

If rules which prohibit lying and stealing may both, in excep-tional circumstances, be superseded by the obligation to preserve human life, it is clear that the latter comes very high on a hierarchy of duties. Some Christians (among others) would say that it ranks so high as to deserve absolute status. Since it is grounded in a notion of the sacredness of human persons, it is certainly a fundamental obligation which should always weigh heavily upon us. But it will already be evident from views which I have expressed earlier that I do not see preservation of life as an absolute command. When death is offering merciful release, it is wrong to try to preserve human life at any cost (and in the long run, because human beings are mortal, the attempt is bound to fail).[9] In certain circumstances, even innocent human beings may have to be sacrificed in order to save other humans with a better chance of survival or those to whom one owes a prior obligation.[10] And finally, in other circumstances it is conceivable that, just as individuals may forfeit the right to know the truth, they may also forfeit the right to life itself. If this is the case, then my principle of never directly harming innocent persons does not apply, because we are actually dealing with guilty (seriously guilty) parties.

The most obvious such case is where an individual has committed first-degree murder, one where there seems to be little or no diminution of personal responsibility. Genesis 9:5–6 suggests that by wilfully taking human life, life created in the image of God, the person who has committed murder deserves to die. He or she *has* forfeited the right to live. The Old Testament goes on, of course, to prescribe the death penalty for a considerable number of offences, not simply that of murder but also others which were seen as particularly serious.[11] In the New Testament Paul *probably* gives backing to the institution of capital punishment when he speaks of the governing authority who 'does not bear the sword in vain' (Rom. 13:4), though this may be pressing the lethal characteristics of a sword too hard. However, the Bible also provides us with examples of the death penalty being remitted. God stamped his mark of protection upon that most callous of murderers Cain (Gen. 4:1–16); and Jesus resisted the Pharisees' invitation to judge that an adulterous woman should be stoned (John 7:53–8:11). The implication would seem to be that though individuals may sometimes deserve to die, fellow-members of the human race are not bound to carry out the ultimate judgment. There is a place for mercy (and as Jesus taught, an appropriate humility) as well as justice.

Every society must make up its collective mind about capital punishment. I do not regard the death penalty *in principle* as barbaric, though particular ways of carrying it out are certainly that. But it will be more appropriate in some societies than in others. This is not just a matter of saying it will be a more effective deterrent in one place than another, though doubtless that is true. More fundamental is the significance which the institution of capital punishment is thought to convey. While in one society it may *underline* how valuable human life is viewed by saying that someone who has taken it is no longer fit to live, in another society it may be seen to *undermine* the value of human life by destroying another person as well.[12] Allied to this is the possibility that the valid principle of retribution may be confused with the sinful desire for revenge. If the retribution involved in capital punishment (i.e., giving someone his just deserts) is equated with revenge (i.e., venting one's feelings of loathing), then it is better that society does not execute its murderers. I suspect that British society is in this muddled condition. On the one hand we see the frightening displays of hatred which are directed by members of the public at individuals who are charged with notorious murderers; on the other hand we have the Hattersleys, representatives of fashionable liberal opinion, who see nothing in the retributive principle of punishment at all.[13] The sober administration of capital justice could scarcely be entrusted to either.

The other type of situation where killing may be viewed as an act of judgment on guilty parties is that of war. I believe that this is an important and appropriate element in the sort of just-war theory for which I have indicated sympathy.[14] If in a military conflict one genuinely believes one's own cause to be just, the implication must be that the soldiers against whom one is fighting are representatives of a cause which is unjust. Admittedly, it is extremely unlikely that they bear much, if any, responsibility for the outbreak of hostilities or for the oppressive tyrannical system whose extension one is battling to resist. The parties which are most transparently and directly guilty (usually the political leaders) rarely make themselves accessible to the executors of justice by appearing on the battlefield! But the armed forces of a tyrant or aggressor bear an indirect, partial and representative responsibility. Without their contribution, the unjust cause cannot be carried forward. Those who resist this cause have no choice but to make these forces their target. However, the latter remain a legitimate target only for so long as they constitute an actual threat (i.e., are active representatives of the unjust cause). If enemy soldiers are captured and disarmed, then their lives should be respected; their association with a guilty regime is both linked with and limited by their capacity to cause lethal harm.

The foregoing discussion reinforces the point that specific prohibitions (such as those forbidding lying, stealing and killing) need to be understood and evaluated in the light of the more fundamental principles of justice and love. Moral rules are both ranked according to their centrality to one's underlying principles, and to some extent relativised by them. Love and justice bid us regard the life of our fellow-human as sacred but also – in rare circumstances – permit the lifting of that protection.

In speaking of a *hierarchy* of duties, I am not seeking to imply that ethical analysis can ever be as precise as a mathematical science. It would be impossible to draw up a league table of obligations, so that one could confidently rank one particular duty in sixth spot and another in twenty-second. This is partly because some of these duties (unlike football teams in the same division) never seem to come into competition with each other, so that it is difficult to compare them: when has anyone ever had to choose *between* committing incest and betraying their country, for instance? It is also because the respective duties cannot be taken out of context and evaluated in isolation: we need to know the specific details of a dilemma situation before making a judgment. There is, moreover, a tremendous variety of situations involving a conflict of duties; we cannot anticipate them all in advance. Nevertheless, thinking in terms of rank and rating has its value. It suggests a useful line of approach to a moral dilemma, that of trying to distinguish what one's respective duties are and gaining a sense of proportion about them. And in deciding in favour of one particular duty, one chooses it *ahead* of the other rather than *against* the other. One still recognises that the lesser duty is important, an obligation which would have binding force in normal circumstances.

Competing Loyalties: God, Family, Job

Thus far in this chapter I have been largely concerned with
conflicts of duty which involve the possibility of breaking a
rule which normally holds good. Not all conflicts of duty,
however, take this form. On occasion they involve a clash of
loyalties. We owe loyalties to God, our families, our employers, our neighbours, society . . . and sometimes these
demands point in different directions. If the offer of an
exciting new job for a businessman means that for long
periods he will be away from his growing young family, should
he take it? Should a missionary couple jeopardise their son's
educational prospects by keeping him with them in a Gospel-
starved corner of the world, or should they risk the loosening
of family ties by sending him to boarding-school in England?
Should a teenage daughter report her parents to the police if
she knows that they are involved in drug trafficking, or should
loyalty to her parents outweigh the concern she feels for other
members of society who are being introduced to drugs?

Jesus had some striking things to say on the subject of
conflicting loyalties. Some of them are uncomplicatedly
straightforward, though none the less challenging:

> No one can serve two masters; for either he will hate the one and
> love the other, or he will be devoted to the one and despise the
> other. You cannot serve God and mammon (Matt. 6:24).

We live amid a generation which repeatedly makes financial
gain its overriding consideration. It is very hard for Christians
not to be affected by this mentality, yet it is one that we are
called to resist. This is not to say that financial considerations
are irrelevant. A publishing firm which never sold books on
which it made a profit could not survive. The acquisition of
money is necessary to make essential provision for ourselves
and our dependants. But it would be a pity if the publishing
firm was never prepared to take a risk on an interesting book
whose selling power was doubtful; and there is no doubt that
the *love* of money is a consuming obsession which insidiously
disputes God's claim to first loyalty in our lives. Whenever we

consider a change of job which involves a major salary increase, it is worth pondering the question: What is the main attraction here? Is God calling me to a new sphere of work, or is the lure of extra cash and a more comfortable life style taking over?

To Christian people it comes as an even ruder shock to discover that Jesus has some very sharp words which raise questions about allegiance to our *families*. Partly because traditional family structures have come under attack, there has been a recent tendency in some parts of the Christian Church to raise the family to near-idolatrous status. It is salutary to remember that Jesus said the following:

> If any one comes to me and does not hate his own father and mother and wife and children and brothers and sisters, yes, and even his own life, he cannot be my disciple (Luke 14:26).

> For I have come to set a man against his father, and a daughter against her mother, and a daughter-in-law against her mother-in-law; and a man's foes will be those of his own household (Matt. 10:35–6).

> To another he said, 'Follow me.' But he said, 'Lord, let me first go and bury my father.' But he said to him, 'Leave the dead to bury their own dead; but as for you, go and proclaim the kingdom of God' (Luke 9:59–60).

These are spine-chilling words, which remain deeply challenging even when we recognise that the 'hate' in Luke 14:26 is not to be taken literally. Jesus there expresses in exaggerated form the point made in Matthew 10:37–8:

> He who loves father or mother *more than* me is not worthy of me; and he who loves son or daughter *more than* me is not worthy of me; and he who does not take his cross and follow me is not worthy of me (my italics).

Jesus challenges each individual to be his disciple, and within a network of relations response to that challenge will vary. He does not desire a disunited family, but that will be the result if some members decide for him, others against him. Loyalty to fellow-members of one's family is relativised within the context of a greater loyalty to Christ.

As far as we can tell, being one of Jesus's original disciples did involve a temporary leave-taking of wife and family. Peter said on one occasion: 'Lo, we have left everything and followed you.'[15] Accompanying an itinerant Rabbi in his wanderings must surely have imposed a considerable strain on family relationships. Taking up one's cross to follow Jesus *can* involve the pain of feeling one is letting one's closest relatives down. It may indeed entail living apart for a while, lengthy absences from home, not giving one's children all the opportunities in life that one would like.

Yet at the same time as issuing the sternest of challenges in this area, Jesus also warns us against neglect of family responsibilities under the guise of religious fervour. This was how he reproached the Pharisees:

> You have a fine way of rejecting the commandment of God, in order to keep your tradition! For Moses said, 'Honour your father and your mother'; and, 'He who speaks evil of father or mother, let him surely die'; but you say, 'If a man tells his father or his mother, What you would have gained from me is Corban' (that is, given to God) – then you no longer permit him to do anything for his father or mother, thus making void the word of God through your tradition which you hand on (Mark 7:9–13).

The Pharisees appeared to be advocating the right thing, placing one's obligations to God before those to one's parents. But Jesus saw that the practice of setting money or property apart as dedicated to God, so that it was not available for use in the family, could simply be an excuse for neglecting one's obvious duties. Not every action which has the *appearance* of displaying a primary loyalty to God necessarily proceeds from the right motivation. Even the most zealous and fervent of missionaries can be twisted in his motives or deluded about their true nature. He may think that extended absence from his family is a worthy sacrifice in the Lord's cause, when in fact no such sacrifice is needed; there are ways of doing the right thing by one's dependants at the same time as serving God with a whole heart.

In the final analysis, it is more accurate to say that Jesus plays *up* loyalty to himself rather than that he plays *down* loyalty to one's family. His concern for the permanence of marriage relationships is evident from his reply to the Pharisees' question about divorce.[16] A husband and wife can hardly be said to be living as 'one flesh' if they are always apart. Likewise, Jesus's compassion for children ('See that you do not despise one of these little ones' Matt. 18:10) scarcely leaves room for doubt that he would be severely critical of parents neglecting their offspring. Paul, while accepting that the presence of faith in one partner and its absence in the other can cause tensions which make separation a possibility, believed that this need not necessarily be the case: even where there is disunity at this profound level, it is possible to maintain one's loyalty both to God and to one's spouse.[17] An unbelieving partner is still to be loved (and hopefully converted), not simply dispensed with. The Christian is called to grapple with the tension caused by competing loyalties, not take an easy way out by abdicating one particular area of responsibility.

If we were to try to place loyalties to God, family and workplace in some sort of hierarchy, that would seem to be the order in which we should rank them. God, as one's Creator and Saviour, an infinite being with whom one has entered upon a relationship destined for all eternity, should come first. Spouse, children and parents, fellow-humans with whom one is engaged in lifelong ties of blood or covenant, should come second. Employers, colleagues and clients, individuals with whom one is involved in significant but less long-term partnerships, should come third. This suffices well as a general statement of principle, but in reality competing loyalties often appear in a more complicated light. Thus it may be that one identifies one's sphere of work with a specific calling by God. Here I do not only have in mind vocations such as missionary, clergyman or member of a monastic community, but any type of job where one believes that God has given one a particular role to play. To be a dedicated Member of Parliament is an extremely taxing job which can take one away from one's family for long periods (and the number of MPs whose marriages break up is indeed worrying). But a Christian might well feel that the tasks of shaping legislation and representing the public are those where disciples of Jesus are especially needed. If Christians are to be the salt of the earth, they need to be liberally sprinkled in different areas, but perhaps particularly in positions where they can act as a savoury and purifying influence. Whether a conscientious MP who spends long hours at Westminster and with constituents is neglecting his obligations to his family cannot simply be measured by how much he does or does not see them; it all depends on his motives, the extent to which his family are committed with him in his political dedication, how he 'redeems the time' when he is with them, and so on.

In deciding between competing loyalties, then, a whole range of circumstantial factors come into play. A television reporter may wonder whether it is right to take up an assignment as foreign correspondent when her widowed father is far from well in an old people's home. Should she not ask for an assignment in this country so that she is near at hand if his condition takes a fatal turn? The answer *may* be 'yes', but there are a number of factors which might enable her to venture abroad with a clear conscience. She may have brothers or sisters living near her father; they can be relied upon to rally round in the event of an emergency. By ensuring that the higher loyalty (that to her father) is fulfilled in alternative ways, she could still be able to meet the lesser obligation (concerning her job). Her employers may agree that if her father's condition does become critical, she can travel home immediately (and in the modern age of air travel, that should not take long). She may have discussed the situation with her father and he is quite adamant that the last thing he wants to live with in his ailing state is the knowledge that she may be blighting her career prospects on his behalf. By reason of her background she might have specialist skills which make her uniquely well equipped to report on events in the particular part of the world to which she is being sent. There are many highly specific features which need to be weighed and considered in making decisions of this kind.

Loyalty to Loved Ones When They're Wrong

Dilemmas involving competing loyalties acquire an additional twist when a party to whom one owes a legitimate obligation is seriously at fault. The illustration cited earlier, that of a teenage girl wondering whether to report her drug-peddling parents, is an example of this. It is a quandary which arises for many a family aware that one of their number is guilty of a serious criminal offence. Dear though our kith and kin should be to us, we also owe a responsibility to the wider community; and this may require, as a last resort, the willingness to do something which looks like the betrayal – turning them in. I say 'as a last resort' because one would hope that within the context of a close relationship the initial attempt to deal with competing loyalties would be by way of reasoned persuasion. The girl should remonstrate with her parents about their way of life, point out the harm that they are doing to themselves and others, and generally appeal to their social conscience. The mother of a murderer or rapist should seek to persuade *him* to give himself up. Nevertheless, if such appeals fall on deaf ears, the good of society may finally warrant testifying against one's offending relatives. This might well involve considerable cost to oneself: certainly the risk of being misunderstood, and in the case of the girl the possibility of being taken into care (her imprisoned parents no longer being in a position to look after her),[18] but that is often the price of doing the right thing.

What reduces some of the pain involved in this type of decision is the knowledge that action which looks like a choice against one's loved ones may ultimately serve their own best interests. The conviction of the parents for drug offences may lead to their treatment and, hopefully, cure. The life of a fugitive murderer is usually an insecure and unhappy one. Again we come back to the importance of acquiring a long-term perspective.

However, what separates and strains relationships between relatives and friends is not necessarily something so clear-cut as a crime. The dilemma may be posed by a serious difference of opinion. A miner genuinely believes that a call to strike is mistaken, but finds himself isolated in a pit-force which has come out solidly in favour of such action. He has always preached the importance of miners' solidarity. Now that he finds himself in the minority, should he brave the picket-line? A socialist husband believes that private education is wrong; his wife has no strong political views on the subject, but in the absence of good state schools in their area is convinced that this is an avenue they owe it to their children to pursue. How do they resolve this one?

What characterises both these situations is the fact that arguing the rightness or wrongness of a particular course of action is not a mere theoretical issue; if there is a failure to arrive at agreement, a decision must be made one way or the other. They also highlight the issue of being loyal to *oneself*, as well as to other people. This demands a high degree of honesty and perception in one's self-dealings! As far as the miner is concerned, he is likely to experience a tension of loyalties between his fellow-miners, with whom he has always identified closely, and his family, for whom he wants to continue bringing in a wage, as well (possibly) as the mine-owners, against whom *he* has no significant grievance on this occasion. He finds it very difficult to resolve the dilemma when viewed in terms of a choice between these different groups. The answer would then seem to lie in being true to himself. At first sight this appears to decide matters in favour of his continuing to work, because that coincides with his analysis of this particular industrial dispute. But he can hardly forget that he has always upheld the principle of miners' solidarity, i.e., that one should support the democratically-arrived-at decisions of one's colleagues even if one disagrees with them. Loyalty to oneself demands consistency, and this should surely be the decisive factor for him in this case.

By the same reckoning, loyalty to one's professed principles means that it would be quite improper for an ardent proponent of comprehensive education to send his own children to private schools. But that apparently straightforward resolution of the parents' dilemma is subject to two major qualifications. First, encountering the lean side of the state system may have a useful effect in leading the father to reconsider his political views: it could be that these are based more on dogmatic ideology than a measured assessment of rival educational systems. I am not seeking to imply that he *should* change his views, only that he ought to evaluate them afresh, and if he does decide to educate his children privately, then he should publicly abandon his previously stated views on education. Second, they are his wife's children, not his alone. (And the children themselves will doubtless have views on where they want to go to school; these are not irrelevant.) The couple should take each other's views into account and try to come to a common mind. If this is still elusive, then the deadlock should be broken by using whatever method has already been agreed for resolving such dilemmas – and that assumes that couples should establish this in theory before they encounter the problem in practice. Methods will vary from couple to couple. It may be that the wife has promised in her marriage vows to obey the husband, and the couple understand that this implies her readiness to accept his decision when they are in disagreement over an important matter. Or it may be that a couple delegate to each other decision-making authority in different areas of family life. As the parent who may have been more closely involved in the children's schooling from the outset, it could well be that education has been deemed to be the wife's province. Either way, loyalty to oneself (and one's partner) would mean adhering to a method of procedure which has already been agreed and established. Refusing to stick by it in testing circumstances would be personally inconsistent and amount to a betrayal of trust. I shall say more about the virtue of consistency in the final chapter.

Duties to Animals

Some readers of this book may feel that, thus far, it has been too people-centred. Nearly all of the dilemmas which I have considered involve choices concerning *human* welfare. But what about obligations we may owe to non-humans? What about the world of birds, animals, plants, trees, land and sea?

Are there not significant moral dilemmas concerning the way in which we treat *them*?

Indeed there are, and I shall consider some such dilemmas shortly. How human beings treat the animal, vegetable and mineral creation is not a matter of moral indifference. The environment in which we live possesses intrinsic value. Human appreciation of its beauty, variety and productivity is widespread; and it should be especially evident in Christians who believe that God created the earth and every living organism in it – and declared them all good. Nevertheless, cruelty to animals and pollution of the environment are frequent phenomena, and the influence of specifically Christian beliefs has allegedly contributed to the sorry record of humanity (particularly Western humanity) in this respect. Defenders of animal welfare have argued that the doctrine of the image of God in man has led to an exaggerated notion of the value of man at the expense of the animals from which he evolved.[19] Some ecologists, likewise, maintain that the instruction purporting to come from God:

> . . . fill the earth and subdue it; and have dominion over the fish of the sea and over the birds of the air and over every living thing that moves upon the earth (Gen. 1:28).

has encouraged human beings' exploitative and destructive instincts.[20] It is certainly true that the 'dominion' implied in this verse and spoken of explicitly in Genesis 1:26 has often been understood in terms of absolute rule, a freedom for man to do as he likes. The moral theologian R. C. Mortimer, defending the practice of fox-hunting on the grounds that it reinforces 'man's high place in the hierarchy of being',[21] is a rather ghastly example of this.

Christians should not abandon the tenets which have come under criticism, but they should be careful about the conclusions which they draw from them. *Homo sapiens* does have a higher place in the hierarchy of creation than animals, birds or fish, and the duties which he owes to his fellow-humans do therefore take precedence over those which he owes to other creatures. Such a judgment does not – or need not – proceed

from human egocentricity, the natural tendency of a particular species to rate its own interests as the most important. It is
based partly on recognition that human beings are rational,
morally responsible and inventive creatures, in a way that
animals are not, or certainly to nothing like the same extent.
In possessing developed capacities of this sort, human beings
reflect the nature of God – though the biblical notion of the
image of God probably also includes the idea that human
beings have a spiritual capacity which enables them to have a
relationship with God. This, too, seems to distinguish humanity from the animals. But the Bible never precisely defines the
content of the *imago Dei*; the Christian should be content to
accept that God does love and value him or her in a way which
exceeds his concern for the rest of creation, without pressing
the question why unduly.

Jesus expressed this relative weighting in some beautiful
words:

> Look at the birds of the air; they neither sow nor reap nor gather
> into barns, and yet your heavenly Father feeds them. Are you not
> of more value than they? . . . Consider the lilies of the field, how
> they grow; they neither toil nor spin; yet I tell you, even Solomon
> in all his glory was not arrayed like one of these. But if God so
> clothes the grass of the field, which today is alive and tomorrow is
> thrown into the oven, will he not much more clothe you, O men
> of little faith? (Matt. 6:26–30; cf. Matt. 10:29–31).

Nevertheless, though Jesus says that human beings are of
greater value in the eyes of God, he still insists that God cares
for the birds and flowers. Another, almost comical witness to
God's subsidiary concern for the animal creation is found at
the end of the book of Jonah:

> And should not I pity Nineveh, that great city, in which there are
> more than a hundred and twenty thousand persons who do not
> know their right hand from their left, *and also much cattle*?
> (Jonah 4:11; my italics).

If God values non-human aspects of his creation in this
way, it is scarcely likely that he desires human beings to

display a ruthless attitude in their dealings with animals and the environment. The exercise of *dominion* should be understood in terms of a responsible discharge of office which has the welfare of one's subjects in mind. Significantly, the picture of Adam exercising dominion in Genesis 2 exudes a friendly paternalism! However, matters do change somewhat after the fall. Cultivation of the land becomes difficult and arduous; and an atmosphere of *threat* becomes characteristic of the relationship between the human and animal worlds. It is symptomatic of this disturbed relationship that in God's covenant with Noah permission is given, probably for the first time, for human beings to eat the flesh of animals:

> Every moving thing that lives shall be food for you; and as I gave you the green plants, I give you everything (Gen. 9:3).

This divine permission is not remitted in the New Testament. Yet it is interesting that one of the most vivid eschatological passages in the Bible is a vision of the restoration of harmony *both* between the animals themselves *and* between the animal world and humanity:

> The wolf shall dwell with the lamb, and the leopard shall lie down with the kid, and the calf and the lion and the fatling together, and a little child shall lead them (Isa. 11:6; see also vv. 7–10).

Similarly, Paul in Romans 8:18–23 suggests the inclusion of the wider creation in God's plan to release the world from suffering. In the light of these passages, a decision not to eat meat could be justified as a sort of pointer to the last things, a symbolic gesture which betokens a desire to recover the harmony between human beings and animals which was lost after the fall. But vegetarianism cannot be said to represent a necessary implication of such passages, only an imaginative application. And in virtue of the fact that the Bible clearly does rate human life as more valuable than animal life, a Christian vegetarian surely has to concede that where animals offer the *only* feasible source of sustenance, man is entitled to kill to eat.

222   DILEMMAS

It also appears that the sacrifice of animal life is justified where this may have a significant part to play in the restoration of human *health*. This is one possible implication of the rather bizarre story of Jesus's transferring the legion of unclean spirits from the Gadarene demoniac into a herd of swine.[22] Presumably the gulf between human and animal worth is such that the peace of a man's mind weighs favourably in proportion to the lives of a large quantity of animals; the pigs acting in a crazy manner would serve to convince the man that the spirits really had left him!

In contrast, there can be no justification for killing animals when this is simply a case of pandering to desire for pleasure. The fact that some animal-hunting sports (e.g., beagling) derive their attraction from a fear-inducing chase, and that other animals are used in the pursuit, marks them out as gratuitously cruel, but even the apparently innocent pastime of outwitting fish looks suspiciously like an act of bullying on the part of the angler! Granted that animal suffering is not directly comparable with human suffering, and that it lacks the pain associated with *long-term* anticipation or memory, it is clear from the nature of animals' reactions that their suffering can be intense. In an important respect it is likely to exceed human suffering, because animals cannot be expected to understand any point to the agonies they are going through, whereas human beings, at least some of the time, can. This consideration, as well as the fact that we rate human life more highly, explains our readiness to 'put down' cats and dogs which are suffering from incurable diseases, steps which we would not take with members of our own species. What then of a form of animal suffering whose purpose is readily comprehensible to humans, but not to the animals themselves: the frequent use of rats, mice, hamsters, guinea-pigs and rabbits, as well as other animals, in scientific experiments? The practice of animal experimentation can pose a considerable moral dilemma. Employees with strong convictions about the treatment of animals may wonder whether to protest (even resign) if they work for one of the many companies which habitually use animals to test new products.

In line with principles established earlier, I believe that experiments on animals should be evaluated according to how directly and how centrally they contribute to human well-being. The testing of medical drugs on animals is surely justified, because it would be irresponsible for a pharmaceutical firm to launch a new drug without testing whether it has deleterious side effects on human health. The testing of cosmetics and perfumes on animals is not justified, because the absence of these artificial aids to beauty would not impoverish human life significantly (in any case, more natural aids are available). Often experiments by rival cosmetic companies duplicate each other, thereby adding to the number of animal lives squandered. A more borderline case is the testing on animals of the toxic effects of new types of paint. Is paint a vital contributor to human well-being? In the strictest sense of the word 'vital', it is not, but clearly buildings, vehicles and implements would rapidly become very dilapidated without it. We do need paint. But an animal-respecting employee in a paint company might justifiably query whether a new *type* of paint represents a significant step forward, or doesn't rather have the character of an unnecessary gimmick, when the cost in animal suffering is borne in mind. Evaluation of the morality of animal experiments in such a case will therefore be a delicately balanced judgment, requiring detailed knowledge about the worth of the product – worth measured in practical rather than commercial terms.

Environmental Dilemmas

Dilemmas concerning environmental issues are extremely varied. The building of a reservoir in a rural locality may serve the purposes of replenishing water supplies, improving the service to nearby industry and employing local people in its actual construction. The reservoir might also be developed as a tourist attraction. On the other hand, the local inhabitants may treasure the natural beauty of the area, and botanists claim that flooding the area will irreversibly destroy a number of rare types of plant (including one that is unique).[23] On the face of it, putting the needs of humanity first would seem to justify the construction of the reservoir, but only after a thorough investigation of alternative locations (i.e., a search for a suitable spot with more mundane types of vegetation) and only if every attempt is made to reduce the environmental damage to the minimum. The rich variety in God's world is something to be treasured and preserved as much as possible, partly because it is dangerous to disrupt the ecological balance of nature, but also because of the intrinsic fascination of different species.

Aesthetic considerations enter into some of the dilemmas associated with conservation. It is congenial to have beautiful surroundings, but should such factors be allowed to stand in the way of answering human need? Does it matter if the erection of a new multistorey carpark to serve a busy shopping and office area spoils the popular view of a city cathedral? How much adjacent clear space can one continue to guarantee an ancient building? Clearly, it is desirable that aesthetic considerations are not forgotten. By careful and tasteful urban planning, it should be possible to bring the causes of utility and conservation into harmony. There may well be alternative locations for the carpark which do not interfere with the view of the cathedral. Yet if the only plausible alternative was the land occupied by four terraced streets, which represented the one area of cheap housing in the city centre, the local inhabitants could justifiably object to their homes being demolished. In a clear either-or situation, conservationists should be willing to accept that concessions have to be made. On the other hand, if fewer commuters and shoppers insisted on using their cars and were more willing to use public transport, there would be no need for the erection of the carpark, and then both the house-dwellers and the architectural devotees could be happy. That is a big *if*, because trends such as that towards more use of the motor-car have an inexorable character. But it is a trend which contributes to another major environmental problem, the rapid rate at which human beings are using up non-renewable sources of energy.

However, when we turn for help to a source of energy

which appears limitless, we encounter a yet more momentous dilemma: the controversy about nuclear power. Unlike resources of oil and natural gas, those of uranium are not in dwindling supply, and by harnessing nuclear techniques to develop them man can now make electricity more cheaply than with any other fuel. But where should society dispose of the nuclear industry's unwelcome side-product, the radio-active waste? The most dangerous material is stored on the industry's sites, and that itself is worrying for those who work at or live near those plants. But locations are needed for the vast quantities of low- and intermediate-level waste. It is difficult to find them. Whenever an area is suggested as a suitable spot for burying it underground in steel containers, local opposition invariably mounts. Though the health hazard of radiation-linked illness from low-level waste buried underground appears to be negligible, no one wants to take any chances, for themselves, their children or their children's children. This appears to be a far-sighted response, but one wonders whether it really represents a realistic assessment of the risks compared with risks which are readily accepted in today's world. Coal-mining is expensive in its cost both to human life and human health, and chemical waste *above* the earth's surface poses a more dangerous threat than nuclear waste below. The dangers connected with nuclear energy receive a disproportionate amount of attention. Part of the explanation for this is that the word 'nuclear' has such sinister vibes for the present generation; it has overwhelmingly negative connotations because of the use to which nuclear energy is put in the manufacture of deadly weapons. I suggest that it would be a pity if the opportunity to put nuclear energy to *positive* use was not developed because of this. It is tempting for Christians to be on the side of fashionable protest, but not necessarily right.

Again, however, such a judgment is necessarily provisional. One can only judge on the most reliable facts and figures available to one, and these are rarely produced by those with an obvious stake in the resolution of the argument. There is nothing shameful about reserving judgment on a particular moral dilemma because one needs to know more.

The risks to which the use of nuclear energy exposes us certainly need to be kept under constant review.

Duties concerning the environment are no trivial affair. Compared with our responsibilities to our fellow-humans, a little bit of pollution might not seem to matter, but in the long run fouling the atmosphere and squandering natural resources *does* affect people (in particular, future generations). We owe it to each other and the God who has delegated dominion to us not to abuse the environment. And in an age when humanity is coming perilously close to exceeding the divine command to *fill* the earth, and when some energy resources are running out fast and others are potentially lethal, that is a demanding challenge indeed.

Notes

1 See in particular pp. 159–161.
2 2 Samuel 11.
3 See pp. 63–4.
4 See my earlier discussion, p. 142.
5 Keith Graves of the BBC and President Reagan have both shown an unhelpful tendency to talk of Gadaffi in this way.
6 See my examples of dilemmas on pp. 13–15.
7 I have here adapted some material found in Thielicke's *Theological Ethics*, A. & C. Black, 1966 vol. I, pp. 524–7.
8 The phrase 'appropriate age' might give the impression that I am ducking a vital question – when should children be given discretion of this sort? – but the answer will rightly be affected by all sorts of cultural factors, so generalisations are not in order.
9 See discussion, pp. 193–6.
10 See discussion, pp. 189–90.
11 Notably the offences of kidnapping, adultery, homosexual acts, the worst forms of incest, blasphemy, idolatry, witchcraft, false prophecy, profanation of the Sabbath and persistent disobedience by children to their parents.
12 For an excellent discussion of the ambivalent nature of capital punishment, see Oliver O'Donovan, *Measure for Measure: Justice in Punishment and the Sentence of Death*, Grove Booklet on Ethics No. 19, Nottingham, 1977.
13 See p. 40 for an earlier citation of Mr Hattersley's views.

14 See my earlier discussion, pp. 191–3.
15 Mark 10:28.
16 See Mark 10:2–12, and my earlier comments on this passage, pp. 59–60.
17 See 1 Cor. 7:10–16.
18 This actually happened in a case which attracted widespread attention in the United States.
19 See e.g., Peter Singer, *Animal Liberation*, Jonathan Cape, 1976, pp. 209–10.
20 See e.g., Ian L. McHarg, *Design with Nature*, Doubleday, 1969, p. 26.
21 This remark is cited by Herbert Waddams in *A New Introduction to Moral Theology*, SCM, 1972 (revised edn), p. 205.
22 See Mark 5:1–20.
23 This was the nub of the controversy which surrounded the building of the Cow Green Reservoir in Upper Teesdale in the late 1960s.

11

THE SEARCH FOR CONSISTENCY

Principles and Priorities

It is time to review where this exploration of moral dilemmas has led. What I have advocated is a middle way between the deontological and consequentialist approaches to ethics. But in doing so I have not suggested that the appropriate course of action in every dilemma situation is one which embodies compromise. Rather, the most fruitful way forward is to think in terms of principles and priorities. This does not remove the need to consider rules and consequences, for some rules follow naturally from certain principles, and the likely consequences of our actions will affect how we evaluate our priorities. But principles and priorities are more fundamental, and it is therefore crucial to attempt to unearth the particular ones which are relevant to the dilemma with which one is struggling.

Principles provide the connecting link between an ethic which focuses on human goodness on the one hand, and one which concentrates on actions' rightness on the other. Love and justice are central to answering both the questions 'What ought I to be like?' and, 'What ought I to do?' They are virtues to which we should earnestly aspire, qualities which are characteristic of God and which he desires to see in the people whom he has made. They are also principles which provide the starting-off point when we come to consider the rights and wrongs of specific issues.

Principles help us to see how much weight should be attached to different rules. It is unhelpful to talk about rules (or even God-given laws) as being absolute and inviolable in a general way. There are rules and rules, some being much more binding and important than others. The test of a rule's inviolability lies in how closely it is connected to some fundamental ethical principle like respect for human dignity. It can be unkind to flirt with someone, as it can be to tease; but neither flirting nor teasing violates human dignity in the way that raping or torturing does. The latter two activities warrant total prohibition; the former two simply a warning that one should be sensitive about indulging in them!

Of course, many difficult moral problems concern activities which are neither relatively trivial nor obviously horrific. What sort of status do rules which are applicable to this intermediate area have? A prohibition of bribery, relevant to the type of problem which Bill was wrestling with in the example cited in Chapter 1,[1] is a possible example of such a rule. This seems to me a category of rule which carries considerable moral force, but not so great that one need feel obliged to desist from all action which contravenes it immediately. Bill's scruples about bribery suggest that in the long term he should not remain in the position of sales executive (or only if he can effect a real change in trading practice), but in the short term he has his responsibilities to colleagues and workforce to consider. Having embarked on the deal with the government agent, he should take whatever steps are necessary to see it through to a satisfactory conclusion – and then take stock of the wider question.

It may be recalled that I suggested a similar two-stage approach to the issue of polygamy.[2] Polygamy falls short of the God-given ideal for marriage, but it is not a wholesale deviation from this ideal. A polygamist has responsibilities to each wife with whom he has entered into a covenant relationship. Recognition that monogamy is a better way should lead the husband not to enter into *another* marriage relationship, should one of two wives die; it does not mean that he should simply discard his less favoured wife *now*.

Thinking in terms of priorities helps to throw fresh light on the much-asked ethical question: 'Does the end justify the means?' Superficially, consenting to bribery or polygamy in the short term looks like a case of saying 'yes'. But I suggest that is the wrong way to view such action. It is more a case of trying to order one's priorities aright. One is setting one's responsibilities to people with whom one has made a specific contract ahead of one's responsibilities to the wider community. Nevertheless, because one is still mindful of the reality of the latter, one does not intend to let an unsatisfactory state of affairs continue indefinitely. The ultimate aim is to make the two sets of responsibility coincide, e.g., to be able to compete for trade deals in an atmosphere uncluttered by demands for bribes. The aim is to make means more and more conformable to ends, so that the tension between the two disappears – but this side of eternity that tension will always be present to some extent.

Similarities and Dissimilarities

Perhaps the most important characteristic which should mark our encounter with dilemmas is an attempt to be consistent. To be inconsistent in one's moral thinking is to be irrational and raises questions about one's personal integrity. The vice for which Jesus reserved probably his harshest words was that of hypocrisy.[3] Hypocrisy can mean a failure to practise what one preaches; it can also entail an attitude of rigorous moral scrupulosity in one area co-existing with an attitude of libertarian indifference in a comparable area. Hypocrisy may consist in a failure to carry through the implications of one's moral stances consistently.

As such it is a very easy fault to fall into. It is therefore important to check whether the reasoning one employs across a wide range of moral issues is mutually coherent. If one objects to the portrayal of explicit sexual scenes on television, does one also object to excessively violent scenes? Does the position one takes towards the taking of human life in the context of issues of war and peace tie in with one's attitude to life-taking in the context of medical issues? If one is adopting a significantly different position, are there sound reasons for this? There may be, but one needs to be clear what they are.

Using the method of analogy, of pointing to factors which are common to different issues, can certainly help one to maintain consistency. It is a method which I have just used in comparing the situations of the businessman and the polygamist. It is one which some Christians have used in a systematic way with regard to certain issues. The just-war criteria are an example of this. They have been applied not only to the question of international conflict, but also (admittedly less often) to the issue of internal conflict within a state. Some theorists have been willing to countenance the possibility of a *just revolution* in the face of an oppressive, tyrannical government. They have applied the same criteria: just cause, last resort, minimum of violence, etc. The criterion which obviously fits uneasily with the idea of revolution is that which insists that the use of force should be approved by constituted authority. Nevertheless, this criterion, too, is applicable if a government is held to have acted in such a way as to forfeit its claim to be the constituted authority, and if the people who originally authorised the government have clearly withdrawn their consent.[4]

The same criteria have also been applied by some to the question of strikes.[5] Has a projected strike action been democratically approved by the workforce? Does it have a just cause? Have all possibilities of a negotiated settlement been exhausted? Will the good achieved outweigh the damage caused? Is there a reasonable chance of success? Will innocent parties suffer as a result of the strike? This is a promising line of enquiry. The question of conscientious objection is also relevant to both wars and strikes. In recent years there has been increasing recognition that it is unfair to force someone who believes it is wrong to fight to do so against his will. In a similar way, picketing which takes the form of actively preventing someone who believes it is wrong to strike from working appears equally open to objection. In both cases the advocates of coercive action should have the freedom to try to persuade their countrymen or colleagues otherwise; but to coerce other people into being coercive shows no respect for their moral integrity.

Analogies, then, can be very illuminating. But they also have their limitations. We need to be aware of the dissimilarities between different ethical areas as well as the points of comparison. Thus it is important to remember that war is a life-or-death issue, whereas a strike (in the vast majority of cases) isn't. Because war is more lethal in its effects, it seems fitting that one should be that much more reluctant to resort to it. A sense of perspective needs to be kept about strikes. They should not be indulged in for trivial reasons, but most last only a short time and do not have very damaging effects. War is on a different plane. Also, with regard to conscientious objection, if a worker has had the chance to vote in a strike ballot, there is a moral onus on him to abide by decisions which have been arrived at democratically.

Awareness of dissimilarities is again important when pondering the implications of an example I used earlier. Approving the act of shooting a mortally wounded soldier might *seem* to be consistent with a policy of euthanasia, i.e., ending the lives of people suffering from agonising and incurable illnesses who desire to die. But two significant facts distinguish such people from the dying soldier. In the former case, but not the latter, medical aid is usually available, so the suffering can be mitigated to some extent; and the fact that death is not imminent means that there is a possibility of patients rediscovering elements of purpose and satisfaction in life. It is important to observe appropriate distinctions. Far from being incompatible with a search for consistency, this is part of it: we must be consistent both in following rules and in making exceptions to them.

Looking to the Spirit

Dilemmas can be fiendishly difficult: let us make no bones about that. But Christians can rejoice that in wrestling with them they are not alone. In Chapter 1 I pointed out various sources of guidance which are available to them, and in writing this book I have repeatedly drawn on these resources: the Bible, with its rich vein of ethical material; the Christian tradition, a heritage replete with wisdom and insight; the present-day community of Christians, in their writing, speaking and doing; and the testimony of nature, which seems to shed some light on sexual issues even if its direction is less clear in other areas. Christians are also promised the help and guidance of the Holy Spirit. When Jesus promised the disciples a Counsellor, who is the 'Spirit of truth' (John 14:17), the word truth presumably includes the idea of *moral* truth.

Christians often think of the Spirit's guidance in terms of sudden inspiration or direct prompting to perform particular courses of action. I do not dispute that the Spirit may guide us in this way. But I believe that he is also lending his help to us when we are engaged in the midst of serious reflection on moral issues and sustained analysis of them. Christians who resolve their dilemmas in an inconsistent manner and on spurious grounds should not abdicate responsibility by claiming direct dependence on the Spirit. Dilemmas are a call and a challenge to do some hard thinking. I hope that some of the ideas which I have begun to work out in this book may assist in the ongoing task of grappling with moral dilemmas; and I pray that in this, as in other areas, the Christian community may become increasingly one 'in the Spirit'.

Notes

1 See pp. 18–19.
2 See my earlier discussion, pp. 162–4.
3 See especially his attack on the scribes and Pharisees in Matthew 23.
4 For a helpful exposition of the idea of a just revolution, see Richard Harries, *Should a Christian Support Guerillas?*, Lutterworth, 1981.
5 See e.g., R. H. Preston in the symposium edited by him, *Industrial Conflicts and their Place in Modern Society*, SCM, 1974, p. 135.

INDEX

War 31, 76, 78, 81, 97, 136–7,
    153–4, 209–10, 230–2; *see also*
    Just-War tradition
Warnock Committee 185–6

Wisdom 121, 233
Wisdom literature 62–3
Wordsworth, William 38
Work 103, 211–5